Income Distribution and Development

Income Distribution and Development
Theory, Evidence, and Policy

Arne Bigsten

HEINEMANN · LONDON

Heinemann Educational Books Ltd
22 Bedford Square, London WC1B 3HH

LONDON EDINBURGH MELBOURNE AUCKLAND
HONG KONG SINGAPORE KUALA LUMPUR NEW DELHI
IBADAN NAIROBI JOHANNESBURG
EXETER (NH) KINGSTON PORT OF SPAIN

British Library Cataloguing in Publication Data

Bigsten, Arne
   Income distribution and development.
   1. Underdeveloped areas—Income
   I. Title
   339.2'09172'4   HC79.I5

   ISBN 0-435-84086-X
   ISBN 0-435-84087-8 Pbk

Typeset by Colset Private Limited, Singapore
Printed by Biddles Ltd, Guildford, Surrey

Contents

Preface

During the 1970s a mass of research got underway about the evolution of income distribution in the LDCs. A systematic assessment of this great effort is long overdue, and this study is an attempt to provide just that. I hope that it will be of use both to students doing courses in development and researchers interested in an assessment of the progress in the search for explanations of income distribution change in LDCs.

This study has been made possible by a research grant from the Swedish Agency for Research Cooperation with Developing Countries (SAREC), which is gratefully acknowledged. The book has been written over a period of several years, while I have been a research fellow at the Department of Economics at the University of Gothenburg and the Institute for Development Studies at the University of Nairobi. I am very grateful for all the help I have received from friends and colleagues at both these institutions.

An earlier version of the manuscript has been read by Carl Hamilton of the Institute of International Economic Studies, University of Stockholm, Mats Lundahl of the Department of Economics, University of Lund, and Rolph van der Hoeven of the ILO, Geneva. I am very grateful to them for their very helpful comments. For comments on parts of the manuscript and useful suggestions I am also much indebted to Magnus Blomström, Harald Dickson, Björn Gustafsson, Lennart Hjalmarsson, Per Lundborg, Henrik Lutzen, Bo Sandelin and Håkan Persson of the Department of Economics, University of Gothenburg; Göran Hyden of the Ford Foundation, Nairobi; David Court of the Rockefeller Foundation, Nairobi; Jan Gunning of the Free University, Amsterdam; Paul Collier of the Institute of Economics and Statistics, the University of Oxford; Dharam Ghai of the ILO, Geneva; Martin Godfrey of the Institute of Development Studies, University of Sussex; and Jan Essner of SIDA.

The typing of various versions of the manuscript has been done very efficiently by Ann-Marie Brisman, Greta Fridmar, Karin Hane, Maj-Britt Mattsson and Samson E. Otieno.

The language and presentation has been much improved by Betty

Low to whom I am much obliged. I would also like to thank David Hill and Robin Frampton of Heinemann for their assistance in the publication of the book.

Of course, all remaining shortcomings of the book are my own responsibility.

Arne Bigsten
Gothenburg, May 1982

1 Introduction

The purpose of this book is to give an overview of the present state of the arts with regard to the analysis of income distribution in LDCs. Therefore it has a broad scope and deals with theoretical issues, empirical findings, and policy.

The degree of inequality is of interest for at least two reasons. First, a relatively equal distribution may be necessary to keep the poorest strata of the population above a certain poverty line because of scarcity of resources. Second, people may desire, for reasons of justice, to live in a society with a certain distribution of income or welfare.

The latter issue has been discussed on a theoretical level by many, but few attempts have been made to analyse this problem empirically (at least within the discipline of economics). Morawetz *et al.* (1977) argue that they have made the first empirical study of the effect of the income distribution on human happiness. They study two similar, closed communities in Israel which differ in their income distribution. They reach the conclusion (p. 522) that 'the more unequal the income distribution, the lower the individual's self-rated happiness'. However, no generalizations can be made from such limited evidence. Nevertheless, it is reasonable to infer from the political debates in various countries that there is a widespread desire for measures that make the distribution of welfare more even than would otherwise be the case.

The book is laid out as follows. In Chapter 2 I review standard income distribution theory and discuss its usefulness for analyses of income distribution in LDCs. There are three problems which need to be confronted. First, which factors determine the ownership and supply of factors? Secondly, how is demand for these factors determined? Thirdly, how is factor supply equated with factor demand? Traditional income distribution theory forms an essential part of our toolkit, when we set out to analyse income distribution also in LDCs. However, since these countries have structural characteristics which are different from those of the DCs, the analyses must be adjusted accordingly. In Chapter 3 I therefore look to development theory to see what that branch of economics can contribute to the analysis and understanding of income distribution in LDCs. It is found that there is a strong emphasis on the disintegrated structure and other specific traits of these economies in development theories. Analytical tools from the structuralist tradition therefore are needed to complement the tools of standard economic theory.

In Chapter 4 I discuss the concepts of inequality and poverty and how best to measure the extent of inequality and poverty. The Gini and Theil indices are identified as the most useful inequality measures. An index proposed by Sen is found to be the most appropriate to measure poverty. In Chapter 5 the empirical knowledge that has by now been gained about the evolution of income distribution in LDCs is pulled together. Factors found to be important are economic system, ownership of assets, sectoral, regional and social structure, factor proportions and technology, education, wage determination, and various aspects of economic policy.

In Chapter 6 the results and analytical methods of the most important large model analyses of income distribution in LDCs are compared. The model analyses show that the size distribution of income is very resistant to single-policy interventions. To achieve a significant improvement of income distribution one needs to put together a package of mutually supporting policies; that is, to have a conscious strategy. A simple one-sector model is presented to high-light some theoretical assumptions underlying the analysis in the very complex, large-scale equilibrium models.

In Chapter 7 the income distribution policies pursued in some countries in East and Central Africa, namely Kenya, Tanzania, and Zambia, are discussed. Major problems with regard to income distribution policy in the Third World or, for that matter, anywhere are discussed. Some general conclusions are drawn from this discussion. First, there is need for a whole-hearted political backing, if the policy is to be successfully implemented. Secondly, one must be aware of the fact that there may often be a trade-off between equality and other goals such as efficiency and long-term growth. Thirdly, there must be congruence between ends and means. With regard to all these aspects one may run into obstacles.

References

Morawetz, D. *et al.* (1977), 'Income distribution and self-rated happiness: some empirical evidence', *Economic Journal*, Vol. 87.

2 The Relevance of Income Distribution Theory to the LDCs

2.1 Introduction

In this chapter I shall discuss the extent to which general income distribution theory can be useful in the context of poor countries. Development theory proper will not be discussed here, but in the following chapter.

There seems to be a widespread feeling among economists that the state of income distribution theory is unsatisfactory. Many surveys of the subject start off by bemoaning it. Economics has not been able to come up with clear-cut answers as to what determines the distribution of income. A main reason for this, of course, is that income distribution is the end result of the workings of the entire economic process; it is thus the result of the totality of economic (and other) influences.

Moreover, economic characteristics and institutions vary among economies. One must take this fact into account when trying to predict the end result of the economic process. To be able to produce a reasonable analysis of the determinants of income distribution in a specific country, one must therefore first identify its most important characteristics and then search for appropriate analytical tools. Ideally, one would want a theory that simultaneously explains prices of factors of production, functional shares and the size distribution of income. So far, no such comprehensive theory exists. To be able to give a good explanation of the distribution of income it may also be necessary to differentiate among sectors and regions, but this will not be discussed in this chapter. However, when analysing distribution in LDCs such breakdowns are often crucial.

2.2 The classical school

The classical economists wrote quite extensively about the issue of income distribution. Adam Smith discussed the division of what was produced among wages, rent, and profit, but he really had no theory about what determined the proportions of that division. Ricardo wrote in *Principles* that the main problem of political economy is to explain the laws that govern the distribution of income among labour, capital, and land. He was the first economist to derive a meaningful income distribution theory.

The land rent plays a crucial role in Ricardo's model. Income is divided between land rent and a composite dose of capital and labour. It is assumed that in the long run equilibrium wages are at the subsistence level and the profit rate is just high enough to maintain the capital. In the short run the sum of profits and wages can exceed this minimum, but this makes the system expand with capital accumulation and parallel population growth until the long-run equilibrium is reached. Following Samuelson (1978, p. 1428), one could say that Ricardo's system overplays the law of diminishing returns and underplays the forces of technical change. Therefore, the pattern of change in the DCs has not followed his prediction.

One characteristic trait of Ricardo's system is that the theory of production and the theory of distribution are integrated. Distribution is prior to exchange; thus, the demand for final products has no influence on the determination of the income distribution. Ricardo regards the relationship between the conditions of production and the prices as a causal one, an idea which was taken over by Marx.

In the Marxian system, the capitalists extract surplus value. They attempt to increase their surplus value by accumulating constant and variable capital. The workers are paid what is needed for their reproduction in a specific society, that is a socially determined subsistence wage. Wages are prevented from rising permanently above this level by the existence of a reserve army of labour; this army is continually replenished by workers who are displaced from handicrafts, or by the labour-saving innovations of the capitalists. There is assumed to be a long-run tendency for the rate of profit to fall and for the crises to become more and more severe. The capitalist system is assumed eventually to collapse as a result of its inherent contradictions.

The classical ideas about subsistence wages etc. were revived by Lewis (1954) when he formulated his dual economy model, but the hypothesis of long-run stagnation was not accepted. Elements of the classical school have via Lewis been incorporated in analyses of the structuralist tradition in development economics. These developments will be discussed in Chapter 3.

2.3 The marginalist school
During the last few decades of the nineteenth century the marginalist revolution introduced a drastically different view of the problem of distribution. All factors were assumed to be paid according to the value of their marginal product. The residual approach of the classical

economists was given up. The scarcity of factors came to be considered the determining factor. The distribution of income from then on was regarded by mainstream economists as a part of the general pricing process in the economy. The prices of factors and goods were assumed to be determined simultaneously by the market process. (The neoclassical model or the 'Good Old Theory' is presented in detail in Bronfenbrenner, 1971; see also Johnson, 1973.)

In the neoclassical model the demand for factors is a derived demand – derived, that is, from the demand for products. The elasticity of demand for factors is dependent on a number of things, such as the elasticity of demand for the final products, profit rates in branches demanding labour, the share of the factor in the price of the final products, the elasticity of substitution of factors, and the link between factor prices. The firms will hire labour until the wage is equal to its marginal revenue product. Thus, the marginal revenue product curve is the labour demand curve of firms. The supply curve shows how much labour the labour force is willing to supply at different wage levels. A theory of labour supply can be based on the hypothesis of equal net advantage, i.e. that a person strives to allocate his time among different uses, e.g. work and leisure, so that the net advantages are equalized.

In the neoclassical model pure production relationships and factor supply conditions together determine the distribution of income in a competitive market. The adding-up problem is related to this theory. If there are constant returns to scale or if the economy is in competitive long-run equilibrium, factor rewards do exactly exhaust the product. However, if these conditions are not fulfilled some factor must obtain a residual.

The sum of payments to the factors of production possessed by an individual determines his income. Factor shares are determined by the prices paid for the factors. The development of prices over time is dependent on changes in the relative factor quantities, elasticity of substitution, changes in the demand for products, and the character of the technical change. Obviously, these characteristics are of importance also in LDCs. The problem is that market imperfections are more important and this complicates the analysis.

2.4 The Kalecki model
Neoclassical analyses utilizing the aggregate production function have received much criticism from a group of Cambridge (England) economists. The main argument is that it is not possible to measure adequately aggregate capital. Because the value of capital is dependent on the rate of interest that is used to discount future profits, it is

circular reasoning to argue that the interest rate at the same time is equal to the marginal product of capital.

The Cambridge controversy has been extensive (see Harcourt and Laing, 1971), but the criticism has been essentially negative. The aim of the critique has been to end the use of the concept of marginal productivity of capital. Little in terms of positive income distribution theory has come out of the debate. However, it has been shown that in a properly disaggregated model it is logically correct to use the concept of marginal productivity of capital. Moreover, even economists who do not approve of the neoclassical production theory (e.g. Taylor *et al.*, 1980, p. 141) have to admit that it is difficult to do away completely with neoclassical methods in empirical work. So even if Taylor and his colleagues are ill at ease, they use neoclassical production functions in their model of Brazil. In their pedagogical one-sector model they use capital as one of the factors of production.

Two interesting alternative approaches to income distribution theory avoid the problem of measuring the capital stock: those of Kalecki (1950) and Kaldor (1956).

In Kalecki's model monopoly analysis is used to determine the sizes of functional shares. Kalecki assumes that firms set their prices by applying a mark-up to its average variable costs. Wages and expenditures on raw materials together are assumed to constitute total variable cost. The difference between total revenue and total variable costs covers fixed costs and net profits. Kalecki assumes that the more monopolistic a market is, the greater is the mark-up. The lower the degree of monopoly power, the greater the share of wages. The extent of market imperfections thus determine the functional shares.

Some aspects of the Kalecki model seems to be of great interest as far as LDCs are concerned. The character of market is an important determinant of the outcome of the economic process. It is desirable that differences in the pricing behaviour of firms in different sectors is taken into account in an analysis of income distribution in LDCs.

2.5 Neo-Keynesian theory

The model proposed by Kaldor is in the Keynesian tradition. Its basic assumptions are that the level of investment is exogenously determined and that workers and capitalists have different propensities to save. To make savings equal to investments, a necessary requirement for equilibrium, total income must be distributed between workers and capitalists in a certain proportion. If investments increase from an equilibrium position, savings must also increase to restore equilibrium. Since capitalists are assumed to have a higher propensity to save, this can only be brought about by an increase of the share of profits in the national income. Such an increase can be accomplished through an increase of the price level.

Many models along these lines have been developed, but it is not possible to review different variants of them here. (For a discussion of the issues of interest here the reader is referred to Sen, 1963; Eichner and Kregel, 1975; Tarshis, 1980; Crotty, 1980.) Only a few points of observation will be made. First, the central feature of the theory is that investment is exogenously determined and that savings adjust to bring about equilibrium. It is emphasized that investment decisions are made in situations with uncertainty and ignorance. 'In this uncertain world it is ephemeral expectations, unpredictable waves of optimism and pessimism and "animal spirits" which decisively influence investment.' (Crotty, 1980, p. 22). Because expectations govern investment decisions, the model would need a theory of expectations formation to be satisfactory. However, neo-Keynesian theorists suggest that this is very difficult. Eichner and Kregel (1975, p. 1302) argue that the favoured model is one where new capital formation is a function of past profits, but also that the accelerator model may be used. However, the model is compatible with several different investment determination mechanisms. In this model, the real wage is determined by the level of investment expenditures and the income distribution that this level requires. The neo-Keynesian theory thus emphasizes the distributive role of factor prices in adjusting savings to investment, while the neoclassical theory emphasizes the allocative role of the factor prices as signals of relative factor scarcity to entrepreneurs (Crotty, 1980, p. 21).

In the neo-Keynesian theory changes in income distribution depend on the growth rate. For one reason or other capital accumulation is going on, and the micro-conditions necessary are created during this process. The empirical question with regard to income distribution analysis is whether this dominance of macro over micro adjustments gives the best explanation of what is actually happening.

A neo-Keynesian approach along these lines has been tried as an alternative to a neoclassical approach in an analysis of Brazilian income distribution (Taylor *et al.*, 1980). Two alternative specifications of a one-sector macromodel are used to simulate the development during the 1960s. The neo-Keynesian specification in this case compares favourably with the neoclassical specification. This will be further discussed in Chapter 6.

2.6 Theories of the size distribution of income
The theories discussed so far have been concerned with the functional distribution of income rather than with personal or size distribution of

income, even though the neoclassical theory also can make some contribution to this. Yotopoulos and Nugent (1976, p. 247) argue, however, that the neoclassical theory is 'uninformative as far as personal income distribution is concerned and most likely wrong'. They feel that the income differences in LDCs are much too large to be explained by differences in factor endowments. Moreover, the theory does not provide any explanation of how these differences in endowments were created in the first place.

The ultimate aim of a study of income distribution must be to go further than the functional distribution, and a number of authors have presented (mostly partial) theories about the determination of the size distribution of income. Blinder (1974, p. 163) concludes his book on the subject with the observation that 'the theory of size distribution is indeed still in its infancy'. This field is less developed than the field of functional income distribution theory.

An extensive survey of theories of personal income distribution has been presented by Sahota (1978). I shall just try to identify the main trends and select what may be useful for a study of income distribution in poor countries. A very old idea is that incomes are distributed among persons according to ability. Differences among workers in productivity and incomes are thus assumed to be a result of differences in ability. It is usually assumed that ability is normally distributed, and one therefore also expects incomes to be normally distributed. Therefore, it came as a surprise when Pareto (1897) presented evidence that incomes tended to be log-normally distributed. Many theorists have since then tried to explain the difference between the assumed distribution of abilities and the observed distribution of incomes.

Pigou (1932) suggested that the skewed distribution was due to the fact that wealth was inherited and that there existed non-competing groups (or a lack of mobility among groups). These conjectures have received some support from empirical studies. He also emphasized (pp. 647–55) that 'Pareto's law' is no law. Income distribution can be changed. Altered inheritance laws would certainly have some effect, although one can to some extent avoid these taxes by investing in the human capital of one's children. It has also been suggested that if there are different components of ability and if these determine productivity in a multiplicative fashion, the distribution may be log-normal. Sahota thinks (1978, p. 4) that despite its intuitive appeal, 'ability theory is rather too simplistic and mechanistic' to be able to provide a satisfactory explanation of income distribution. There has been a reaction against the ability theory in the form of screening and filtering theories of various kinds, which will be dealt with below.

Another major type of analysis that also emerged early was the stochastic theory of income distribution. In this type of approach the skewed distribution was explained by the workings of random factors. Gibrat (1931) showed that if, from a given initial income distribution, the incomes are subject to random percentage changes, independent of income level, the random process will generate a log-normal distribution of income. This is known as Gibrat's 'law of proportionate effect'. Gibrat's model was shown to have the defect that aggregate income gradually increases. To correct the model for this defect, Champernowne (1953) used the assumption that the size of the random shocks decreases with income level. This can assure constancy of variance.

Even so, to assume that the income distribution is determined through a random process contributes very little to our understanding of the determinants of income distribution and of the policies that can be pursued to change it. Blinder (1974, p. 7) emphasizes the traditional standpoint of economic theory that the income distribution should be viewed as the end result of deliberate choices by decision-makers.

Reder (1969, p. 206) argues in a survey on the subject that it is the purpose of size distribution theory to explain how the income distribution is determined by the structural characteristics of the economy. The most important parameters according to him refer to 'technology, tastes, and the distribution of natural abilities', but he also emphasizes the importance of 'the degree of resource utilization, rate of economic growth, and degree of monopoly power'.

Sahota (1978, p. 9) points out that *ad hoc* auxiliary hypotheses have continually been added to the original framework to make the stochastic theory accommodate new facts. This is a dubious scientific procedure, and Sahota finds that 'the old stochastic theory of distribution is apparently in disrepute'. A theory of this type is thus not satisfactory from the point of view of economic analysis, or, for that matter for policy making.

2.7 The human capital school and its critics

Friedman (1953) was a forerunner to the human capital school. He presented a theory that is referred to as the individual choice theory. This combines stochastic influences with optimizing behaviour on behalf of the individuals. Each individual is assumed to maximize his expected utility. People choose among occupations that yield different expected income streams and different risks. The attitude towards risk is assumed to differ among individuals, and in a society composed of risk-averters choices will be less risky and hence the *ex post* spread of incomes will be less than in a society composed of risk-lovers.

According to this theory one might expect incomes to be more equal in LDCs than in DCs, since the poor dominate and may be assumed to be more risk averse than the rich. Since inequality is greater in LDCs this explanation seems dubious, at least in general. If the range of possible choices is very limited, structural factors take on greater importance.

Friedman's approach is more general than the human capital theory which followed, but the latter has more or less taken over and is more thoroughly developed (Sahota, 1978, p. 10). The human capital theory is developed on grounds similar to those of Friedman's model. It is based on the assumption of optimizing individuals. These are assumed to determine how much to invest in themselves in terms of, say, education on the basis of calculations of the probable present value on the discounted future income streams in alternative occupations. The alternative that maximizes lifetime discounted earnings is chosen. 'Human capital theorists accept the principle of equalizing differences and competitive labour markets and pay scant attention to the principle of non-competing groups.' (Sahota, 1978, p. 13). It is pointed out by Cline (1975, p. 366) that in Mincer's (1958) model 'all incomes are in reality equal'. Differences in annual incomes are assumed to be attributable to the fact that people with longer education have to be compensated for this with higher annual incomes during their correspondingly shorter worker period (see also Becker, 1964 and Mincer, 1974). Blinder (1974) argues that two weaknesses in the approach are that it is not clear what human capital really is and that it appears as if leisure had no value.

Sahota (1978) lists the five main objections that have been raised against the human capital theory. The critique has led to a mass of interesting work on the determinants of income distribution. The aspects that are of interest to the study of inequality in LDCs will be considered here.

Objection 1 'The discounted-value maximization behaviour is too far-fetched.' (Sahota, 1978, p. 14).

An individual's capacity for correct calculation of this magnitude is limited. Moreover, in the context of the LDCs today, the economic structure is undergoing rapid change, so it is very difficult for any individual to foresee his economic lifecycle. This is obviously easier in the DCs, where career patterns are more stable. On the other hand, the differences in earnings among alternatives are usually much larger in LDCs, and therefore very crude calculations may be sufficient to guide the choices of individuals in the right direction. To assume that educational preferences are implicitly based on such calculations may therefore be reasonable. The problem is, however, that the freedom of choice is considerably less for most youngsters in LDCs. Even if a youngster prefers a certain level of education, he may be unable to get it for many reasons. Imperfections in capital markets which are common in LDCs mean that it is not possible for most individuals to realize the optimal allocation of their time between education and work. Opportunities to borrow money are definitely unequal. One may also add that there is a skewed distribution of the knowledge of what training and education imply, i.e. the risk is judged differently depending on your background. Thus, even if the human capital approach contains some important truths, it must be supplemented by additional factors to make useful analysis of inequality in LDCs possible.

Objection 2 'The theory studies human capital as a source of earnings and more recently, too, the sources of human investment, but scarcely analyses the causes of human investment.' (Sahota, 1978, p. 15).

That economic opportunities for education are unequal has already been pointed out.

Objection 3 'It is a partial and piecemeal theory.' (Sahota, 1978, p. 16).

The point made here is that the theory as it was first developed was only concerned with the supply of human capital. The demand side was not explicitly taken into account. This criticism is an important one as far as the applicability of the theory in LDCs is concerned.

For example, Cline (1975, p. 366) is critical of the model with regard to its relevance to LDCs, because of its failure to acknowledge a causation that runs as follows: '(i) family background determines level of schooling; (ii) given the state of the economy there is a certain distribution of high and low paying jobs with remuneration determined by a combination of status and marginal productivity considerations; (iii) the education filter screens out a limited number of candidates to be placed in the limited number of high income jobs'. Implicit in this critique is the notion that wage levels in LDCs are determined from the demand side of the labour market. Since the human capital theory is essentially a supply-side theory, it may be of dubious value if Cline's conception of reality is correct. We shall return to this issue in the two subsequent sections and in Chapter 3.

Objection 4 'Schooling is merely a screening device.' (Sahota, 1978, p. 17).

The screening theories were developed in reaction to the over-emphasis of the human capital theorists of the role of education. Sahota distinguishes between two types of theories. The first is theories that attack mainly schooling (the early version of the Becker – Mincer theory). According to this school (Arrow, 1973; Stiglitz, 1975) education mainly serves as a filter which sorts out people with attributes that are demanded by employers. It does not, according to Arrow's hypothesis, increase either cognition or social-ization. Or, to put it differently, the educational system screens per-sons and points out the most productive ones. These are then paid higher wages than the less productive ones.

According to Arrow (1973, p. 194) 'the filter theory of education is part of a larger view about the nature of the economic system and its equilibrium. It is based on the assumption that economic agents have highly imperfect information. In particular, the purchaser of a worker's services has a very poor idea of his productivity.' Therefore, Arrow just assumes that the employer has good statistical information.

There has also been a strong Marxist critique of human capital theory. According to Bowles and Gintis (1975) the function of formal education is to preserve the existing class structure and to create docile workers. Carnoy (1974) argues that education in LDCs is aimed at upholding the existing economic organization and at maximizing the income of the elite. These authors doubt that more education leads to a higher rate of economic growth.

The second type of approach is segmented labour market theories, i.e. 'theories that emphasize the demand side and are more critical of the on-the-job training aspect [the late version] than the formal schooling aspect of human capital theory'. 'Generalized education may influence the potential productivity of workers, but actual productivity depends on on-the-job experience which, it is alleged, is not open to the underdog even with credentials.' (Sahota, 1978, p. 17)

These types of analyses are of importance to the economies in the Third World. An interesting approach in this context is the job com-petition model attributable mainly to Thurow (see e.g. Thurow, 1975; Thurow and Lucas, 1972). This approach is based on the assumption that the labour market does not function in the smoothly equilibrating way often assumed, and this means that people with identical skills may be paid different wages. In the neoclassical model wage competi-tion is assumed, i.e. employers are assumed to adjust wages according to supply and demand conditions in each sub-market. In the job competition model it is instead the characteristics of the job which determine the wage level. Workers are allocated jobs according to their place in the labour queue. 'Marginal product of the labourer is not set by his education-acquired skills, but by the skills he learns on the job after successfully passing through the labour queue.' (Cline, 1975, p. 367). The position of a worker in the queue should be dependent on the potential cost to the employer of training the worker. It is possible that the employers attempt to determine this with the help of some screening device such as education.

Cline (1975, p. 367) asks critically why, in equilibrium, 'any job would have a marginal product different from that of any other job'. He argues that since the employer has the possibility of training any individual in the labour queue for the job and should be willing to accept costs equal to the sum of the training cost and the net wage paid to the worker, there should be equalization. This holds, however, only if the employer knows that he can keep the worker in the job. Cline thinks that only sociological factors remain to determine relative wages, but he seems to overlook the fact that it is one of the basic assumptions of the model that the labour market is not in full equilibrium. Moreover, it is quite possible that you may have to pay more than the market-clearing wage to keep the worker working efficiently because of nutrition requirements. You may also choose to pay more to stabilize the labour force, that is reduce labour turnover which is costly.

Still, also Cline (1975, pp. 367−8) finds the job competition approach useful for a number of reasons: '(i) its implication that formal training and human characteristics provide the information for an ordinal ranking of applicants, but not the basis for a cardinal ranking for relative remuneration among them; (ii) its emphasis on the expansion of job opportunities; (iii) its implication that collapsing non-germane wage-differentials is a principal means for equalization; (iv) its strong caveat against the human capital approach of equalizing education as a means of equalizing income. These strengths apply *a fortiori* to the developing economy, in which it is the structure of the economy that generates the profile of job openings characteristically associated with the vastly differing wage levels; organized industrial jobs paying high wages; relatively high wages for the civil service; and very low income for the large portion of the labour queue of workers left to fend for themselves in the unorganized urban services sector or rural wage and tenant labour sector.'

Cline thus emphasizes the structure of the economy as the most important determinant (see also Cain, 1976). This type of approach is of considerable importance to the analysis of income distribution in economies, where imbalances and market imperfections abound.

Other discussions that are of interest in this context concern the 'internal labour markets', i.e. labour markets within a firm which are largely insulated from outside competition. The points of entry to this labour market are at the bottom of the hierarchy. Positions higher up are filled with people from within the firm. This theory has been developed by Doeringer and Piore (1971); they emphasize that skills are often firm-specific and thus on-the-job training becomes very important. This restricts the scope for competitive forces. Since competitive forces cannot determine the relative wages, factors such as custom and status take on importance.

The place in the internal hierarchy is the factor emphasized by Doeringer and Piore. Others have suggested that the level of managerial salaries is determined by the place of the job in the hierarchy (Simon, 1957; Lydall, 1968). The salary of a person in the hierarchy is assumed to be some multiple of that of his subordinates. The hierarchy organization approach has been used to explain the skewness of the upper tail of the income distribution. Calvo and Wellisz (1978) have shown that hierarchies can generate wage differentials, even if labour is homogeneous.

Objection 5 'There is some incongruence between percept and practice, even among human capitalists.' (Sahota, 1978, p. 18).

The main point emphasized by Sahota is that there, as yet, does not exist any comprehensive test of the human capital theory of income distribution. Too little has been attempted in the way of falsification of the theory.

2.8 Supply and demand theories

It has been pointed out already that in the human capital theory incomes are determined from the supply side. There have been reactions to the over-emphasis of supply factors in the form of theories that concentrate instead wholly on the demand side.

Recently, there have been extensions of the human capital model, which constitute more complete theories (Blinder, 1974; Tinbergen 1956, 1970, 1975). In Tinbergen's model (1970) incomes are regarded as prices of productive services from land, capital, and work. The labour market is not homogeneous but compartmentalized. The factor payments on each market are determined by supply and demand. The employees offer their services and attempt to maximize their utility at the given wage structure, while the employers try to maximize their profits with wage scales and production functions as restrictions. According to Tinbergen the remunerations must reflect the relative scarcity of different factors of production, equal earnings are therefore not likely within this system. The income scale is the unknown function of the problem which must be determined in such a way that demand and supply is equalized in all compartments.

The utility functions of individuals include three types of arguments (Tinbergen, 1970, p. 223): '(i) quantities consumed of all goods and services; (ii) parameters representing the nature of the job taken; and (iii) parameters representing the nature of the individual'.

An essential point in this context is that the level of utility decreases as the tension between the skill parameters of the individual and the job parameters increases. The theory is therefore sometimes referred to as Tinbergen's tension theory (Bjerke, 1970, p. 245). The theory is formulated in such a way that the resulting income distribution can be described by the log-normal distribution. The theory therefore is consistent with the observed distributions.

In his (1975) book Tinbergen develops these ideas. He tries to integrate ideas from the human capital school, relating to the supply side of the labour market, with ideas from the education planning school, relating to the demand side, in a supply – demand framework along the lines already done in his previous articles. He regards the process of evolution with regard to inequality as a race between education, which tends to decrease inequalities, and technological change, which tends to widen them.

The absence of homogeneity on both the demand and supply sides of the labour market is certainly of great interest to the analysis of LDCs. The practical problem comes when one must try to represent both job and worker characteristics in vector form. No complete representation is possible, and one may even be forced to make such simplifications that a return to more traditional theory becomes inevitable.

2.9 The importance of wealth

The size distribution theories discussed so far have mainly been concerned with the distribution of earnings. Of course, there are also incomes from property, but this is almost neglected in income distribution theory. People obtain wealth either through inheritance or through current savings. The Kaldor model discussed above emphasizes the differences in savings behaviour of capitalists and workers, and because the former do save a larger proportion of their income, the concentration of wealth may increase. One must also assume that in the first place it is the inheritance of wealth which makes someone a capitalist. The model in its original form is too restrictive to give an adequate explanation of the size distribution of income. The distinction between only two socioeconomic categories is too restrictive for this purpose. Third World economies are disintegrated, with large differences in the productivity of the various segments of the economy. However, as will be seen in Chapter 6, this neo-Keynesian approach can be extended and quite successfully applied.

Meade (1976, Chapter 9) discusses the intergenerational transmission of endowments. He point out that in a perfectly competitive *laissez-faire* society it is only inequalities in endowments which can explain differences in income. Meade identifies four different types of endowments which are transmitted from parents to children; (i) a certain genetic make-up; (ii) income-earning property; (iii) a certain level of education and training; and (iv) some less tangible advantages emanating from the kind of social contacts that follow with the social background. However, the income that a person eventually gets is also dependent on the choices he makes and the luck he has in his career. The end result is thus a result of the initial endowments, the choices made by the individual and the character of the society.

Lydall (1968, p. 135) comes to a similar conclusion about the determinants of the earnings of an individual. He lists the following six factors: (i) inherited qualities; (ii) socioeconomic class; (iii) type of school attended; (iv) changes in abilities, health, strength during the first 20–30 years in employment, and personality characteristics; (v) willingness and opportunity to take a managerial position; and (vi) luck.

Meade (1976, pp. 157–8) emphasizes the positive feedbacks among the factors he discusses. Because of these there are 'powerful built-in tendencies for the rich to sustain their riches and the poor their poverty', and 'that the various endowments passed from parent to child are likely to become highly correlated with each other'. Obviously, these problems are very intricate and definitely the least developed part of what one would like to incorporate in a 'complete' income distribution theory. There are not only theoretical problems, but the data situation is also very problematic in most countries as far as wealth is concerned. There are also many historical and institutional differences among countries which in part explain the distribution of wealth. One must therefore, with regard to wealth distribution, carefully consider the historical dimension. Moreover, the distribution of property income is of greater importance to income distribution in LDCs than in DCs.

2.10 Conclusions
In this chapter I have reviewed the major income distribution theories

and tried to indicate the extent to which different approaches can be useful in a Third World context. Definite conclusions cannot be drawn on the basis of a brief survey of the income distribution literature. The theories must first be confronted with the empirical situation in a specific country. Different theories may be appropriate in different contexts. Therefore it is useful to be aware of the contents of the tool-kit.

There are basically three problems to solve. First, what factors determine ownership and supply of factors? Second, what factors determine demand for factor services? Third, how is supply equated with demand? This is a very old problem within economics, but there are, in many cases, no definite and satisfactory answers, and even if one may be found on the theoretical level, the empirical problems still remain to be solved.

Obviously, both human and material capital are important for the determination of the distribution of income. Therefore, ideas concerning human capital, as well as inheritance and savings, should be incorporated. Still, the structure of the economies is basic to the determination of income distribution in LDCs, and in this context screening hypothesis as well as the job competition model are of great interest.

A satisfactory analysis of income distribution in a LDC requires that the compartmentalized character of LDC labour markets is taken into account, and the structure of the economy must play a large role. The job competition model may be useful because it seems to give a reasonable description of many LDC economies. It also makes it possible to link very easily changes in the structure of employment to changes in the structure of production.

Of course, the job competition model is mainly concerned with the demand side of the labour market, while a complete analysis should also take the supply side into account. The labour force should be differentiated by skills, for this obviously is a very important earnings determinant. At least, it determines the place of a worker in the labour queue.

It seems evident that it is the background in terms of education etc. which determines a person's life-time income rather than his risk or time preferences. Freedom of choice is restricted. Of course, every individual chooses within existing restrictions, but if the scope for choice is very restricted it may be unneccessary to go too deep into the choice behaviour of the individuals. It may suffice to consider the situation in which the choice is made.

The maximizing behaviour of both firms and individuals must in a poor and disintegrated country, where markets are far from perfect, be constrained to a larger extent than in a developed country. The rules of price determination may differ between different sectors, at least between those exposed to external competition and those protected from competition from abroad. The dynamic pattern of the economy may be described, as was done in Adelman's and Robinson's (1978) model, as one of 'lurching equilibrium'. It gradually adjusts towards a full equilibrium which it may never reach.

The treatment of wealth constitutes a great problem in any empirical analysis. Analytically, it is fairly straightforward, if feedbacks are disregarded; what matters is the rules of inheritance and the savings rate. If the ownership of wealth interacts with other factors the situation becomes more intricate, but to come to grips with this may be too difficult. The analysis of the role of wealth in the theory leaves much to be desired.

There are also the problems of the distributional consequences of the public sector and its activities, and the importance of unions and their bargaining power. These are, however, not discussed in this chapter. Some evidence about this will be presented in the discussion of the empirical evidence in Chapter 5.

Sahota (1978, p. 40) points out that today there are two major directions in income distribution theory: the human capital-oriented group which considers inequalities to be individually made, and the environmentalists, who consider them to be society-made. A comprehensive theory certainly would have to incorporate traits from both these sides, but an analysis designed for LDCs would have to lean more in the environmentalists' direction than would a corresponding analysis for DCs. Still, even there, the latter approach has much to contribute.

References

Adelman, I. and Robinson, S. (1978), *Income Distribution Policy in Developing Countries. A Case Study of Korea*, Oxford University Press, London.

Arrow, K.J. (1973), 'Higher education as a filter', *Journal of Public Economy*, Vol. 2.

Becker, G. (1964), *Human Capital*, National Bureau of Economic Research, New York.

Bjerke, K. (1970), 'Income and wage distributions. Part 1: a survey of the literature', *Review of Income and Wealth*, Vol. 16.

Blinder, A.S. (1974), *Toward an Economic Theory of Income Distribution*, The MIT Press, Cambridge, Mass.

Bowles, S. and Gintis, H. (1975), 'The problem with human capital theory – a Marxian critique', *American Economic Review*, Vol. 65.

Bronfenbrenner, M. (1971), *Income Distribution Theory*, Aldine, Chicago.

Carnoy, M. (1974), *Education as Cultural Imperialism*, David McKay, New York.

Cain, G.C. (1976), 'The challenge of segmented labor market theories to orthodox theory: a survey', *Journal of Economic Literature*, Vol. 14.

Calvo, G.A. and Wellisz, S. (1978) 'Supervision, loss of control and the optimum size of the firm', *Journal of Political Economy*, Vol. 86.

Champernowne, D.G. (1953), 'A model of income distribution', *Economic Journal*, Vol. 63.

Cline, W.R. (1975), 'Distribution and development: a survey of literature', *Journal of Development Economics*, Vol. 1.

Crotty, J.R. (1980), 'Post-Keynesian economic theory: an overview and evaluation', *American Economic Review*, Vol. 70.

Doeringer, P.B. and Piore, M.J., *Internal Labour Markets and Manpower Analysis*, Heath, Lexington, Mass.

Eichner, A.S. and Kregel, J.A. (1975), 'An essay on post-Keynesian theory: a new paradigm in economics', *Journal of Economic Literature*, Vol. 13.

Friedman, M. (1953), 'Choice, chance, and the personal distribution of income', *Journal of Political Economy*, Vol. 61.

Gibrat, R. (1931), *Les Inégalités Economiques*, Recveil Sirey, Paris.

Harcourt, G.C. and Laing, N.F. (eds.) (1971), *Capital and Growth*, Penguin, Harmondsworth.

Johnson, H.G. (1973), *The Theory of Income Distribution*, Gray-Mills Publishing, London.

Kaldor, N. (1956), 'Alternative theories of income distribution', *Review of Economic Studies*, Vol. 23.

Kalecki, M. (1950), 'The distribution of the national income', in American Economic Association, *Readings in the Theory of Income Distribution*, Allen & Unwin, London.

Lewis, W.A. (1954), 'Economic Development with Unlimited Supplies of Labour', *Manchester School of Economic and Social Studies*, Vol. 22.

Lydall, H. (1968), *The Structure of Earnings*, Clarendon Press, London.

Meade, J.R. (1976), *The Just Economy*, Allen & Unwin, London.

Mincer, J. (1958), 'Investment in human capital and personal income distribution', *Journal of Political Economy*, Vol. 66.

Mincer, J. (1974), *Schooling, Experience, and Earnings*, National Bureau of Economic Research, New York.

Pareto, V. (1897), *Cours d'Economie Politique*, Rouge, Lausanne.

Pigou, A.C. (1932), *The Economics of Welfare*, 4th edn., Macmillan, London.

Reder, M.W. (1969), 'A partial survey of the theory of income size distribution', in Soltow (ed.).

Sahota, G.S. (1978), 'Theories of personal income distribution: a survey', *Journal of Economic Literature*, Vol. 16.

Samuelson, P.A. (1978),'The canonical classical model of political economy', *Journal of Economic Literature*, Vol. 16.

Sen, A. (1963), 'Neoclassical and neo-Keynesian theories of distribution', *Economic Record*, Vol. 39.

Simon, H.A. (1957), 'The compensation of executives', *Sociometry*, Vol. 20.

Soltow, L. (ed) (1969), *Six Papers on the Size Distribution of Wealth and Income*, National Bureau of Economic Research, Columbia University Press, New York.

Stiglitz, J.E. (1975), 'The theory of "screening" education and the distribution of income', *American Economic Review*, Vol. 65.

Tarshis, L. (1980), 'Post-Keynesian economics: a promise that bounced', *American Economic Reivew*, Vol. 70.

Taylor, L., Bacha, E.L., Cardoso, E.A., Lysy, F.J. (1980), *Models of Growth and*

Distribution for Brazil, Oxford University Press, New York.

Thurow, L.C. (1975), *Generating Inequality: Mechanics of Distribution in the US Economy*, Basic Books, New York.

Thurow, L.C. and Lucas, R.E.B. (1972), *The American Distribution of Income: A Structural Problem*, Joint Economic Committee, Congress of the United States, Washington, DC.

Tinbergen, J. (1956), 'On the theory of income distribution', *Weltwirtschaftliches Archiv*, Vol. 77.

Tinbergen, J. (1970), 'A positive and normative theory of income distribution', *Review of Income and Wealth*, Vol. 16.

Tinbergen, J. (1975), *Income Distribution. Analysis and Policy*, North-Holland, Amsterdam.

Yotopoulos, P.A. and Nugent, J.B. (1976), *Economics of Development. Empirical Investigations*, Harper and Row, New York.

3 Development Theory and Income Distribution

3.1 Introduction
In Chapter 2 I mentioned that the standard theory had to be adjusted before it is applied to LDCs. In this chapter, I provide a review of theories of economic development and try to identify the elements that can be useful for an analysis of the income distribution in LDCs. In sections 3.2 and 3.3 I describe how development economics emerged as a subject in its own right and the main trends within the field. From this mini-survey I then conclude that development economics can complement traditional income distribution theory mainly with regard to sectoral and functional distribution. In section 3.4 I look in greater detail at some grand development theories. I find that one must be cautious with generalizations about long-run development. The grand theories of development are too imprecise to be analytically useful.

In sections 3.5 and 3.6 I discuss in more detail the dualism and dependency theories and their relevance in this context. They can be regarded as the major structuralist and neo-Marxist alternatives to the standard neoclassical model. Both analyse intersectoral differences, which are of fundamental importance to income distribution.

In sections 3.7, 3.8, 3.9, and 3.10 I give some remarks on the analysis of capital formation, multisectoral analysis, foreign trade analysis and labour market analysis. The conclusions are summed up in section 3.11.

3.2 The emergence of development economics
Before the Second World War, the discussion of the problems of the less developed countries was limited. Naturally, there were some discussions going on within the colonial administrations about how best to use their possessions, and there was some discussion of the relations between the developed and underdeveloped countries. However, both with the general public and among economists in the DCs the interest in the poor nations of the world was limited. During the Second World War, interest in the development of the less developed countries grew

concurrently with the discussion of the problems related to the reconstruction of the war-torn industrialized economies.

At that time the knowledge about the workings of underdeveloped economies was very limited. It was not considered to be any problem to apply directly the analytical tools and theories that had been developed in the industrialized countries in an analysis of the growth problems of the less developed countries.

During the 1950s most economists saw the development problem as a problem of maximization of the growth of GDP. To achieve this end sufficient investment funds should be created, through domestic savings or through loans, aid or direct investments from abroad.

The long-term goal was usually specified as the creation of a process of self-sustaining growth, i.e. a growth process which could be maintained without funds from abroad. It was believed that growth and modernization would lead to the elimination of dualism and reduction of inequalities. It was also often argued that to break their stagnation, the LDCs should have large, coordinated investment packages – a 'big push' – of mutually supporting projects. To be able to achieve this kind of concerted effort, most LDCs started to carry out 'development planning'. This did not mean that they became planned economies of the Soviet type (with a few exceptions). Most of them retained much of the private enterprise economy, although attempts were made to direct development to a larger extent than before. The areas emphasized, at this time, were industrialization, import substitution and investment in infrastructure.

By and by, knowledge about the process of change in the LDCs was gathered, and economists realized that there were particular problems related to development and growth in these countries. It is now obvious that it is not just the lack of investment capital which hinders growth in the LDCs, as can be seen from the experiences of OPEC countries such as Nigeria and Indonesia. There is a whole spectrum of restrictions which must be attacked simultaneously. Yotopoulos and Nugent (1976) point out that far too much attention has been paid to various fundamentalist dogmas, not only capital fundamentalism, but also sectoral fundamentalism (industry or agriculture), import-substitution fundamentalism, or planning fundamentalism. The linkages between different problems have often been obscured or overlooked. There has also been 'too much emphasis on development as a uniform, smooth, and equilibrating process of continuous marginal adjustments. Conversely, too little attention has been devoted to the study of structure and discontinuous processes and disequilibria . . .'. 'Yet to a large extent development is the study of disequilibrium and structural change, the causes of which must be understood.'

(Yotopoulos and Nugent, 1976, pp. 12−15).

Moreover, it has also become clear to development economists that it is not sufficient to concentrate on the goal of maximizing the growth of GDP. Many people have gained very little from the increase in aggregate production, and the situation of some has even deteriorated. Thus the issues of income distribution and poverty eradication have come into focus.

3.3 On methodology

During the period since the Second World War development economics has gradually emerged as a subject in its own right, although, by its very nature, it is a combination of elements from other fields of economics (as well as other sciences, in some cases).

Development economics differs from other branches of economics mainly with respect to its domain. It deals with a type of economy other than that of mainstream economics, which is mainly concerned with the developed, capitalistic market economies. These analyses cannot be applied on Third World countries without adjustment.

If we consider, for example, short-run macroeconomics and monetary policy (Reynolds, 1971, pp. 266−8), we find that they must be of a different character in an underdeveloped economy because of the different setting. Fluctuations in the industrialized countries are often associated with changes in private investment, for example, while in the LDCs the sources would more likely be fluctuations in export proceeds, poor harvests, or large budget deficits. The standard macro model assumes a certain degree of homogeneity in behaviour and working markets, which makes aggregation possible. These preconditions are not present in most underdeveloped economies. The same goes for the prerequisites of monetary theory. The supply of financial assets is very limited, and habits of holding money and securities are poorly developed, as is the network of financial institutions. The consequence of this is that the standard policy instruments are difficult to use.

Economic science can be regarded as a tool-kit, where the usefulness of different tools in different settings in each case has to be determined on the basis of the criteria of realism and relevance. The art of development economics is very much the art of imaginative use and adjustments of the tools of standard theory.

Yotopoulos and Nugent find that contributions to the field of development economics have tended

> towards one of two poles − introspective generalization and immanent empiricism − both of which fall short of scientific analysis. Contributions of the former type have mainly reflected the paradigm of evolution of the

now developed countries, which may not be wholly applicable. The immanent empiricists, on the other hand, give infinite weight to deviations from the special case of the DCs. Instead of looking for a theory, the immanent empiricist looks at the data hard enough and long enough until some 'general principles' become clear, less by formal logic than by insight.

(1976, p. 11)

Because of the recentness of the subject and its eclectic nature, development economics must be considered less developed than other branches of economics with an old and established tradition. This has also meant that there is less agreement as to what constitutes the accepted body of theory within the field. A variety of approaches can be found in the literature.

Chenery (1975) argues that from a methodological standpoint most approaches within development economics can be grouped under one of three headings: neoclassical, neo-Marxist, and structuralist. These approaches, however, do not form completely distinct sets, and each contains elements that ought to be incorporated in a 'general theory of development', if such a theory can ever be achieved. Since the 1960s very few attempts have been made by traditional development economists to formulate a 'general' theory of development, since it has been very difficult to find factors and relationships that are sufficiently stable at different times and in different countries.

During the same period, however, the so-called dependency school grew in importance. Proponents of this school argued that it provided the general explanation of the underdevelopment of the Third World. We shall come back to this below, and see that also among dependency theorists the claims are much more modest today.

Thus, as yet, the great synthesis has not emerged – and it may well never do so. Even within the different schools there is much bewilderment, and the claims about explanatory power are very modest. None of the above mentioned paradigms can be wholeheartedly accepted as a basis for a study of income distribution and development. Eclecticism is necessary to give an adequate representation of an LDC. Chenery (1975, p. 310) notes that the structuralist approach 'attempts to identify specific rigidities, lags, and other characteristics of the structure of developing economies that affect economic adjustments and the choice of development policy'. If this very general definition of structuralism is accepted, it may incorporate traits from the other traditions as well.

The pattern of structural change is a fundamental determinant of the development of inequality and the incidence of poverty in an underdeveloped economy. It is, therefore, essential that it is viewed as an economy with sectors with very different characteristics – as a fragmented or disintegrated economy – and the relationships and relative development of these are of central interest. A model for the analysis of income distribution in an underdeveloped country should therefore ideally incorporate both the structural disequilibria that exist and features of equilibrium to guarantee the consistency of the solution of the model. Yotopoulos and Nugent argue (1976, p. xxii) that 'the most important area for synthesizing lies in the combination of neoclassical equilibrium analysis with structural disequilibrium approaches'.

To determine income distribution in an LDC one must first explain income distribution by sector, secondly the distribution by factors, and lastly map the distribution obtained in the two first steps into a household income distribution. It is mainly for the determination of sectoral and functional distribution that development theory can make a contribution. To take the last step to the size distribution of income one must look at income distribution theories for guidance.

3.4 General explanations of development
In this section a brief discussion of some important attempts at explaining development will be presented. Their usefulness for the study of income distribution will be ascertained. The dualism and dependency schools will not be discussed here, but in the following two sections.

To formulate a theoretical approach to development which incorporates all aspects of some importance is impossible because there are so many. Moreover, a number of factors, which have been suggested to be important, are decidedly difficult to quantify and incorporate in a scientific analysis. There is therefore a trade-off between the broadness of the scope and the precision of the analysis. Of course, precision won at the cost of neglect of the most essential factors is of little value. One must therefore try to find a balance between completeness of coverage and precision. Studies that go too far in either direction give little insight or knowledge.

Adelman and Morris (1967) have used multivariate analysis to find out what social, political and economic variables are important for economic development. This type of analysis is mainly a sort of hunt for correlation and the theory is more or less absent. This means that one must be careful about jumping from correlation to causality. Yet, the analysis may be suggestive and give ideas for further research. Adelman and Morris conclude that social factors seem to be very important determinants of the level of GDP, particularly among countries at the lowest per capita income levels. They therefore draw the tentative conclusion, which seems reasonable, that particularly for economies in the very poorest category development requires both social and economic transformation. The problem is that a general model of social and economic development is beyond reach. The question therefore is: What social factors can and should one try to incorporate in a model for the analysis of development or income distribution?

Let us briefly consider how economists of various periods have dealt with the problem of development. The classical economists were much concerned with the causes of growth and the long-run evolution of society. Smith, Ricardo, and Marx all presented more or less systematized 'grand' theories encompassing the whole of society. Smith viewed the evolution as a gradual transition through hunting, pastoral, agricultural, commercial, and manufacturing stages. Ricardo anticipated stagnation in the long run as a result of diminishing returns to land. Marx saw evolution as a transition, first from feudalism to capitalism, and then finally to socialism. The neo-classical economists who later came to dominate economics had less to say about growth and development.

One of the few economists who did have something to say about development during the pre-second World War period was Joseph Schumpeter, who considered growth and stability to be contradictory concepts. He defined development as 'the carrying out of new combinations', such as the introduction of new goods, new methods of production, opening of new markets, finding new sources of supply of raw materials or the carrying out of a new organization of industry. Schumpeter emphasized the importance of the entrepreneur or innovator. This type of idea was taken over by Hagen (1962) and McClelland (1961), who argue that the entrepreneur is the engine of growth in LDCs. The social climate and attitudinal factors obviously are of importance, but to model such factors is extremely difficult.

Since the Second World War, starting with Harrod and Domar, a lot of effort has been devoted to research on growth theory. The theories developed within this tradition have, however, mainly been concerned with abstract economies, which resemble the DCs more than the LDCs. In the latter there are disequilibria and imperfect markets, and the structure itself is undergoing rapid change.

Rostow (1960) presented a stage theory inspired by the Harrod – Domar model which was supposed to constitute an alternative to the Marxist scheme. Rostow argued that societies pass through five different stages: (i) the traditional society; (ii) the long period during which the economic and social preconditions for growth evolve; (iii) the take-off, when there is a rapid rise in productive investment, high rate of growth of manufacturing production, and political, social and institutional frameworks conducive to growth emerge; (iv) the drive to maturity; and (v) the era of high mass consumption. This theory is one of the most thoroughly criticized theories of long-run development, and Rostow gradually introduced a number of qualifications, which meant that the theory no longer prescribed any definite sequence of development. A number of patterns were assumed to be possible.

For example, Kuznets (1961) denied that there always is a take-off, with a discontinuous jump in savings and growth rates. On the contrary, many countries have gone through a very gradual process. Fishlow (1965, p. 116) pointed out that it is not possible to determine whether an actual economy is really at the take-off stage or not. Statements about this would amount to nothing more than sheer guesswork. Rostow's model is basically a classificatory scheme, but since it is not possible to determine at what stage an economy really is, its usefulness is little.

A theory on this level of generalization may, even if it is not operational, give insights and raise important questions, but Rostow's theory hardly does that either. It does not tell how and why a country moves from one stage to another, which would be its most interesting contribution. The theory is therefore of little analytical interest.

Grandiose theories are always difficult to verify empirically. Gerschenkron (1962, pp. 31−51) has made extensive historical comparisons of economic development in different countries, and he is impressed by the diversity of experiences as far as industrial development is concerned. It may therefore be concluded, both on theoretical and empirical grounds, that grand theories such as Rostow's are much too general to provide a basis for an empirical analysis of development and income distribution in a less developed country.

There are also differences between the situation of the now developed countries and the LDCs, which means that care must be exercised when comparing the problems of the LDCs with the earlier experiences of the now developed countries. Meier (1976, pp. 93−9) emphasizes the following differences between the LDCs of today and Europe of yesterday:

1. The LDCs have a different relationship with the rest of the world.
2. They start from a lower income level in their attempts to accelerate growth.
3. They may be in a sequence of growth different from that of Europe.

4. They have as yet not experienced any significant agricultural improvements which can serve as a basis for industrialization.
5. The population pressure is worse.
6. There are socio-cultural and political differences.

A number of factors thus make it necessary to be careful with historical parallels, even if all the experiences of the DCs certainly are not irrelevant.

Meier goes on to list a number of advantages and drawbacks that follow from being a late developer. First, there are a number of consequences, which have made it more difficult to develop in a world with more developed countries. These factors are:

1. Rapid reduction in death-rates, which aggravates the population pressure.
2. Introduction of labour-saving technology developed in countries where labour is scarce has aggravated the underutilization of labour.
3. The organizations and skills that are developed in the DCs are ill-adopted to the needs of the LDCs.
4. Technical progress has harmed trade prospects. Synthetic products have been substituted for raw materials produced by the LDCs.
5. There can be very little emigration from the LDCs compared with what was possible from Europe during the nineteenth century. Moreover, it is mainly the best educated people who leave the LDCs.

One might also add that we today have a situation with fierce superpower competition and enormous military expenditure, which diverts resources to unproductive uses. The lack of mutual trust and cooperation also hinders concerted efforts to assist LDCs.

Of course, there are also things on the positive side:

1. The LDCs can draw on the larger accumulated stock of knowledge.
2. The LDCs may benefit from a flow of resources from the DCs.
3. The example of the DCs has created a consciousness and desire for development in the poor countries.

It is not easy to determine if positive or negative factors dominate, but at least in aggregate terms the growth of many LDCs during the last twenty years has been rapid. It is when the position of the poorest strata is considered that the picture becomes less bright.

It may be concluded from this section that the grand, general theories which were much discussed a few years ago are of little use as a theoretical basis for an empirical analysis of income distribution in LDCs. The differences among countries in experience are too large and the theories lack precision. To analyse income distribution one requires considerable disaggregation; macro-oriented approaches are therefore of little help.

Another conclusion that can be reached is that one must be careful not to make too much of historical parallels with other countries at other times. The situation today is naturally not totally unique, but the present combination of forces has never existed before. However, tools developed in another context may certainly be useful if properly adjusted to take the differences in context into account.

3.5 Dual economy theory
One of the most influential approaches to the analysis of development problems is the dualism theory. In the basic dualistic model, it is assumed that the economy is divided into two sectors, which are largely independent of each other and very different. They are linked to each other mainly through the flow of labour from the subsistence sector to the modern sector. The traditional sector is assumed to be stagnant and producing for subsistence. The modern sector is assumed to constitute the dynamic element in the economy. The dualistic structure is a consequence of the introduction of a modern element in a traditional economy. The creation of export enclaves under colonialism is a typical example of this.

Advocates of a neoclassical approach argue that market imperfections such as dualism will disappear fairly rapidly, while the proponents of a dualistic (or structuralist) approach assume that the segmentation will prevail for a long time. Of course, the assumption of a lack of communication between the sectors is vital for the continued existence of the cleavage.

Much has been written that can be characterized as dualism analysis, but basically three different types of approaches can be distinguished, namely theories of social, technological, and economic dualism. The concept of social dualism was first introduced by Boeke (1953), who describes a dual society as one in which two parallel social systems with completely different ways of life exist. The concept of technological dualism is mainly attributable to Eckaus (1955), who argues that the elasticity of substitution between factors of production is zero in the modern sector, while it is large in the traditional sector. The modern sector thus produces with fixed technical coefficients and a comparatively capital-intensive technology which provides little employment. In the subsistence sector, where there is scope for substitution, much labour will be used.

The model of economic dualism incorporates features of both these variants. It is based on the assumption of the existence of two distinct sectors with limited contact, as was mentioned above, and emphasizes the need to increase the savings rate. Lewis's (1954) model is the classic one in the field.

In his famous 1954 article W.A. Lewis formulated a model of the development process which came to influence very strongly the views of a whole generation of development economists and policy-makers. Lewis distinguishes between two different sectors of the economy with very different characteristics. Development is equivalent to the gradual swelling of one of the sectors – the modern one – and the gradual decline of the other – the traditional one. Development is conceived of as a process whereby the modern sector absorbs the surplus labour of the traditional sector, and the transformation of the traditional sector will not start until its labour surplus has been eliminated. When this stage is reached neoclassical analysis can be used.

The dualistic model in its pure form has been criticised by many. For example, Griffin attacks the model on the grounds that it is at variance with facts.

> Indeed it now seems most unlikely that the assumptions of the model of economic dualism – and particularly the assumptions about the extent of rural unemployment, the relationship of wages to the marginal product of labour, the willingness of peasants to save, and the response of workers and farmers to economic incentives – can withstand empirical scrutiny.
>
> (1969, pp. 24–5)

The use of the concept of disguised unemployment or surplus labour means that there is a risk of overlooking the changes that are necessary to raise productivity of those remaining after the so-called surplus has been removed. Another problem in Lewis's approach relates to the demand side of the investment process. Lewis was concerned with increasing savings through increased profits, and thus assumed that there would be no problem of investing the money once it was there.

Still, this presupposes the existence of capitalists (or government organizations) willing to invest, conditions conducive to investment and that the investments are made in the activities with the highest returns. It is argued that the modern sector pays a relatively small part of total income in wages, and this in turn implies that effective demand is kept down and little further investment is stimulated, unless the economy is competitive in foreign markets.

The sequence of development predicted by Lewis has, in many countries, not been realized, since the modern sector has not been able to expand employment to the degree predicted. It has barely managed to keep pace with the growth of the labour force; in many countries the share of modern sector employment in total employment has hardly increased in spite of the rapid growth of GDP.

Yotopoulos and Nugent point out that

> if the mechanisms that lead to equilibrium are weak, or if the development is a disequilibrium process, integrationist policies, such as the labour surplus strategy based on development of the industrial sector, will accentuate dualism and therefore be selfdefeating. A more appropriate policy in the same context would be to invest in agriculture and to plug up the leakages to the non-agricultural sector. (1976, p. 256)

If dualism and market imperfections persist inequality will also be persistent.

Are the underdeveloped countries then doomed to live for a very long time with a subsistence sector, which constitutes a drag on development? The agricultural sector will certainly remain dominant in terms of employment, at least in the foreseeable furture in most LDCs. Still, there seems to be a process of commercialization coming about, in African economies such as Kenya, in a way different from the one predicted by, for example, Fei and Ranis (1964). There the peasant economy is in a state of transition from subsistence production to semi-monetary and monetary production. Monetary production gradually encroaches on the peasant sector, and it is that, rather than labour being shifted out of the sector, which transforms it. This kind of transformation has gone further in non-African LDCs.

Lewis, Fei and Ranis all predicted that in the long run both agricultural and industrial sectors will adjust to relative factor endowments and prices, and that the dualistic structure will thus disappear. Until this happens their approach is relevant.

To sum up: A number of elements in the dualistic model have been shown to be at variance with facts. Still, the theory emphasizes that the economies in the Third World are disintegrated, i.e. that they contain sectors with greatly varying levels of productivity; this must be taken into account in the analyses of these economies. The division of the economy into only two sectors may be too restrictive to capture the complexity of these economies, but in a theoretical analysis it may be acceptable to simplify.

The emphasis of the persistence of 'dualism' is important. Yotopoulos and Nugent (1976, p. xxx) argue that this 'is explained by the persistence of the market imperfections that originally gave rise to dualism. These imperfections usually result from the efforts of individual groups to establish rent-maximizing positions', and once such positions are established, they tend to be perpetuated. 'In this way, dualism and the unequal distribution of income are intimately interconnected and both are perpetuated.' (See also Lundahl and Ndlela, 1980.)

3.6 The dependency paradigm

During the 1960s an alternative school of thought on development emerged — the so-called dependency school. This was an outgrowth of earlier Marxist theories and of ideas developed within the so-called ECLA school. In a survey article Palma (1978) describes the theoretical background and the different variants of this approach.

The Marxist debate on underdevelopment has centred on the concept of imperialism. On a general level imperialism can be defined as 'a relationship of a hegemonical state to people or nations under its control' (Lichtheim, 1971, p. 10). However, such a definition does not imply that imperialism is a phenomenon that refers to the capitalistic system. This is implied in Marxism, where the concept is used to describe relations between developed and underdeveloped countries within the capitalistic system. Later on, the concept came to denote a specific phase — the monopolistic phase — of the development of this system. Thus, the concept has been used in two somewhat different connotations. If imperialism is considered from the more restrictive viewpoint, i.e. as something referring to the relations between the developed and the underdeveloped nations within the world capitalistic system, three different phases can be distinguished (Sutcliffe, 1972, p. 172).

1. Plunder (of wealth and slaves) and export of manufactured goods to the periphery (Marx and Engels).
2. Export of capital, competition about raw materials and growth of the monopolies (Lenin).
3. A complex, post-colonial form of dependence for the countries of the periphery, where foreign capital, profit repatriation and deterioration of terms of trade together restrict, distort or stop economic development.

In all three phases the interests of the centre are favoured relative to the interests of the periphery. In the first case the primary capital accumulation is simplified and markets for export of manufactures are created. In the second case the mature capitalism can escape from the tendency for a fall in the rate of profit. It can at least be postponed by a geographic expansion of the economy. In the third case it is possible for the developed capitalistic countries to protect themselves against competition which could threaten the stability, organization and growth of the capitalistic system.

Palma tries to show that there is a specific analytical approach corresponding to each of these variants. The first one, represented by Marx and Engels, views capitalism as a historically progressive system which is spread from the developed to the underdeveloped countries through a continuous process of destruction and elimination of the pre-capitalistic structures. The second one is represented by the classics in imperialism analysis (e.g. Lenin). This group sees the process as more complex with interdependence between external and internal structures. They emphasize the difficulties of 'late' industrialization, the role of foreign capital, and the great capacity for survival of pre-capitalistic structures. However, it was predicted that once the colonial ties were severed, an industrialization would take place, i.e. the underdeveloped countries would go through a development process similar to the one of the now developed countries. The third approach, which to a large extent emanates from Baran (1957), accepts, almost like an 'axiomatic truth' (Palma, 1978, p. 886), that no country in the Third World can break out of its economic dependence and eventually reach a level of development comparable to the one of the now developed industrial economies. Capitalism is here no longer considered to be a historically progressive force. It is from this starting point that the so-called dependency school has evolved.

Because so much has been written on dependency theory it is difficult to determine exactly what it is. A reasonable attempt to sum up the main elements has been made by Leys (1977, pp. 92–3). He summarizes what he means by dependency theory:

1. The state of underdevelopment in the Third World is the result of the same process that created development in the industrialized countries.
2. The prime mover of the system is capital seeking profits. The global pattern of investment determines the pattern of growth.
3. This meant that capitalists accumulated capital where profits were the highest. This led to the extraction of surplus from the Third World , which perpetuated the low levels of productivity and the structure of dependence. The economies remained externally oriented.
4. This meant that local initiatives were blocked, and no autonomous

development path could be followed because of, for example, the smallness of the market.

5. There emerged classes in the periphery with interests common to those of the bourgeoisie of the centre.
6. The concept of underdevelopment refers to this self-perpetuating process, its structure and result. Dependency sometimes means the same thing, but sometimes it refers to the non-autonomous character of the processes governing development in the periphery.

The dependency school is by no means a homogeneous movement. Different writers emphasize different aspects, and some consider capitalistic development to be totally impossible for underdeveloped countries; others think that some capitalist development is possible, but that it must remain of a subordinate nature. Palma suggests the following classification of the existing approaches:

1. The first group tries to construct a theory of underdevelopment, where the dependent character of the economies is the factor determining the entire process of change (e.g. Frank, 1967).
2. The other group tries to reformulate the ECLA analysis, which strongly emphasizes the irrelevance of trade theories.
3. The third category, with which Palma sympathizes, abstains from presenting a mechanico – formal theory of dependency. Instead concrete cases of dependency are studied. This school is considered by Palma (1978, p. 899), to constitute a sound reaction to 'the excessive theorizing in a vacuum characteristic of other analyses of dependency'. He also notes that 'the theoretical reasoning which can be developed at present concerning capitalist development in Latin America is strictly limited by the lack of case studies; the need at the moment is for "analytic" rather than "synthetic" work'.

The first school was initiated by Baran who argued that development in the periphery was inimical to the dominant interest in the centre. To impede such development, the centre capitalists formed coalitions with the pre-capitalist elites in the periphery. These coalitions then made it possible to extract economic surplus, and this, in turn, reduces the chances of economic development in these countries. The surplus that actually is created either leaves the country, or is squandered by the elite. Moreover, the problem is not just that the size of investments is kept down, but that the investments that actually take place have a relatively small stimulating effect on the local economy, since much of the investment goods have to be bought abroad.

Andre Gunder Frank (1967) starts from this and concludes that the only alternative left is socialist revolution. Within the present system only underdevelopment is possible. He argues first that the periphery has been incorporated in the world economy since the first days of colonialism; secondly, that this incorporation immediately transformed these economies into capitalistic economies; thirdly, that this was accomplished by an unbreakable centre – periphery chain, through which surplus gradually is transferred to the centre. The only way out of the situation of structural underdevelopment, according to Frank, is through a break of the centre – periphery relations. Within the system no development is possible.

Palma criticizes Frank on a number of points, but the one that is of most interest in this context is that it has been shown that capitalist development actually can occur in the Third World. Thus, progress is not completely blocked.

Lall (1975) has presented a very thorough critique of the dependency school. His main point is that the dependency theorists emphasize traits that tend to be characteristic of capitalistic development in general and thus cannot be considered to be characteristics of a special process of capitalistic underdevelopment. Further, he argues that it has not been possible to find a causal link between these characteristics and underdevelopment. If the dependency school is to have any analytical function, it must satisfy two criteria according to Lall:

1. It must specify certain characteristics that exist in dependent countries, but not in non-dependent countries.
2. These characteristics must be shown to affect development in the dependent countries in a negative way.

This has not been done and Lall (1975, p. 800) notes that 'one sometimes gets the impression on reading the literature that "dependency" is defined in a circular manner: less developed countries are poor because they are dependent, and any characteristics that they display signify dependency'.

Thus, Lall does not deny that many of the factors about which the dependency theorists talk actually do exist in the LDCs, but he argues that these factors together cannot be taken to define a separate category of dependency. Lall discusses the different characteristics and finds that it is extremely difficult to define a state of dependency from them. He looks at (i) dependence on foreign capital; (ii) use of foreign technology in a small industrial sector; (iii) specialization on export of raw materials and labour-intensive goods; (iv) unequal exchange; and (v) increasing inequality.

Lall thinks that what many really want to say is that capitalism as such is undesirable rather than that capitalistic development, on its own terms, is impossible. The concept is often applied to factors that have always accompanied capitalistic development in certain stages. Thus, these are not a consequence of the fact that the countries are dependent, but of the choice of a capitalistic development path. Attempts at definition have been arbitrary and analytically useless.

Leys (1977) points out that it is necessary to remain on a very high level of abstraction if the fundamental difficulties of using the concept of dependence are to be avoided. Some of the problems he points out are that:

1. The concept of development is unclear.
2. Concrete typologies of centres and peripheries are seldom presented.
3. The theory incorporates only economic variables and is static and underdevelopment is considered to be inevitable.
4. It has not been possible to explain what causes underdevelopment.

The theory cannot explain why more capital is not invested in the Third World to exploit the cheap labour available there. The theory only gives a general description of the existing situation and has no theoretical explanation of why certain mechanisms develop at certain times.

Palma sums up his views on the first group with the conclusion that their statements are contrary to facts, and that the theories are static and ahistorical. He admits that there is capitalistic exploitation in Latin America, but 'to deny . . . that capitalist development is taking place in some countries in Latin America and in some parts of the rest of the periphery is no less than absurd' (Palma, 1978, p. 904).

The second group of dependency theorists took their starting point in the ideas of Prebisch. Since the import-substitution policy did not succeed as expected, this group also tended to arrive at pessimistic conclusions about the inevitability of underdevelopment and stagnation. However, just as they were starting to publish their findings, international trade started to expand, terms of trade improved for Latin American countries, and some countries could benefit from this and experience rapid growth in GNP.

Palma is of the opinion that it is about time to give up the stag-nationist thesis and to go on to analyse concrete situations of underdevelopment. This is what is done within the third group. Also within this group the Latin American countries are considered to be integrated in a world capitalistic system, where the dynamism lies outside the countries in the periphery. To understand the dynamism of the world capitalist system is essential, says Palma. Multinationals have started to invest in Third World countries, and dependency and industrialization no longer necessarily contradict each other. This third group also tries to emphasize the analysis of internal factors such as inequality in the income distribution. To state that a country is dependent is not sufficient, if one is interested in coming to any useful conclusions with regard to income distribution.

Leys writes in his survey article that

> it is becoming clear that 'underdevelopment' and 'dependency' theory is no longer serviceable and must be transcended. The evidence for this is (i) theoretical repetition and stagnation in the literature on underdevelopment and dependency theory; and (ii) the existence of fundamental problems of analysis which UDT (underdevelopment theory) cannot solve, or even formulate, and central problems of development strategy which are linked with these, and about which UDT is either silent – or ambiguous; an evident lack of practical impact in favour of the popular force in the struggles in Third World countries, but on the contrary, a marked tendency for the Underdevelopment/dependency perspective to be co-opted by developmentalists allied to international capital.
>
> (1977 p. 92)

Like theorists within the other schools of development analysis advocates of the dependency analysis now make more modest claims than before. Few people today argue that a general development theory exists which is applicable in all circumstances. More time must now be devoted to concrete studies aimed at accumulating scientific knowledge before any meaningful generalizations can be made. Maybe it will never be meaningful to generalize about development? At the least, one must be very cautious.

Both dependency theory and dualism theory emphasize the cleavage of the underdeveloped economies. One part has a lot of contact with the developed countries, but is only to a minor extent integrated with the rest of the economy in the periphery. Thus, both theories agree, to a considerable extent, in their description of the actual situation, although some writers argue that the two theories are completely different. Sunkel (1973) has written an article in which he discusses the transnational integration within the world capitalistic system, which is combined with national disintegration. Some segments are integrated with the world market, while the rest of the economy is left more or less to itself. According to him, the advancement of modernization introduces a wedge between the integrated and segregated elements (Sunkel, 1973). This very much resembles earlier discussions of export enclaves and the lack of secondary spread effects from these.

Both the dualistic theory and the dependency theory underline that the structural characteristics of the economies in the Third World are vitally important. As long as the disintegrated structure of these economies remain, there will be no far-reaching price equalization of factors employed in different sectors. Segmented markets will therefore prevail with very decisive effects on the income distribution.

3.7 Analysis of capital formation

The savings and investment process is important for income distribution. The process of capital formation consists of three phases: (i) the act of saving in real terms; (ii) the channelling of savings from saver to investor through the credit market; and (iii) the act of investment itself.

Savings can be increased through voluntary restrictions of consumption, through taxation or compulsory lending to the government, or merely as a by-product of inflation. Of course, foreign resources can also increase the availability of funds. Determination of investment demand is more complicated, and will not be discussed here.

Savings rate and capital formation are important determinants of the rate of growth of an economy, even if other factors also play a considerable role. Investments determine the pattern of growth, which in turn generates a certain pattern of income opportunities. The pattern of savings also strongly influences income distribution, through its effects on the distribution of the ownership of wealth. Incomes from wealth constitute a large share of GDP, particularly in LDCs.

In a fragmented capital market the rate of return on investment in physical capital may be expected to vary, and it is often much higher than the interest rate paid on bank deposits. It is possible that investment in human capital gives a return between these two levels. If that is the case, wage-earners who can only get the bank rate will tend to save very little, while capital owners who can get a high return on real investments will have a high saving propensity. This point is the reason for McKinnon's (1973) advocacy for liberating capital markets and increasing bank deposit interest rates as a means of capital accumulation in the process of economic development. It would also be beneficial as far as income distribution is concerned, since money is now transferred from small savers to often well-off borrowers. The analysis of savings behaviour in different socioeconomic categories is one important aspect of the study of income distribution, particularly its development over time. Mikesell and Zinser (1973) have surveyed the literature on savings functions in LDCs, but they find that little is known about the savings behaviour of different categories.

3.8 Multisectoral analysis

Income distribution analysis in LDCs need to be disaggregated. As long as the great differences among sectors in productivity and in other aspects remain, these cannot be aggregated, since that would make the differentiation, which really is the object of the analysis, disappear.

Structural change is the essence of development, and there are a number of economic forces that generate such change. Changes in the composition of demand, as a result of differences in income elasticities of demand, lead to changes in the relative size of different economic sectors. There is substitution on the input as well as the output side of the production process. Due attention must also be given to intersectoral resource transfers and the creation of markets for output. The input-output linkages must be taken into account. To come up with realistic results the analysis must encompass the entire system of production, and it must also incorporate the most relevant institutional characteristics of the economy.

The interdependence between agriculture and industry has been intensively discussed among development economists. It has been emphasized that early development in the DCs took place, among other things, because of the development of agriculture, which is important also for industrial development and the whole economy. An efficient agricultural sector provides food and raw materials. It provides an investible surplus, it provides demand for the output of the industrial sector, and it may help easing the foreign exchange constraint.

Meier strongly underlines the importance of agriculture and writes that if there is to be structural transformation in the long run, there must, in the short run, first be a transformation of agriculture to make it possible for the sector to make the above mentioned contributions. He also notes that

> misallocation of resources between agriculture and manufactures is probably rarely a major cause of poverty and backwardness, except where government through tariffs, discriminatory taxation and expenditure policies, and failure to provide on a regionally non-discriminatory pattern facilities for education, health promotion, and technical training, is itself responsible for this misallocation   (Meier, 1976, p. 567)

However, this is what has happened in many cases. The import-substitution policy implied a systematic discrimination of agriculture relative to industry, and this certainly made the income distribution more uneven in many countries. The vast majority of the poor belong to the agricultural sector and their incomes were lowered by this policy (relative to what it would have been with a more neutral policy). Thus, agricultural development needs to be emphasized not only because of its instrumental value in the respects mentioned above, but also because it generates incomes directly for the main poverty target group, the peasants and landless labour (see Lipton, 1977).

The sectoral pattern of growth and the intersectoral interdependencies are very important determinants of the evolution of the income distribution pattern. It is mainly with regard to this part of the income determination process that development theory has something to contribute to the analysis. Once the functional and sectoral distribution has been determined and the final step to the individual level is to be taken, development theory can provide no answer. When determining income distribution within each factor category, it is necessary to consider the ownership of physical capital as well as human capital or other factors operating at the micro level.

3.9 Foreign trade analysis
It is also of great importance to understand the relationship between foreign trade and income distribution. Whether prices are determined domestically or on the international market has considerable income distribution consequences, and institutional knowledge about the character of the trade policy pursued is here essential. If a country faces promising trade prospects, for example because of an abundance of natural resources of some sort, it may find it beneficial to adjust its output according to its existing comparative advantage and trade as much as possible. This means that the country may delay or abstain from the course of structural change that it would otherwise consider optimal. In such a case it may pay to have an 'unbalanced' or very specialized production structure.

Whether it is beneficial in the long run to adjust to short-run comparative advantage has been discussed by many since the days of Friedrich List, who argued the case for 'infant industry' protection. No general answer can be given to the question. The circumstances may differ considerably between countries and over time. The debate on balanced versus unbalanced growth which raged during the 1950s and early 1960s more or less disregarded foreign trade, on the assumption that the income elasticity of demand for LDC exports was very low. There was an almost universal application of import-substitution policy in the LDCs. However, in recent years several LDCs have shown that they can compete successfully on the world market. The theory of balanced growth emphasized the smallness of the market, indivisibilities and external effects of investments. One obvious way to overcome the market limitation is to sell on the world market.

3.10 Labour market analysis

In the explanation of size distribution of income the analysis of the labour market is also very important. However, this is one of the areas of development economics, where much remains to be done. To start with there are conceptual problems (see Bigsten, 1980, Chapter 8). Then there are disintegrated markets or markets in disequilibrium, while for analytical reasons one would prefer to treat the problem as a general equilibrium problem.

Basically, there are three types of employment problems, namely (i) the shortage of work opportunities; (ii) inadequate income from work; and (iii) underutilized labour resources. The first and last problems are reflections of market imbalances, while the second reflects the generally low level of productivity in the economy.

The labour market in the LDCs, at least the organized, or modern labour market, is often characterized by underpriced capital and over-priced labour. This, together with an import-substitution policy that has constituted a levy on agriculture, has led to increasing pressure on the urban economy, with open unemployment and a swelling informal sector. The migration flow to urban centres is explained by Todaro (1969) by a comparison of expected incomes in rural relative with those in urban areas. The urban – rural link is thus of great importance in the analysis of income distribution. Urban development cannot solve the urban unemployment problem in a situation with very low incomes in the rural areas. Expansion of employment opportunities in urban areas only attracts new migrants. Todaro's model is a very simple job-search model. It explains migrant behaviour and selectivity, but it may be more interesting to have a model that relates to the demand side of the labour market. The job-competition model as developed by Thurow (1969) is such a model.

The automatic mechanism of wage competition has in most cases not led to an equalization of wages between agriculture and the rest of the economy. In the wage-competition model it is assumed that workers compete against each other on the basis of wages, while in the job-competition model they compete for jobs on the basis of their individual characteristics. In this model it is not the marginal productivity of the worker which determines the wage rate of the job, but instead the marginal productivity of the job which determines the wage rate. The firm is on its demand curve, while the households (workers) are off their supply curve.

In the job-competition model wages are paid on the basis of job characteristics. These can be of different kinds, e.g. with regard to the amount of capital per worker. The characteristics of the workers only determine their place in the labour queue. The employer fills the vacancies from the top of the queue. Employers use the individual characteristics as a proxy for the trainability of the workers. By employing workers with a good background the employer minimizes his training costs.

In this model on-the-job training is essential. Since marginal productivity of capital is a function of the amount and quality of the labour with which it is employed, it is in the interest of the employer to pay for on-the-job training, even if the individual himself would not be willing to undertake it and pay for it himself.

According to this model,

> the labour market is not primarily a place for determining the wage-rate endogenously, by matching demand and supplies of different kinds of skills. Instead, the labour market matches trainable individuals with jobs that have training opportunities, the amount of on-the-job training required to bring a worker up to the marginal productivity of the job being endogenously determined.   (Yotopoulos and Nugent, 1976, p. 232)

The conclusion that follows from this model is that it is not possible to reduce wage differentials and inequality by increasing the supply of job skills as a result of either educational investments or investments in migration from farms to the urban sector.

The emphasis on capital accumulation in the early development literature, e.g. in models of economic dualism (Lewis, 1954), led to an over-emphasis on capital accumulation in development policy. This was reflected in distorted factor prices – i.e. in this case undervaluation of capital: from 'overvalued exchange rates, accelerated depreciation allowances, negative effective rates of protection for imported capital goods, tax rebates, and tying foreign aid to the importation of the donor country's capital goods' (Yotopoulos and Nugent, 1976, p. 233). This led to increased capital intensity in production, and the marginal productivity of labour in employment increased. This in turn led 'to more on-the-job training for the skilled workers in this subsector, bringing them up to the marginal productivity of the job'. This tended to increase the wage-rates of modern sector employees, and led to a gradually increasing income gap between employees in this sector and labour outside it.

What would be the result of increased education in the job-competition model? Trickling down of skills certainly, but how would this affect inequality? If rural – urban migration is selective (i.e. it is the best educated and most efficient workers who move), which seems to be the case, it is not the marginal individuals in the rural areas who move to urban areas. Then migration will lower the average quality of labour in the countryside. This might retard the growth of productivity in the rural areas, and thus further increase the gap between urban and rural areas. Increased education in the countryside may therefore be an unfeasible policy of equalization, unless it is combined with other policies aimed at increasing access to employment opportunities in rural areas.

The way to increase employment according to this model is to increase the demand for skills rather than the supply of skills, e.g. by decreasing the costs of training to employers, say through wage subsidies. 'The wage, in other words, is the independent variable in the economic model, and it is exogeneously determined by considerations of status and prestige, in accordance with the value judgements of society.' (Yotopoulos and Nugent, 1976, p. 234).

The job-competition model is of great interest in the context of underdevelopment. It is congruent with the imbalances and disintegration emphasized in the development theories discussed above. The model may therefore be a useful tool in development analysis.

3.11 Conclusions

The purpose of this review of development economics was to find out what it could contribute to the analysis of income distribution analysis in Third World countries. I have argued that the development problem is a multidimensional one and that a structuralist approach would be the best alternative. It has also been argued that one should be wary of generalizations with regard to the development process. Specific traits of individual countries must be taken into account.

Both dual economy analysis and dependency theory emphasize the disintegrated character of Third World countries. The economic structure must obviously be given a central role in the analysis.

Several studies have shown the danger of partial analysis of income distribution. The links between sectors and regions must therefore be considered within some kind of consistency framework.

Finally, to be able to analyse the link from functional and sectoral distribution to household distribution, labour market analysis is vital. Before specifying the model to use in the analysis, the strength of competitive forces in a given country needs to be empirically investigated.

References

Adelman, I, and Morris, C.T. (1967), *Society, Politics, and Economic Development*, Johns Hopkins University Press, Baltimore.

Baran, P.A. (1957), *The Political Economy of Growth*, Modern Reader Paperbacks, New York.

Bigsten, A. (1980), *Regional Inequality and Development. A Case Study of Kenya*, Gower, Farnborough.

Boeke, J.H. (1953), *Economics and Economic Policy of Dual Economies*, Institute of Pacific Relations, New York.

Chenery, H.B. (1975), 'The structuralist approach to development policy', *American Economic Review*, Vol. 65.

Eckaus, R.S. (1955), 'The factors proportions problem in underdeveloped areas', *American Economic Review*, Vol. 45.

Fei, J.C.H. and Ranis, G. (1964), *Development of the Labor Surplus Economy: Theory and Policy*, Irwin, Homewood, Ill.

Fishlow, A. (1965), 'Empty economic stages', *Economic Journal*, Vol 75.

Frank, A.G. (1967), *Capitalism and Underdevelopment in Latin America: Historical Studies of Chile and Brasil*, Monthly Review Press, New York.

Gerschenkron, A. (1962), *Economic Backwardness in Historical Perspective*, Belknap Press, Cambridge, Mass.

Griffin, K. (1969), *Underdevelopment in Spanish America*, Allen & Unwin, London.

Hagen, E.E. (1962), *On the Theory of Social Change*, Dorsey Press, Homewood, Ill.

Kuznets, S. (1961), 'Quantitative aspects of the economic growth of nations: part 6, long-term trends in capital formation proportions', *Economic Development and Cultural Change*, Vol. 9.

Lall, S. (1975), 'Is dependence a useful concept in analysing underdevelopment', *World Development*, Vol. 3.

Lewis, W.A. (1954), 'Economic development with unlimited supplies of labour', *Manchester School of Economic and Social Studies*, Vol. 22.

Leys, C. (1977), 'Underdevelopment and dependency: critical notes', *Journal of Contemporary Asia*, Vol. 7.

Lichtheim, G. (1971), *Imperialism*, Penguin, Harmondsworth.

Lipton, M. (1977), *Why Poor People Stay Poor. Urban Bias in World Development*, Temple Smith, London.

Lundahl, M. and Ndlela, D.B. (1980), 'Land alienation, dualism and economic discrimination: South Africa and Rhodesia', *Economy and History*, Vol. 23.

McClelland, D.C. (1961), *The Achieving Society*, Van Norstrand, Princeton.

McKinnon, R.I. (1973), *Money and Capital in Economic Development*, Brookings Institution, Washington.

Meier, G.M. (1976), *Leading Issues in Economic Development*, 3rd edn., Oxford University Press, New York.

Mikesell, R., and Zinser, J.E. (1973), 'The nature of the savings function in developing countries: a survey of the theoretical and empirical literature', *Journal of Economic Literature*, Vol. 11.

Owen, R., and Sutcliffe, B. (eds.) (1972), *Studies in the Theory of Imperialism*, Longman, London.

Palma, G. (1978), 'Dependency: a formal theory of underdevelopment or a methodology for the analysis of concrete situations of underdevelopment?', *World Development*, Vol. 6.

Reynolds, L. (1971), *The Three Worlds of Economics*, Yale University Press, New Haven.

Rostow, W.W. (1960), *Stages of Economic Growth: A Non-Communist Manifesto*, Cambridge University Press, Cambridge.

Sunkel, O. (1973), 'Transnational capitalism and national disintegration in Latin America', *Social and Economic Studies*, Vol. 22.

Sutcliffe, B. (1972), 'Imperialism and industrialization in the Third World', in Owen and Sutcliffe (eds.).

Thurow, L.C. (1969), *Poverty and Discrimination*, Brookings Institution, Washington, DC.

Todaro, M.P. (1969), 'A model of labor migration and urban unemployment in less developed countries', *American Economic Review*, Vol. 59.

Yotopoulos, P.A. and Nugent, J.B. (1976), *Economics of Development. Empirical Investigations*, Harper and Row, New York.

4 The Measurement of Inequality and Poverty

4.1 Introduction
In this chapter I shall discuss the concept of inequality and alternative approaches to its measurement. I shall first, very briefly, consider some contributions from traditional welfare economics to the discussion of income distribution. Then I shall specify the properties that an inequality measure should have, and, on the basis of these, try to select one or a few measures that can be used in empirical work. Finally, I shall extend the discussion and consider ways of measuring the extent of poverty. A poverty measure gives more direct information about what is happening to the poor, constituting the target group in, for example, the basic needs strategy.

4.2 Welfare economics and distribution
In this section I shall review some approaches of traditional welfare economics to the normative question: How should economic welfare be distributed? Pen (1971, Chapter 7) presents 21 different answers to this question, so the choice is not easy.

When analysing this question economists usually want to consider both resources and preferences. The individual is assumed to choose among alternatives, given resources and preferences. He can, for example, make choices with regard to the time-profile of incomes, its risk, income vs. leisure, income vs. environment, consumption vs. savings, and the composition of the consumption bundle (Söderström, 1977).

Differences in material welfare that result from differences in taste with regard to factors such as those just mentioned should ideally be disregarded in the analysis of the distribution of welfare. One should, for example, compare life incomes rather than annual incomes in income distribution studies to eliminate the effect of differences in time preferences.

Of course, to get data about life incomes in an empirical analysis of an underdeveloped economy is very difficult. It may therefore be necessary to accept the use of annual income as a proxy for what one ideally would like to measure. Besides, in an underdeveloped economy most people have limited possibilities of determining the time profile of their incomes. Because of the lack of an efficient credit system it is also more difficult in underdeveloped countries to have a consumption profile which differs significantly from the income-profile over time. The choice of annual income or annual consumption as the measure of economic standard is therefore more acceptable in an underdeveloped country.

The issue of income distribution became important in the political debate during the eighteenth and nineteenth centuries. Many welfare economists at that time advocated utilitarianism, i.e. the maximization of the sum of the welfare of all individuals. This meant that everyone's welfare counted, but the criterion did not necessarily imply that it should be equally distributed. However, if it is assumed that everyone has the same utility function and that it is concave, the criterion means that an equal distribution maximizes social welfare. If utility is not measurable or comparable among individuals, it might be argued that it is a reasonable assumption that the welfare of an individual increases with income at a decreasing rate. This might then be taken to imply that to maximize expected utility, income should be distributed equally among all citizens.

One criticism that can be directed against the utilitarian criterion is that if utility really were measurable and comparable among people and if the capacity of individuals to derive utility from resources differed, the criterion would support a policy of transfers to the individuals with the greatest capacity for pleasure. This is certainly anti-egalitarian! Instead, it might be argued that if someone has a low capacity for pleasure, for example as a result of some physical handicap, he should be given more resources to make up for this, i.e. enough to make his utility equal to everybody else's.

A question that has been extensively discussed in welfare economics is how to derive a social welfare norm with desirable properties directly from the rankings of the individuals. An attempt to deal with this problem was made by Pareto, who formulated a norm which gave everyone power to veto any change that he considered to be detrimental to his interest. This means that only changes that benefit someone without hurting anybody else can be accepted. Of course, such a norm is of little use in practical policy-making. Its acceptance would tend to hinder all attempts to redistribute income.

To make this norm somewhat more useful welfare economists devised compensation tests. The idea of these was that a change would be acceptable if those gaining would be able to compensate those losing, while at the same time remaining on a higher welfare level than in the initial situation. It is thus a test of potential welfare gains. However, if the new situation really is to be considered superior according to the Pareto criterion one must see to it that the compensation is actually paid out. Then we are back to the original type of Pareto comparison, which says that no one should lose welfare in comparison with the initial situation.

Thus, the Pareto criterion is barren as far as analysis of income distribution is concerned. The theory of collective choice (see e.g. Arrow, 1951, 1967; Sen, 1970), which addresses the issue whether it is possible to make rational collective choices based on contradictory individual preferences, is of more interest. In these analyses it is first assumed that each individual ranks all possible alternative states of the society. Then these individual orderings are to be weighted together according to some given rule. The problem is to determine what this rule should be. Naturally, the first and most obvious choice is majority rule. However, when this method is used to rank three or more alternative distributions, it may produce different results depending on the order in which the alternatives are compared. For example, one may get the cyclical result that distribution A is preferred to B, B to C, and C to A. Arrow (1951) showed with his impossibility theorem that a collective decision rule cannot at the same time meet the following four desirable requirements: (i) collective rationality (which means that the social choice function is derivable from an ordering for any given set of individual orderings); (ii) the Pareto principle; (iii) independence of irrelevant alternatives; and (iv) non-dictatorship. A lively discussion followed Arrow's seminal contribution. In general, however, very little of interest can be said about the distribution of income on the basis of individual orderings without both cardinality and interpersonal comparisons.

Harsanyi (1955) has gone beyond the completely individualistic framework and suggested that people do not let issues relating to the entire society, e.g. the income distribution, be determined on the basis of individual preferences which imply that each individual is only interested in maximizing his own personal welfare. He argues that one should distinguish between subjective preferences, relating to choices within a given society, and ethical preferences concerning the organization of society. In a given society, an individual may very well prefer to be rich rather than poor, while he at the same time prefers an egalitarian income distribution in that society.

It seems reasonable to assume that people have ethical preferences. The problem is to get an individual to reveal his true ethical preferences about income distribution. Rawls (1971) has suggested that each individual should be made to choose among different hypothetical distributions of welfare (or income) among the members of society, without knowing what his own position in that society would be. Rawls believes that in such a situation everyone would tend to agree on the maximin rule of choice, which says that one should try to maximize the welfare of the worst-off individual. This means that differences in welfare are acceptable only in so far as they lead to the best possible situation for the worst off citizen.

Thus, Rawls's criterion has very egalitarian implications. The question naturally is just how egalitarian a society it would produce. Some inequalities would still be accepted if there were a trade-off between equality and efficiency as argued by Okun (1975), for example. However, even if Rawls's criterion is not necessarily an argument for a completely equal distribution of welfare or income, it probably implies a society with considerably less inequality than the present one.

To sum up these remarks on some issues in welfare economics I think one might say that they can provide no definite basis for the choice of an inequality measure. Utilitarianism focuses on the sum of utilities rather than their distribution. The Pareto criterion is useless as far as distributional judgements are concerned. The theory of collective choice has shown the difficulty in devising a social ordering on the basis of individual orderings. It seems reasonable to let valuations of income distribution be made on the basis of the ethical preferences of people rather than their subjective preferences. However, the problem of aggregating preferences remains; no definite theoretical conclusion can be reached about how one should specify a just distribution, given that individual orderings are known.

In the search for a reasonable measure of inequality value judgements are unavoidable. What can be done in a discussion on the choice of inequality measures is to specify the ethical bases on which the choice is made. The measure should be chosen in such a way that it can gain the widest possible acceptance. People must not necessarily agree on the desirability of equality, but it is a good thing if they agree on what inequality is before they argue about it.

4.3 Choice of inequality measure
A considerable number of measures have been proposed in the literature. Comprehensive surveys are provided by, for example, Sen (1973), Szal and Robinson (1977), and Cowell (1977). The problem is to find a measure that can gain wide acceptance and is suitable for the analysis at hand. If the choice of measure is not to be made in an *ad hoc* manner there are two possible approaches available. The first

approach is to derive the measure from a social welfare function. If the measure is to have a normative basis, the social welfare function must be assumed to subsume the values of society with regard to distribution. The alternative approach is to specify a set of axioms that the measure ought to satisfy. To make it possible to get the measure widely accepted, the axioms must, naturally, be acceptable to most people.

The social welfare function (SWF) approach will be considered first. A SWF is used to find one figure that characterizes the level of welfare of the society on the basis of individual levels of welfare. Just one example of this approach will be given. This is due to Cowell (1977, p. 42) who presents the following list of properties that a social welfare function can have:

1. The SWF is *individualistic* and *non-decreasing*, if for any state A: $W_A = W(y_{1A}, y_{2A}, \ldots, y_{nA})$ and if $y_{iB} \geq y_{iA}$ implies, *ceteris paribus*, that $W_B \geq W_A$, which in turn implies that state B is at least as good as state A.

y_{iA} is the magnitude of person i's 'economic position' in social state A, where i is a label that can be any number between 1 and n inclusive.

2. The SWF is *symmetric* for any state if it is true that $W(y_1, y_2, \ldots, y_n) = W(y_2, y_1, \ldots, y_n) = \ldots = W(y_n, \ldots, y_2, y_1)$. That is, the value of W does not depend on the particular assignment of labels to members of the population.

3. The SWF is *additive* if it can be written $W(y_1, y_2, \ldots, y_n) = \sum_{i=1}^{n} U_i(y_i) = U_1(y_1) + U_2(y_2) + \ldots + U_n(y_n)$, where U_1 is a function of y_1 alone etc.

4. The SWF is strictly *concave* if the welfare weight $(dU(y_i)/dy_i) = U'(y_i)$ always decreases as y_i increases.

5. The SWF has *constant elasticity*, or *constant relative inequality aversion* if $U(y_i)$ can be written $U(y_i) = \frac{1}{1-\epsilon} y_i^{1-\epsilon}$ (or in a cardinally equivalent form), where ϵ is the inequality aversion parameter.

A few comments need to be made about these assumptions. The first assumption simply states that if someone's income increases, so does his welfare, and that social welfare increases as the welfare of an individual increases. The second condition means that the income measure used gives the same welfare to anyone. Differences in needs etc. are assumed away. The third assumption is utilitarian and thus quite strong, but Cowell argues that this is not as restrictive in terms of choice of inequality measures that one would suspect. The fourth assumption represents the society's valuation of a man's income. Assumption five, finally, means that 'the proportional decrease in the welfare weight U′ for a given proportional increase in income should be the same at any income level' (1977, p. 45). A 1% increase in a person's income will decrease his welfare weight by ϵ% independently of his income level. The parameter ϵ indicates how strong our preferences for equality are *vis-à-vis* uniformly higher income for all.

There is one important result which does not require assumption five (Cowell, 1977, p. 49).

Theorem: Let the social state A have an associated income distribution $(y_{1A}, y_{2A}, \ldots, y_{nA})$ and social state B have income distribution $(y_{1B}, y_{2B}, \ldots y_{nB})$, where total income in state A and in state B is identical. Let W be any SWF satisfying assumptions 1 to 4. Then the Lorenz curve for state B lies wholly inside the Lorenz curve for state A, if and only if $W_B > W_A$ for every SWF satisfying assumptions 1 to 4.

This shows that the Lorenz diagram is a powerful tool, and it points to the criterion of Lorenz domination, which will be discussed below. Moreover, since the Lorenz criterion intuitively is sensible, this theorem also indicates that the set of characteristics chosen makes sense. Yet, this theorem is not sufficient. We may also want to compare situations where Lorenz curves intersect. The Lorenz criterion can only say whether inequality has decreased or increased in certain situations. A numerical inequality measure is therefore often needed. A numerical measure also makes it possible to make comparisons of magnitudes of change in income distribution in different cases. Cowell shows how such a measure can be derived on the basis of a social welfare function with the characteristics listed above.

Given that we have agreed on the form of the social welfare function and on the strength of society's inequality aversion (ϵ), the degree of inequality can be determined according to two alternative measures. The first one, Dalton's inequality index, measures how far actual average social utility falls short of potential average social utility (if all income is equally distributed). The other one, attributable to Atkinson (1970), is a variant of the Dalton index, and it can be written

$$A = 1 - \frac{y_e}{\bar{y}} \tag{4.1}$$

where $\bar{y}$ is the mean income of the population and y_e is the level of income per capita, which, if equally distributed, would give the same level of social welfare as the welfare generated by the existing distribution.

The size of y_e depends on the size of the parameter ϵ, i.e. the degree of inequality aversion. When this is taken into account, the formula (for grouped data) becomes (Atkinson, 1975, p. 48)

$$A = 1 - \left[\sum_{g=1}^{m} \left(\frac{y_g}{\bar{y}} \right)^{1-\epsilon} p_g \right]^{\frac{1}{1-\epsilon}}$$

(4.2)

where y_g = mean income of those in the gth income range;

$\quad\quad\ p_g$ = proportion of population with incomes in the gth range;

$\quad\quad\ m$ = number of groups.

Sen (1973, pp. 38−9) criticizes this measure on two grounds. First, it is based exclusively on a normative formulation and has thus lost some of its descriptive content. Secondly, the measure is based on a utilitarian framework, that is the addition of individual welfare components. The welfare of an individual is determined without consideration of the welfare of others. The concept of inequality here is completely determined by the form of the utility function, which may be a drawback with regard to the desire to find a measure that can gain the widest possible acceptance.

Atkinson (1970), on the other hand, claims that behind every measure of inequality there must be some type of conception of welfare. He argues that statistical measures of inequality necessarily have a normative character, since they always, explicitly or implicitly, contain a valuation of how much weight one should give to income differences in different ranges of the income scale.

Regardless of this, Sen (1973) does not agree that a measure of inequality should be derived from a social welfare function, since this may mean that the concept loses the descriptive character it has in ordinary usage. Sen does not feel that it is necessary to, a priori, specify the welfare loss caused by inequality in income distribution. Another problem is that the social welfare function is not empirically known, but has to be specified by someone, for example the planner. This approach is therefore not necessarily better than the alternative to be discussed below as far as how well it reflects the inequality in the society.

I will now consider another way of deriving inequality measures. To find measures with desirable properties I shall instead start from a set of axioms that should be acceptable to many as a relevant basis for inequality comparisons.

Fields and Fei (1978) start from a discussion of ordinality versus cardinality. If the Lorenz curve of one distribution lies wholly inside the curve of another distribution, it may unambiguously be stated that the first distribution is more equal than the latter (as has already been pointed out above). However, if the Lorenz curves cross each other, the Lorenz domination criterion is not sufficient. Some cardinal measure must be derived. It is the choice of such a measure which is the object of Fields and Fei's article. They start by specifying a number of properties that they feel a good index of inequality should have; then they examine whether various measures that have been proposed satisfy these properties.

They first assume that there are n families in an economy, whose incomes can be represented by a non-negative row-vector:

$$X = (y_1 y_2 \ldots y_n) \geq 0$$

in the non-negative orthant of the n-dimensional income distribution space Ω^+. They assume a complete pre-ordering of all points in Ω^+, i.e. a binary relation defined on ordered pairs must then satisfy the conditions of comparability and transitivity.

Then Fields and Fei introduce their three axioms for inequality comparisons:

A1: *Scale irrevelance* – The measure should be independent of the level of income.
A2: *Symmetry* – All families (or whatever the units being compared are) should be treated the same.
A3: *Rank preserving equalization* – This says that a transfer from a richer family to a poorer one that does not change the ranking of families should always reduce the inequality measure.

Next they investigate whether the three axioms are sufficient to allow us to compare any two points in the income distribution space. They first show that it is justified to use the criterion of Lorenz domination for inequality comparisons. This is almost self-evident, since a transfer from a richer person to a poorer one gives both a higher Lorenz curve and a distribution of income that everyone must consider to be more equal.

However, the Lorenz criterion is not complete; that is, it is not possible to compare all pairs of distribution on the basis of this criterion. Completeness is normally and usually achieved by cardinality. Fields and Fei therefore investigate what measures satisfy the axioms proposed. They find that the coefficient of variation (CV), the Gini coefficient (G), Atkinson's index (A) and the Theil index (T) satisfy all three axioms.

The formulas for these indices are given below (except for Atkinson's index, which was presented above). The notation is the same as before, plus that the number of individuals or families is denoted by n.

The coefficient of variation for grouped data can be written

$$CV = \frac{\sqrt{\sum\limits_{g=1}^{m} (\bar{y} - y_g)^2 p_g}}{\bar{y}} \tag{4.3}$$

The Gini coefficient can be written

$$G = \frac{1}{2n^2\bar{y}} \sum\limits_{i=1}^{n} \sum\limits_{j=1}^{n} |y_i - y_j| \tag{4.4}$$

There exist approximate methods of computing the index if the data are given by groups only. In such a situation one can define

$$G = 1 - \sum\limits_{z=1}^{m} p_z (Q_z + Q_{z-1}) \tag{4.5}$$

where Q_z is the cumulated income share of income group z.

After the groups have been ordered from the poorest ($z = 1$) to the richest ($z = m$), the respective cumulated income shares can be derived as

$$Q_z = \frac{\sum\limits_{g=1}^{z} y_g}{\sum\limits_{g=1}^{m} y_g} \tag{4.6}$$

for each $z = 1, \ldots, m$.

The Q_z values are then inserted in (4.5) and the Gini value is obtained.

For the Theil index we need some further notation:

ysh_g = the share of group g in y, which is total income;
n_g = number of people in group g.

The Theil index (see Theil, 1967, 1972) in its decomposed form can be written:

$$T = \sum\limits_{g=1}^{m} ysh_g \ln \left[\frac{ysh_g}{P_g} \right] + \sum\limits_{g=1}^{m} ysh_g \left\{ \sum\limits_{i=1}^{n_g} \frac{y_i}{ysh_g} \ln \left[\frac{\frac{y_i}{ysg_g}}{1 \, /n_g} \right] \right\} \tag{4.7}$$

This can be rewritten

$$T = T_b + \sum\limits_{g=1}^{m} ysh_g T_g \tag{4.8}$$

where T = the total Theil index;
T_b = the Theil index of inequality between groups;
T_g = inequality within group g.

The measures give the same ranking as the Lorenz criterion of distributions whose Lorenz curves do not intersect. However, when they do, these measures may give different results. Further valuations are then called for in the choice of index. By extending the system of axioms it might be possible to eliminate some more alternatives, but very restrictive and special axioms would have to be introduced in order to reduce the number of alternatives to one. We then have the problem that the more axioms you introduce, the less hope there is for general acceptance of the set of axioms. It is therefore not done.

The analysis of Fields and Fei thus leads to the conclusion that there are at least four alternative cardinal measures of interest. What will be considered now is whether there are any arguments that may justify the use of any one of these rather than the others. Cowell (1977) performs an analysis similar to the one presented by Fields and Fei, but specifies another set of criteria that he feels an inequality measure should satisfy. He suggests the following ones:

1. *Income Scale Independence* – same as A1 above.
2. *Principle of Population* – This means that the measure should be independent of the number of income receivers.
3. *Weak Principle of Transfers* – An inequality measure is satisfying this principle, if the following always holds. Consider two individuals with incomes y and $y + d$, where d is positive. If an amount $\triangle y < \frac{2}{2}d$ is transferred from the richer to the poorer man, the inequality measure should decrease.
4. *Strong Principle of Transfers* – An inequality measure satisfies this stronger principle, if the amount of the reduction in inequality depends only on the distance between the income shares of the two individuals, no matter which two individuals are chosen.

Most measures satisfy the two first criteria. On the basis of these it is not possible to eliminate any of the measures found useful by Fields and Fei. The last two axioms, however, are of greater interest. It is shown that all these measures actually satisfy the Weak Principle, which means that they rank distributions in the same order as the Lorenz criterion, given that the Lorenz curves do not intersect. This is naturally because the Weak Principle essentially is the same as A3.

However, only one of these four measures satisfies the Strong Principle of Transfers and that is the Theil index. That the Gini coefficient does not satisfy the principle is obvious, since the effect of a redistribution on the index depends on the positions of the individuals on the income ladder. The distance concept for the coefficient of variation is absolute differences, which means that this index does not meet the Strong Principle. The same goes for Atkinson's index, where the distance is the difference in marginal utility.

Therefore, the Strong Principle of Transfers indicates that the Theil measure is a good one. In a measure that satisfies the Strong Principle the change in its value is dependent only on the distance between the income shares of the individuals concerned and nothing else. This is certainly an attractive cardinal property. Another attractive property is that it is possible to decompose the Theil index into inequality within groups and inequality between groups.

Sen (1973, p. 43) points out that the Theil index 'is almost strictly in the form of a utilitarian social welfare function, which make the individual welfare components equal to $x_i \ln \dfrac{1}{x_i}$, where x_i is the share of income going to person i'. Sen thinks that this is a rather peculiar welfare function (see also Sen, 1974a).

He has criticized both the Theil index and Atkinson's index on the grounds that they are in the utilitarian tradition. In his own discussion (1973, p. 31) of alternative measure he argues that three measures that would be useful are the Gini coefficient, the coefficient of variation, and the standard deviation of logarithms. The last one does not meet the criterion that a transfer from a richer person to a poorer should always reduce the inequality measure. This means that this index has not passed the tests set up above for the choice of good measures. The other two indices are the two that remain of the four indices suggested by Fields and Fei. They do not meet the Strong Principle of Transfers as indicated above, but on the other hand they do not suffer from the utilitarian bias of the Theil-index criticized by Sen. Given that there are problems with the utilitarian framework, as indicated in section 4.2, these measures might thus be useful alternatives to the Theil index.

According to Champernowne's study (1974) these two measures differ in so far as the coefficient of variation is most sensitive to high relative incomes, while the Gini coefficient is most sensitive to inequalities among the less extreme incomes.

Sen (1973, p. 28) has criticized the coefficient of variation on the grounds that it is based on an arbitrary squaring procedure and only measures incomes *vis-à-vis* the mean. The Gini coefficient does not have this drawback. It compares every pair of incomes and thus is a very direct measure of inequality. On the negative side is, of course, the fact that the Gini coefficient is actually a rank-order-weighted sum of different persons' income shares. The sensitivity of the measure to an income transfer between two persons depends on the number of people between them on the income scale and not on the difference in relative income. The Theil index can be additively decomposed in an empirically useful manner (see the discussion in Bourguignon, 1979; Shorrocks, 1980). No similar, straightforward disaggregation is possible in the Gini index. Bhattacharya and Mahalanobis (1967) and Pyatt (1976) have presented formulas for the disaggregation of the Gini index. In Pyatt's decomposition you get three components, one which is due to differences within groups, one due to differences between groups, and one which is due to the degree of overlapping between groups. Since that last one, in all realistic circumstances, is different from zero, the Gini coefficient can not be decomposed into within group and between group inequality only. This means that it is not a particularly useful index in a decomposition analysis. For such an analysis the Theil index is a better alternative.

The discussion in this section can be summed up as follows. The first norm of inequality comparison that should be applied is the Lorenz domination criterion, which is an ordinal measure. If this cannot be used, for practical reasons or because the Lorenz curves cross each other, some cardinal measure must be chosen. Of the measures discussed in the literature the Theil index and the Gini coefficient seem to be of most interest. The former because it meets the Strong Principle of Transfers and because it can be decomposed in an empirically useful fashion. The Gini coefficient does not have these advantages, but it has other advantages which make it a useful measure. It is a very direct measure of inequality without the utilitarian traits of the Theil index. It is not based on any specific assumption with regard to the form of the income distribution and does not particularly emphasize differences in any specific range. It is thus a fairly 'neutral', much used, and easily understandable measure. Moreover, it forms the basis for the poverty measure to be derived in the next section.

4.4 Poverty measurement

To be able to evaluate the success of a policy of poverty alleviation it is necessary to measure the extent of poverty, rather than the degree of inequality which has been discussed above. This is what will be discussed in this section (see also Szal, 1977).

Essentially, two problems must be dealt with in this context. First, the poor must be identified, i.e. it is necessary to find out what incomes different categories of the population have and then it must be determined who is to be classified as poor. The second problem is to find a reasonable index of poverty.

The problems relating to the collection of data will not be discussed in this context, but a few comments will be made on how to derive a suitable poverty line. Basically, two alternatives can be used, either a relative or an absolute norm. If a relative norm is chosen one might, for example, define the poorest 40% as the poor, or alternatively define everyone who earns less than e.g. half of the average income as being poor. The first alternative is particularly problematic since, a priori, it determines the extent of poverty and makes the elimination of it impossible. The other relative measure does not have this problem. It is a measure of relative deprivation. If society is aiming at satisfying absolute material wants, an absolute measure is more useful.

Several approaches have been used to derive an absolute measure. One might, for example, specify a certain minimum living standard in terms of minimum levels of consumption of certain basic needs; the level of income that is required to sustain that level of consumption is then derived. The most essential part is of course food; one should therefore start by calculating the cost of the minimum acceptable food bundle.

In all realistic circumstances people also need certain non-food items. There are different ways of calculating this part. It is possible to measure how large a proportion of expenditures an average poor household actually spends on food items; the food budget estimate is then divided by this proportion. (The procedure has to be somewhat *ad hoc* since the poverty group has not yet been identified. One might look at the budgets of the poorest 20% of the households.) If the budget is split, for example 50–50, the poverty line becomes twice the minimum food budget. An alternative approach is to choose only certain non-food items that are considered to meet basic needs, and then measure how large a proportion of income the poor actually spend on these items. The food budget is then divided by the share of food in a budget comprising both necessary food and necessary non-food expenditures. The second approach is the one that comes closest to the notion of basic needs. It can thus be considered to be of interest to governments that aim at basic needs satisfaction. Still, it is difficult to determine what is 'necessary' non-food expenditures; it will therefore often be necessary to be satisfied with the first alternative.

Now assume that we have identified the poor and established a poverty line. The problem remaining and the problem on which we focus here is the choice of a poverty measure, that is a measure of the extent of poverty.

A very common index is the percentage of the population in poverty, i.e. below the poverty line. A drawback of this measure is that it gives the same weight to someone who is, say, 1 rupee below as to one who is 100 rupees below the line. The concept of the poverty gap has therefore been introduced. This measures the total income needed to bring everyone who is below the poverty line up to that standard. The shaded area in Figure 4.1 represents the total income shortfall.

Fishlow (quoted in Szal, 1977) has defined four policy-related measures based on the concept of the poverty gap. The measures are:

1. The redistribution potential $= \dfrac{\text{DAV}}{\text{OAP}}$;

2. The marginal taxation rate to alleviate poverty $= \dfrac{\text{OAP}}{\text{DAV}}$;

3. Reallocation of government expenditure potential
   $= \dfrac{\text{Government expenditures}}{\text{OAP}}$;

4. The percentage of government expenditures necessary to alleviate poverty $= \dfrac{\text{OAP}}{\text{Government expenditures}}$;

These variations of the poverty gap measure are of interest to policy-makers, but here I am only interested in finding a general and useful measure of the extent of poverty. Sen (1974b; 1976) has developed an index that is superior to any of the ones so far discussed.

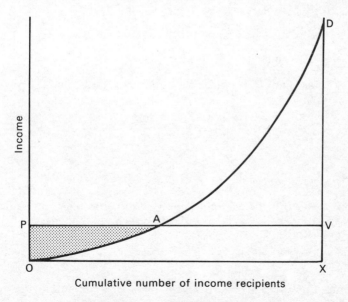

Figure 4.1   The poverty gap

It takes both the number in poverty and each individual's income gap into account. His index can be defined as a normalized weighted sum of the incomes of the poor. To arrive at this measure Sen needs to specify a weighting scheme and a normalization procedure. A rank-order weighting scheme is chosen, i.e. just like the one for the Gini coefficient discussed above. His normalization axiom says that if the poor have the same income, the poverty index is equal to the product of the proportion of people in poverty and the proportionate average gap.

To show, in a more formal way, what the measure implies, the following notation is introduced:

n = total population size;
$\bar{y}$ = mean income of the population;
z = poverty line;
q = number of people in poverty;
m = mean income of the people below the poverty line;
G_p = Gini-coefficient of the distribution of income among the poor.

First the population is ordered according to incomes from lowest to highest:

$$y_1 \leqslant y_2 \leqslant y_3 \leqslant y_4 \leqslant \ldots \leqslant y_n$$

Given that we have determined the poverty line z, we get:

$$y_q \leqslant z \quad \text{and} \quad y_{q+1} > z$$

The proportion of the population in poverty is q/n, and the poverty gap is

$$T = \sum_{i=1}^{q} (z - y_i) \tag{4.9}$$

Moreover

$$T = q(z - m) \tag{4.10}$$

where $(z - m)$ is the average poverty gap. Thus the proportionate average gap is $(z - m)/z$. An index can then be written as

$$P = q/n \left(\frac{z - m}{z} \right) \tag{4.11}$$

Now, this measure is derived on the assumption that the distribution of income among the poor is of no importance. To take this distribution into account Sen introduces the rank-order weights, which are $(q + 1 - i)$ on the income gap of person i. The index with the normalization then becomes

$$S = \frac{2}{(q + 1)nz} \sum_{i=1}^{q} (q + 1 - i)(z - y_i) \qquad (4.12)$$

To illustrate the content of the measure we may separate the effect of the inequality among the poor, as measured by the Gini coefficient. The formula can be written

$$S' = \frac{q}{n} \frac{1}{z} (z - m(1 - G_p)) \qquad (4.13)$$

where G_p is the Gini coefficient of inequality among the poor.

The measure P given above is thus increased by the product of the Gini coefficient and the mean income of the poor. Anand (1977) points out that this correction of the mean income of the poor yields the equally distributed equivalent income of the poor, which is equivalent to the level of income which, if equally distributed, would give the same level of social welfare as the existing income distribution. The weighted income gap is thus derived as the difference between the poverty line and the equally distributed equivalent income of the poor.

The index may vary between 0 and 1. It is equal to 0 when nobody is below the poverty line, and it is 1 when everyone has zero income.

The problematic point with regard to this measure is, as in the case of the Gini coefficient, that it is derived from a rank-order-weighted welfare function, where the welfare a person derives from income is proportional to his rank in the income distribution. Still, as I have argued above, the Gini-coefficient has several attractive characteristics. Moreover, given the situation in the LDCs, this kind of criticism can be taken with a grain of salt. The bias, which the use of this measure may result in, is certainly of limited practical importance. The great advantage of this measure compared with those discussed previously is that it is decreased more by transfers to the poorest of the poor than by transfers to those in the poverty group who are less poor. This together with the advantages of the Gini coefficient mentioned above, i.e. that it is easily understandable and easily applied, seem to more than outweigh the drawback of using a rank-order-weighted welfare function.

References

Anand, S. (1977), 'Aspects of poverty in Malaysia', *The Review of Income and Wealth*, series 23.

Arrow, K.J. (1951), *Social Choice and Individual Welfare*, Wiley, New York.

Arrow, K.J. (1967), 'Values and collective decision-making', reprinted in Phelps (ed).

Atkinson, A.B. (1970), 'On the measurement of inequality', *Journal of Economic Theory*, Vol. 2.

Atkinson, A.B. (1975), *The Economics of Inequality*, Oxford University Press, London.

Bhattacharya, N. and Mahalanobis, B. (1967), 'Regional disparities in household consumption in India', *American Statistical Association Journal*, Vol. 62.

Bourguignon, F. (1979), 'Decomposable inequality measures', *Econometrica* Vol. 47.

Champernowne, D.G. (1974), A comparison of measures of inequality of income distribution', *Economic Journal*, Vol. 84.

Cowell, F.A. (1977), *Measuring Inequality*, Philip Allan, Oxford.

Fields, G.S. and Fei, J.C.H. (1978), 'On inequality comparisons', *Econometrica*, Vol. 46.

Frank, C.R. and Webb, R.C. (eds.) (1977), *Income Distribution and Growth in the Less Developed Countries*, The Brookings Institution, Washington, DC.

Harsanyi, J.C. (1955), 'Cardinal welfare, individualistic ethics, and interpersonal comparisons of utility', *Journal of Political Economy*, Vol. 63.

Okun, A.M. (1975), *Equality and Efficiency. The Big Trade-off*, The Brookings Institution, Washington, DC.

Pen, J. (1971), *Income Distribution*, Penguin, Harmondsworth.

Phelps, E.S. (ed.) (1973), *Economic Justice*, Penguin, Harmondsworth.

Pyatt, G. (1976), 'On the interpretation and disaggregation of Gini coefficients', *Economic Journal*, Vol. 86.

Rawls, J. (1971), *A Theory of Justice*, Harvard University Press, Cambridge, Mass.

Sen, A. (1970), *Collective Choice and Social Welfare*, Holden-Day, San Francisco.

Sen, A. (1973), *On Economic Inequality*, Clarendon Press, Oxford.

Sen, A. (1974a), 'Informational bases of alternative welfare measures', *Journal of Public Economics*, Vol. 3.

Sen, A. (1974b), 'Poverty, inequality, and unemployment: some conceptual issues in measurement', in Srinivasan and Bradhan (eds.).

Sen, A. (1976), 'Poverty: an ordinal approach to measurement', *Econometrica*, Vol. 44.

Shorrocks, A.F. (1980), 'The class of additively decomposable inequality measures', *Econometrica*, Vol. 48.

Srinivasan, T.R. and Bradhan, P.K. (eds.) (1974), *Poverty and Income Distribution in India*, Statistical Publishing Society, Calcutta.

Szal, R. (1977), *Poverty: Measurement and Analysis*, Working Paper no. 60, WEP, Income Distribution and Employment Programme, International Labour Organization, Geneva.

Szal, R. and Robinson, S. (1977), 'Measuring income inequality', in Frank and Webb (eds.).

Söderström, H.T. (1977), 'På jakt efter en rättvis fördelning av välfärden', *Ekonomisk debatt*, Vol. 6.

Theil, H. (1967), *Economics and Information Theory*, North-Holland, Amsterdam.

Theil, H. (1972), *Statistical Decomposition Analysis*, North-Holland, Amsterdam.

5 The Evolution of Income Distribution in LDCs: A Survey of Empirical Evidence

5.1 Introduction

It has become increasingly obvious that the effect of economic growth in most less developed countries has been decidedly uneven. Some groups have managed to increase their standard of living substantially, while others have gained little or, in some cases, even experienced an absolute decline in standards. Ahluwalia *et al.* (1979) estimate that almost 40% of the population in the LDCs in 1975 were living in absolute poverty.* Most of the poor are to be found in southern Asia, Indonesia, and Sub-Saharan Africa.

The growing awareness of the problems of poverty and inequality has led to a surge of interest in the relation between development and income distribution, which has resulted in a vast amount of empirical research on the subject. In this chapter I attempt to systematize the results of this sprawling research.

It is impossible to come anywhere near complete coverage of the literature in this field, but the ambition has been to get a coverage that is sufficiently wide to ensure that the major factors are identified. The survey is also in the main restricted to studies of a comprehensive character concerning the evolution of inequality in LDCs, while results from studies of specific factors are included only as complements. The data problems are notorious in income distribution analyses in the LDCs, but no discussion of these is attempted here. Studies analysing family or personal income distribution are used and in some cases studies analysing the distribution of household expenditures are also included. One must therefore be wary of comparisons between individual studies. The major income distributional factors are not too dissimilar whether analysed on the personal or the household level. It is the identification of these factors which is the aim of this chapter.

*The poverty line was defined as the income needed in India to secure adequate nutrition, given the existing expenditure pattern.

In this chapter I first present the results of some cross-country studies trying to find out to what extent the degree of inequality is a function of, for example, the level of per capita income. After that, I draw on a number of recent country studies on the evolution of inequality and its determinants. The survey in this chapter may hopefully be of help in future income distribution analyses, since it pinpoints the factors which have been shown to be the major determinants of the evolution of income distribution.

5.2 The evidence of cross-country studies

Some indication of how income distribution changes during the development process can be obtained from cross-country studies of countries on different levels of per capita income. These give some insight into the time pattern of income distribution, and will therefore be discussed before we go on to time-series studies of individual countries. The latter give a more detailed and reliable picture of the factors that determine the evolution of income distribution.

The interest in cross-country studies was initiated by a paper by Kuznets in 1955 (see also Kuznets, 1963), in which he advanced the hypothesis that inequality first increases and then decreases with development. The reason for this 'inverted U' pattern is that growth in the early stages of development tends to be concentrated in the modern part of the economy, which initially is small in terms of employment. In the pre-industrial society, where agriculture predominated, there was little differentiation; with the introduction of capitalistic industries the degree of differentiation increased, causing an increase in inequality.

Kuznets's seminal contribution was followed by a number of studies dealing with this issue. Among the earlier ones were Karvis (1960) and Oshima (1962). They presented data supporting Kuznets's hypothesis that early growth increases inequality, and they argue as well that changes in the economic structure cause the increase in inequality. Swamy (1967) showed that the increase in intersectoral differences in India during the 1950s accounted for 85% of the increase in the inequality of size distribution of consumer expenditures during this period, while just 15% of the increase was caused by changes within sectors.

During the last few years a number of cross-country studies of the relation between per capita income and the degree of inequality have been presented. The results from these cross-country studies must be interpreted with great caution, but they still can be assumed to provide an approximation of the development over time.

Adelman and Morris (1971, 1973) have done a cross-sectional

analysis of personal income distribution in 74 underdeveloped countries, which indicates that over a very long period of the modernization process inequality increases, unless there is efficient planning for equity. They find that, with respect to the share of income accruing to the poorest 20% of households, the most important explanatory factors are dualism and various aspects of foreign trade and agricultural policy. They claim that 'economic development is associated with increases in the share of the bottom 20% only after relatively high levels of socioeconomic development have been attained. At the early stages of the development process economic development works to the relative disadvantage of the lowest income groups.' (Adelman and Morris, 1971, p. 12).

Concentration of income tends to increase with dualism,* and they also find that

> once a sharply dualistic development pattern has been initiated, further economic growth actually reduces the share of the lowest 60%. . . . In the absence of government intervention, dualistic growth therefore increases the concentration of income. The extent of cleavage of technology and life style thus exerts a profound influence upon income distribution, not only in itself, but also by influencing the way in which further development affects the distribution of income.   (Adelman and Morris, 1971, p. 21)

One must make some reservations with regard to the type of analysis pursued by Adelman and Morris. In very critical reviews, Higgins (1975) and Little (1976) characterize their analysis as implicit theorizing using variables about which little knowledge exists. Higgins argues (p. 214) that to rank in a correct manner countries in terms of the kind of qualitative variables that are used, a major interdisciplinary research effort for each variable would be required. It should also be pointed out that what Adelman and Morris have been doing is to 'hunt for correlation', and one should not without a theoretical underpinning jump from correlation to causality. Still, the work of Adelman and Morris gives food for thought and provides interesting hypotheses that can be the basis of further research.

The data assembled by Adelman and Morris are used by Paukert (1973) to calculate how the Gini-coefficient changes with the level of per capita income. He finds (p. 116) that 'there is a sharp increase in inequality as one moves from countries in the lowest income group to those in the $101–200 group, and a further but less pronounced

---

*The method of ranking of countries on this variable is somewhat *ad hoc* and not easily summarized. The ranking depends on the extent of cleavage and contrast between the modern, monetized sector and the traditional, non-monetized sector with regard to socioeconomic structure and technology.

increase as one moves on to the $201–300 group. This group and the next ($301–500) represent the peak of inequality' (1965 US dollar).

Chenery and Syrquin (1975) have in another cross-country study of development patterns analysed the development of inequality, and also their results (based on data from 1950 to 1970) are in accordance with Kuznets's hypothesis. They locate the peak of inequality at a per capita income of about $300 (1964 US dollar).

Since there is a very large, unexplained inter-country variation, they also test a number of other explanatory variables. They add proxies for education, dualism and the size of the agricultural sector, and this notably improves the regression results. Still, their main conclusion is that when population growth is high and the modern sector is too small to absorb a substantial part of the labour force, there is a tendency for inequality to increase.

In a survey of the literature on distribution and development, Cline (1975) cites evidence from Ahluwalia that seems to cast doubt on the hypothesis of the inverted U. In two later articles, however, Ahluwalia (1976a, 1976b) presents extensive results from studies on inequality, which support the hypothesis. He cannot, however, find any evidence for the hypothesis that inequality is greater in rapidly growing countries than in slowly growing countries at the same income level. Since Ahluwalia's study (1976b) seems to be the most comprehensive of this type, it might be worthwhile to sum up the results (see also Ahluwalia in Chenery *et al.*, 1974).

Since the results are based on cross-sectional and not time-series studies, Ahluwalia cautions the reader: They should be regarded as 'stylized facts' for which one should try to find a theoretical explanation. This kind of study therefore represents only a starting point in our search for explanations and causal mechanisms.

Kuznets's hypothesis is supported by Ahluwalia's regressions. Moreover, he identifies turning points for different income groups: The share of the top 20% increases up to $364 (1965–1971 US dollar), after which the share of this group declines; the share of the next 40% declines until $291 and then improves, while the lowest 20% have to wait until per capita GNP has reached $600. Ahluwalia's conclusion (p. 310) is that 'the reversal of the "deteriorating phase" of relative inequality begins fairly early, first for the middle income group, and much later for the lower income groups. It appears that if there is a "trickle down" process, then it takes substantially longer to reach the bottom'. The conclusion that the relative decline is most prolonged for the poorest groups accentuates the need for a change of development strategy. In many underdeveloped countries the present rate of growth of per capita incomes is so low that it may take a century before the turning point is reached. Despite the fact that a relative decline does not necessarily mean a decrease of the absolute income level, it usually at least implies a slow rate of improvement.

Like others who have analysed the relationship between per capita incomes and inequality, Ahluwalia finds that the level of incomes explains only a limited part of the variation in the material. He therefore introduces other explanatory variables relating to intersectoral shifts in production, expansion of education and the demographic transition. His conclusion is that these factors contribute considerably to the explanation of the improvement in the distribution, but that they do not explain the early deterioration. The share of agriculture is the only factor of those discussed which is associated with the deteriorating phase, but its effect is ambiguous. On the basis of Ahluwalia's study it is difficult to identify the process that generates increasing inequality in the early stages of development.

Recently, also Lydall (1977) has made a similar analysis of data from 71 countries. The results of his regressions are consistent with those of Paukert and Ahluwalia. Lydall (1977, p. 7) finds that

> on the average (i) the share of the top 5% of income units reaches a maximum among countries which are still at a very low level of economic development (about $200 per capita in 1971 prices); (ii) the share of the bottom 20% of income units reaches a minimum among countries which are at a somewhat more advanced stage of economic development (about $500 per capita); and (iii) the Gini coefficient is at its maximum with a per capita income of about $250. (1977, p. 7)

A slightly different approach is taken by Cromwell (1977) who emphasizes the difference between capitalist and non-capitalist modes of production; the coexistence of the capitalist mode with pre-capitalist modes of production creates inequality.* Cromwell (1977, p. 300) assumes that the share of the labour force working for wages or salaries gives an indication of the relative size of the capitalist sector. He then uses this to explain the degree of inequality. His hypothesis is that this is a better predictor of inequality than the per capita income measure usually employed in this type of analysis, since this

---

*Cromwell (1977, p. 305) claims that socialism as practised in Eastern Europe has resulted in a more equal income distribution than the capitalistic development of the advanced Western countries; the Gini coefficient is 35% lower. This kind of comparison is obviously very difficult, but the evidence by Michal (1978), Chapman (1978), and Wiles (1978, p. 191) supports this assertion. Wiles give data which give some indication of the differences of the countries he compares. North America has the highest inequality followed by Italy ('Catholic Europe'), then Sweden and the UK ('Protestant Europe') and finally the European socialist countries (see also Wiles, 1974).

only indirectly measure the degree of capitalist penetration.

Also he finds an inverted-U pattern, with inequality peaking when the share of the labour force employed for wages and salaries reaches 40%. However, the level of significance is very low ($R^2 = 0.13$) so one cannot conclude that this variable gives a better explanation than per capita income, particularly not because no comparative regression on per capita income is made.

The tentative conclusion that can be drawn from the studies discussed so far is that there seems to be a tendency towards increasing inequality in early stages of development, followed by a period of declining inequality after a certain income level has been reached.

All these studies of the distributional consequences of growth are exploratory. They do not investigate dynamic processes in a historical context for any particular country, which is desirable, if one is to be able to identify clearly the causal mechanisms. The rest of this chapter will therefore be devoted to the survey of the results of country studies, in which a more careful analysis of the dynamics of development has been made.

I shall first present some empirical estimates of the development of income distribution in Latin America, Asia and, to some extent, Africa. Then I shall try to pinpoint the factors that have been found to be the determinants of the development of income distribution in the countries studied.

5.3 The time pattern of inequality
The cross-country evidence regarding the relationship between inequality and per capita income level suggests that inequality first grows and then declines as income grows. However, it is also found that the level of per capita income only explains a limited part of the variation in the material and that other factors together are more important than the level of per capita income. Actually, the reason that per capita income is correlated with inequality must be that it itself is correlated with factors that vary systematically with per capita income. It is those factors which are of interest here.

The country studies surveyed below give an indication of how inequality has changed over time in a number of Third World countries. They show that in many countries growth has primarily benefited the upper or middle classes and that the income distribution has become more unequal.

5.3.1 Latin America
A number of studies have been devoted to the evolution of income distribution in Brazil. The standard conclusion is that inequality has

increased, and that the rapid growth in the late 1960s and early 1970s mainly benefited the top 5% (Fishlow, 1972). This standard conclusion is challenged by Fields (1977, p. 575), who argues that growth reached persons at all income levels and that the incomes of the poor grew faster than the incomes of the non-poor. However, Fields's analysis has been criticized by several authors, and his conclusion about the growth rate of the poor being higher than that of the rich appears to be incorrect and a consequence of misinterpretation of the data (see Ahluwalia and Duloy, 1980; Pyatt and Srinivasan, 1980; Fishlow, 1980; Fields, 1980; Bacha and Taylor, 1978). In reality the share of the poorest seems to have declined, though their absolute income level probably did rise.

Another Latin American country whose income distribution has been thoroughly analysed is Colombia. Berry and Urrutia (1976) have made a very comprehensive study. Urrutia (1976) gives a concise summary of how the Colombian income distribution has developed. He points out that income distribution is very uneven, but no worse than in Mexico and Brazil. Poverty is mainly a rural problem − here as in most places. The average income of the seventh decile in the rural sector is lower than that of the second decile in the urban sector. Most poor families live on small holdings.

Income distribution was about the same in the 1960s as it was in the 1930s. It grew worse up to the 1950s and then improved somewhat. Berry and Urrutia (1976, p. 116) make some tentative estimates of the development of income distribution between 1930 and 1960 on the basis of wage series for groups of workers, and they find that income distribution in agriculture deteriorated throughout the period, while the non-agricultural distribution worsened until the early 1950s and then improved. They feel that overall there is some consistency with the Kuznets hypothesis.

The ones that have benefited most from economic growth seem to be the middle class, that is the eighth and ninth deciles of the income distribution. The poorest may not have become worse off, although the agricultural workers are about as poor in the 1960s as they were in the 1930s.

The income distribution of Brazil and Colombia has been extensively analysed and discussed in the literature. I shall now very briefly point to some evidence concerning other countries on the continent. Foxley (1976) contains a number of papers dealing with income distribution in Latin America. The articles in the volume deal with Peru, Puerto Rico, Argentina, Brazil, Cuba, Chile, Venezuela, and Colombia. Among these Cuba has managed to bring about a redistribution of income; Peru and Chile (before 1973) have attempted to.

Argentina and Brazil have had a pattern of development which has benefited mainly the top 5% of the population, while growth in Mexico, Puerto Rico and Colombia has benefited mainly the middle class (see also van Ginneken, 1980). According to MacEwan (1981, Chapter 12) Cuba experienced a considerable reduction in inequality in the period directly after the 1959 revolution. The major factors were the land reform and the employment policy of the government. The pattern of income distribution that was created in the early 1960s was maintained at least until the early 1970s. It seems clear that there was a shift in income distribution in the early 1960s, but whether inequality has declined or increased since then is unclear. Seers (1974) points to the incentive problem in the late 1960s and the reintroduction of more of material incentives in 1970. There seems to have been a strong conflict between efficiency and equity, and this was resolved by a reduction in the reliance on moral incentives.

To sum up: in the case of Latin America, there is some evidence indicating that Colombia might have passed the turning point, and that Cuba managed to decrease inequality. There is no clear evidence of a widespread deterioration of the absolute incomes of the poor in Latin America.

5.3.2 Asia

For a long time the Asian masses have been considered the poorest of the poor, and as far as the Indian sub-continent goes this definitely still holds. Some countries in the Far East have, however, managed to take a leap forward and substantially raise the living standards of the ordinary citizens.

A very large share of the really poor of the world live in India. The extent of their poverty was extensively documented by Dandekar and Rath (1971). They started from the situation as measured by private consumption expenditures (National Sample Survey) in 1960/61. They found that the consumption expenditure of 40% of the rural population was less than 0.5 rupees per day, while 50% of the urban population spent less than 0.75 rupees per day (which is considered to be the equivalent of 0.5 rupees in the rural areas) on consumption.

The rural poor consist of agricultural labourers, small landholders and village artisans, and the urban poor are mainly an overflow of the rural poor into the urban areas. Dandekar and Rath (1971, p. 17) found that the consumption of the bottom 20% rural poor increased by only 2% between 1960/61 and 1967/68. The conditions of the bottom 20% of the urban poor did definitely deteriorate, and for another 20% of the urban population it remained more or less stagnant. Another computation covering the period 1956/57 to

1967/68 using NSS-data was made by Minhas (1970). He found that the proportion of the rural population living in poverty declined during this period. Rajaraman (1975) has chosen to use the same data base for Punjab, but finds that during the period between 1960/61 and 1970/71 poverty did increase somewhat.

The results of this kind of computations are obviously very sensitive to the choice of starting year. Since 1960/61 was a good agricultural year, analyses starting from that year have a certain pessimistic bias. Still, it seems safe to say that the situation of the poor did not change much during the 1960s, and poverty continued to spread to urban areas from the rural areas through migration.

During the second half of the 1960s, high-yielding varieties of rice and wheat were being introduced on a large scale in rural Asia. The distributional consequences of the Green Revolution has been the subject of heated debates. Griffin (1974), for example, argues that there was a tendency towards increasing inequality.

The empirical basis for his conclusions was rather weak, but Griffin and others joined in a large ILO study (1977), where a number of case studies on rural poverty in Asia were presented. The countries covered Pakistan, the Indian states of Punjab, Uttar Pradesh, Bihar and Tamil Nadu, Bangladesh, Sri Lanka, West Malaysia, Indonesia, the Philippines and China. The main conclusion regarding the seven countries included in the study (excluding China) is that the income distribution has become more uneven. In a number of areas the standard of the poorest in the rural areas has actually deteriorated. It is also shown that the degree of landlessness is increasing.

Since the ILO study was published, Ahluwalia (1978) has presented a systematic time-series analysis of Indian NSS-data which covers more years than other studies (the period 1956/57 to 1973/74). He finds (p. 303) that the percentage of the rural population in poverty declines from over 50% in the mid-1950s to around 40% in 1960/61, then rises sharply through the mid-1960s, reaching a peak in 1967/68, and then declines again. There is no significant time trend over this period, although a constant percentage in poverty implies that the absolute number of poor families has increased. Only two Indian states – Assam and West Bengal – show a significant trend increase in poverty, while Andra Pradesh and Tamil Nadu is showing a decline.

When Ahluwalia analyses the data on the national level, he finds that 'improved agricultural performance is definitely associated with reductions in the incidence of poverty' (Ahluwalia, 1978, p. 310). There thus seems to be a certain trickle-down process. However, when looking at state date the picture becomes more difficult to interpret.

Ahluwalia (1978, p. 319) finds that there were factors operating in the rural economy that tended to increase the incidence of poverty, but that agricultural growth leading to higher output per head tended to offset the adverse effect of these factors. Griffin and Ghose (1979, p. 371) use the same data to show that for the period 1960/61 to 1973/74 poverty increased in 12 out of 14 states. Nayyar (1979) found poverty to be increasing considerably in Bihar during the 1960s.

The empirical picture is rather mixed as far as India is concerned, but it seems safe to say that there has been no significant improvements for the rural poor and that economic inequalities have tended to increase. The absolute number of people living in poverty has almost certainly increased.

Guisinger and Hicks (1978) have used household budget survey data to estimate changes in the Gini coefficient for Pakistan. They find that it probably did decrease during the 1960s, but that it may have increased again during the 1970s. However, neither these household budget survey data, nor wage and earnings data show that there has been any significant change. In a study using household budget data (Lee, 1977) it was found that in Malaysia over the period 1957–79 inequality increased, while it decreased in Sri Lanka between 1963 and 1973.

King and Weldon (1977) have analysed household budget survey data on income distribution in Java during the period 1963–70. They find that there was little change in the relative distribution in rural areas, but a worsening distribution in urban areas. The largest cities accounted for most of the deterioration. The richest 10% of the urban dwellers have increased their share. They conclude that there was a 'deterioration in real levels of living for approximately the bottom 40% of the population, a widening gap between the rich and the poor in urban areas, and an increasing imbalance between the capital city and other areas of Java' (p. 710).

Berry (1978, p. 317) has compared four different family income and expenditure surveys for the Philippines covering a period of 15 years. He finds that these surveys cast doubt on conclusions showing a worsening income distribution. 'The decline in most of the real wage series raises the question of whether they can be consistent with the evidence from the family income and expenditure survey data to the effect that incomes of wage-earning families as well as of all families were rising during the 1960s.' (Berry, 1978, p. 327). Berry's conclusion is that the income distribution changed very little.

A few countries in Asia have recently been able to achieve very rapid growth through industrialization for export. One of these economies is Hong Kong. Hsia and Chau (1978a) have analysed how industrialization has affected income distribution. During the past 15 years the economy has experienced an average annual growth rate of about 10%, and this has transformed the economy from one with surplus labour to one with a labour shortage. The authors find that during the period 1961–71 both income dispersion within industrial and occupational groups and income differentials among these groups narrowed (Hsia and Chau, 1978a, p. 183).

Chow and Papanek (1981, p. 472) draw together the data that are available on overall income distribution and they draw the conclusion that at the very least there does not appear to have been any deterioration in the income distribution during the period of rapid growth. It may have improved.

Another country that has been doing quite well both with regard to growth and income distributions is Taiwan. Fei, Ranis, and Kuo (1978) find that Taiwan reached the turning-point in 1968, whereafter labour became scarce. Just as in Hong Kong, this had a favourable effect on income distribution. The overall Gini coefficient increased up to this time, but then it started to decrease. The development of Taiwan thus fits the inverted-U pattern discussed earlier. During the period before the turning point the Gini coefficient of the rural sector was falling, and this limited the increase in the overall Gini coefficient. Also South Korea has been able to achieve a very rapid economic growth since the mid-1960s, through a labour and skill-intensive export-oriented development strategy (Adelman and Robinson, 1978). The high growth rate has been brought about without any deterioration of the income distribution.

Asia thus provides a mixed picture. There is evidence which suggests that the income distribution in many Asian countries has deteriorated since the 1950s. In some countries there may even have been an absolute decline in the living standards of a considerable number of people during some periods.

However, in Asia, there are also some countries that have done well both in terms of growth and income distribution, namely the so called new industrial countries. Both Hong Kong and Taiwan have experienced an improving income distribution, while South Korea has managed to sustain an extraordinarily rapid growth of GDP without any significant deterioration in the relatively even income distribution.

Data on interpersonal income distribution in China are scarce. Here, as in Cuba, there was a considerable reduction in inequality just after the revolution (see e.g. Perkins, 1980). What has happened since then with the income distribution is less clear. The scattered data which are available seem to suggest that the income differences within firms and in agriculture have remained fairly high. Whether overall inequality has declined or not during the period since the 1950s is very hard to determine (Bigsten, 1975).

5.3.3 Africa
Compared with the mass of research on Asia and Latin America, little has been published on the change over time of income distribution in Africa. There is scattered evidence, e.g. in the ILO report of Kenya (1972), but little in terms of thorough time-series analysis.

Van der Hoeven's study of Zambia (1977) can be mentioned as an example of an attempt in this direction. He finds that incomes are more evenly distributed in urban than in rural areas, that average income is higher in urban areas, and that inequality increased during the 1960s as a result of increasing urban (formal sector) incomes combined with stagnation within traditional agriculture. He emphasizes the importance of the fact that Zambia is a dual economy with few linkages between the two segments of the economy. He also points to a slight deterioration of the domestic terms of trade for agriculture and the strong bargaining power of trade unions.

Paul Collier (1981) has analysed the development of oil-rich Nigeria. His conclusion is that neither the rural poor, nor the unskilled urban wage-earners benefited from the rapid growth during the 1970s. Obviously, the better-off segments of the urban population benefited (greatly); one must therefore draw the conclusion that the income distribution became more unequal.

Therefore the available evidence suggests that there may have been a deterioration in income distribution in many countries on this continent as well. A priori, this seems plausible, if we believe in the inverted-U hypothesis. Most African countries are still very poor.

It should be pointed out that in aggregate the African economies were fairly successful during the 1960s, but during the 1970s per capita income actually fell in about 20 of the Sub-Saharan countries. If income distribution did not improve, the extent of poverty must have increased. The economic prospects of Sub-Saharan Africa at present certainly look bleak.

In the following section I shall discuss the most important factors, which have been shown to influence the evolution of income distribution in the Third World.

5.4 Factors determining the evolution of income distribution

5.4.1 Economic characteristics affecting income distribution
The empirical studies surveyed use different approaches and cover a

large number of countries and a wide variety of factors are touched upon. I have tried to include the major factors discussed. The problem in summarizing the results is to find a structure of presentation which makes it possible to incorporate the major determinants identified in the studies.

I have chosen to summarize what has been learnt from the studies about the determination of income distribution under 11 different headings (sections 5.4.2–5.4.12). Each one of these represents an economic characteristic, which has been found to be of importance to the pattern of income distribution change. It is the nature of these characteristics in an economy which determines the evolution of income distribution there.

The ultimate aim is to explain the change in size distribution of income over time. The characteristics discussed can affect this indirectly through their effect on the functional income distribution, which is then mapped into a distribution among households. Alternatively a characteristic can affect the distribution of the income accruing to a factor and thus affect the size distribution more directly.

The first characteristic discussed is type of economic system, which is a basic institutional trait of an economy. Then we go on to consider the role of factors which primarily affect size distribution indirectly through their effect on functional income distribution, i.e. factor proportions and technology. Sectoral and regional structure as well as the process of wage formation affects the size distribution both indirectly and directly. Ownership pattern and social stratification mainly affect size distribution directly. Finally, the effect of some types of economic policies are discussed. Of course, the purpose of economic policy to a large extent is to change the economic characteristics already listed, and therefore it is difficult to make a clear-cut distinction between the former and the latter sections. Generally, some overlap between sub-sections is inevitable in this presentation of the evidence.

5.4.2 Economic system

The most basic institutional characteristic is the type of economic system. Some LDCs are difficult to classify, but the majority could probably be characterized as capitalist economies (including a considerable number calling themselves socialist). The mix between private and government activity, nevertheless, varies. In general, a large private sector is reflected in a relatively unequal distribution of income, since the return to capital is appropriated by individuals rather than the state.

As far as one can judge from the sparse data available on socialist countries in the Third World, e.g. China (Lardy, 1978) and Cuba (MacEwan, 1981), the income distribution in these seems to be more even than in the capitalistic (or mixed) economies, about which more is known. There is, however, little information available about how income distribution changes over time in the socialist LDCs. Thus, even if there is a difference in the level of inequality, we know very little about what happens to inequality in socialist LDCs as they, move to higher levels of economic development. Since it is mainly non-socialist countries which are covered in the studies surveyed here, the degree to which the points made here are valid for the socialist ones as well is not easily determined. To answer this question further research is required.

5.4.3 Factor proportions

As the first step in the analysis of income distribution determination one wants to determine the functional income distribution. Numerous factors contribute to the determination of this. In this sub-section we shall concentrate on the effects of changes in factor proportions which obviously is very important. In the following sub-sections other determinants of functional income distribution are considered.

A rapid growth of the labour force tends to keep wages down, while land rents and capital incomes increase. A demographic transition is thus one important factor which can hasten the termination of the situation with surplus labour. To end such a situation when there is a high rate of labour force growth, the rate of capital formation will have to be substantially higher than when the size of the labour force is stagnating.

The case of Taiwan is interesting in this context. Ranis (1978, p. 407) argues that its success with regard to income distribution followed from (i) an increasing volume of non-agricultural employment opportunities in the rural areas; (ii) a functional distribution of non-agricultural income which did not turn against labour in the presence of persistently low wage rates; and (iii) an improving distribution of agricultural income. Apart from the land reform and decentralization policies already touched upon, a major factor was the overall economic policy which increasingly forced output mixes and technology choices into greater harmony with changing endowment conditions. The lesson from the Taiwan case is (Ranis, 1978, p. 407) that 'the only sure method of achieving a sustained improvement in equity lies in hastening the advent of commercialization, i.e. the end of the labour surplus condition'.

Similar conclusions have been drawn with regard to Colombia. Berry and Urrutia (1976, p. 70) find that the major causes of the deterioration of income distribution in the rural areas are the sluggish behaviour of real wages and the decline of the wage share. The decline in the real wage resulted from (i) the declining importance of some labour intensive crops; (ii) an increase of the rural proletariat; and (iii) the after-effects of the depression. Labour thus became increasingly abundant, not more scarce.

The factor proportions are affected either by changes in the growth rate of labour or capital. A high rate of capital accumulation helps to increase the demand for labour and contributes to higher wages. The overall effect on income distribution is uncertain.

It may also be pointed out that the productivity of labour may vary with the level of nutrition. Myrdal (1968, p. 754) argues that a more even distribution of income, and therefore higher incomes for the poor, would improve efficiency and labour input. Therefore, the access to food has an instrumental value as well as being an aim in itself. Rodgers (1975) analyses data from the Kosi area in India and finds support for his theory of a nutritionally based wage determination. There it is inefficient for the employer to lower wages below a certain level even if there is surplus labour, because the work efficiency deteriorates so much.

5.4.4 Technology
Apart from the growth in factor quantities, the change in demand for and yields of these are also a consequence of the pattern of technological change. One aspect of this, which has been much discussed, is the influence of the Green Revolution.

Griffin (1974) considers four types of consequences of the new technique: (i) effects on resource allocation; (ii) production methods; (iii) propensity to innovate; and (iv) income distribution. He argues that in rural Asia factor prices are biased; some markets are absent and others are fragmented. These imperfections are a result of immobility of resources, bad communications, lack of information, the policy of the authorities with a systematic bias in favour of certain groups, and the monopoly power of the rich farmers. Wealth gives political power and this, in turn, makes it possible to influence policy in a way that gives this group access to resources. Griffin discusses the price formation for different factors of production and shows that the price structure systematically favours the large-scale farmers.

This has consequences for the choice of production technique. Peasant production becomes too labour-intensive and large farmer production too capital-intensive in comparison with the allocation of resources that would result if prices were the same for both groups. The biased price structure does thus not only lead to an uneven distribution of incomes; it also leads to an inefficient allocation of resources.

Next, Griffin goes on to show that the fact that material inputs are too cheap in comparison with labour biases the process of innovation. The type of innovations that occur are very often dependent on water, pesticides, fertilizers, etc. This together with the biased price system increases the dualism between large-scale farmers and peasants. Because policy-makers have mainly supported this type of innovation the bias has been further aggravated. Thus both market forces and policy factors work in the direction of increasing inequality. The technological bias has thus meant a falling share for labour and a deterioration of the relative income of small farmers and landless labourers (see also Lipton, 1978).

In a paper on the Green Revolution in Mexico, Tuckman (1976) emphasizes that very little is really known about its effects on income distribution. The tentative results, however, seem to indicate that it increased production considerably and increased regional inequality, but it seems to have decreased absolute poverty.

A problem in evaluating the effects of the Green Revolution is the choice of the norm of comparison. The appropriate norm would, of course, be the development path without high yielding varieties. Since this cannot be observed, Griffin uses the development in the period preceding the introduction of the new varieties as a basis for this comparison. It is not self-evident that this pattern of development was possible to sustain. Even if inequalities have increased on the Indian countryside, the extent of poverty there might have been larger without the Green Revolution. Still, Griffin is correct in pointing out that the institutional structure has had distributional consequences, which were not necessary.

It should be emphasized that there are examples of the introduction of new varieties where the indivisibility problem is small. The introduction of hybrid maize in Kenya (Gerhart, 1975) is an example where a new variety has been almost completely adopted also by small farmers. The new maize varieties introduced were a basic factor behind a decade of a successful development of smallholder agriculture in Kenya.

Apart from the biases inherent in technological change in LDCs one must remember that the overwhelming share of technological development takes place in the industrialized countries. This technology is then transferred from the DCs. Since it has been developed on the basis of relative factor prices greatly different from those of the average LDC, it is too capital-intensive with regard to the existing factor endowments in LDCs. This has implied an inefficient allocation of resources and under-utilization of labour, and consequently a more concentrated distribution of labour incomes than that yielded by a more labour-intensive technique. The problem is, however, that such a technique is often not available (see Stewart, 1974, 1978; Tokman, 1975; Bhalla, 1975; Sen, 1975; Baer, 1976; Wehr, 1977; Hamilton and Söderström, 1981).

5.4.5 Sectoral structure

Having considered the importance of type of economic system, factor proportions, and technology we shall now go on to consider the effect of sectoral economic structure. This was emphasized in the cross-country studies presented above as a major factor affecting the change in income distribution over time. It is certainly true that within the framework of institutions and ownership discussed above, the pattern of structural change is a fundamental determinant of the development of income distribution.

Let us look at the development of a country that starts out as a dual economy. What normally happens is that the modern sector increases its relative importance. There is a reallocation of output and labour. Initially, when the modern sector is small in terms of employment, this tends to increase inequality (the Kuznets effect), because average modern sector incomes usually are considerably higher than incomes in the traditional sector.

The fact that inequality in the modern sector is often greater than in the traditional sector also contributes to an increased overall inequality.

This pattern of structural change tends to have the strongest effect in the early stages of development. In Sub-Saharan Africa it has possibly been the major influence on the evolution of income distribution during much of the twentieth century, even if few time-series analyses are available to show it.

Malaysia did not do well with regard to income distribution up to 1970, which was, partly, a result of the imbalanced pattern of development between the modern sector and the rest of the economy.

> Rapid growth of the modern sector exacerbated intersectoral and rural – urban income differentials and the reliance on foreign investment led to a capital-intensive pattern of industrial growth. Productivity and real wages rose in the industrial sector and this, together with a distorted labour market, ensured rising real wages in estate agriculture and the rest of the modern sector at the same time as open unemployment and underemployment, increased in both rural and urban areas.
>
> (Lee, 1977, p. 285; see also Anand, 1977)

Again, this is a rather typical description of a pattern of growth which

Malaysia has in common with many Third World countries. Lee points out that Sri Lanka did do better with regard to income distribution, although not in other respects, because the terms of trade did turn in favour of the peasant sector while real wages fell in the modern sector.

With regard to the not so poor Latin America, the factor of structural change does not appear to be so vitally important by itself as in Africa and Asia. For example, Bacha and Taylor (1978) consider whether the shift of labour from sectors with little differentiation to sectors with more differentiation may have increased inequality in Brazil. They find that this was not so. Instead population movements between regions and between sectors seem to have had an equalizing influence on income distribution.

In conclusion we might say that the pattern of structural change seems to have the largest effect in the early stages of development. Both the existing gap between the modern and the traditional sector and its change over time are very important. There is a need to reduce dualism, if long-run equalization is to be brought about. (This was pointed out already in section 5.2.) Measures to improve the integration of the economy are therefore important.

5.4.6 Regional structure
Apart from sectoral dualism, there are also regional and urban – rural imbalances in most LDCs. This is important also for interpersonal income distribution, since large imbalances between regions in the access to income opportunities as well as in their rewards is a structural determinant of inequality, which is not easily eliminated. It will help keep inequalities up.

Time-series data on regional inequality in LDCs is scarce, but Williamson (1965) has shown in a cross-country analysis that an inverted-U pattern also exists with regard to regional inequality, i.e. it first increases and then decreases. His analysis has been subjected to criticism (Gilbert and Goodman, 1976a), since the empirical basis for the conclusions about the early phase is weak.

Evidence on the time pattern of regional inequality in Kenya between 1967 and 1976 is provided in Bigsten (1980). It is shown that there was a very small increase in regional inequality up to 1974. In 1975 and 1976, regional inequality decreased temporarily as a result of the commodity boom, which raised the price of coffee and tea three to four times in one year. This study shows that regional inequalities are a permanent feature in very poor countries.

The reason for this is economies of scale which lead to a concentration of production to one or a few plants within a given line of production. The location of these plants is then influenced by the location of sellers of inputs and the buyers of the outputs. These factors, together with other forms of agglomeration economies, breed concentration. If there is an agglomeration of producers and wealthy consumers in a certain region at a given time, the cost-minimizing producer very often locates close to this agglomeration. This starts a cumulative process towards concentration, which in the short run can be checked only by an active regional policy.

There is also some evidence of the time pattern of regional inequality in China. Lardy (1978) argues that China has given much weight to the goal of an equitable regional distribution of income. To achieve this end it has been necessary to transfer resources away from the rich regions to the poorer ones. To accomplish this, the state has retained much centralized financial control.

Lardy finds that data on provincial per capita social expenditures and provincial shares in national investments indicate a weak tendency towards equalization. The data base for the 1960s and 1970s is, however, very weak. Still, for the period 1957–74 the population weighted coefficient of variation of provincial industrial per capita output fell by about 5%. This development would have been unlikely without a conscious regional policy.

Lardy's (1978, p. 192) conclusion is that the Chinese have been relatively successful in simultaneously pursuing the two goals of growth and equity. They have achieved a long-run growth rate of about 6%, while moving strenuously to reduce intersectoral and interregional inequalities.

Lipton (1977) argues that the most important class conflict in LDCs is between urban and rural classes. The huge welfare gap that exists today between urban and rural populations is not just inequitable, but also inefficient. Lipton claims that the effect on output of a certain amount of resources invested in agriculture is two to three times larger than in industry. The urban bias in development results, to some extent, from a misconception about the process of development, but basically it rests on the convergent interests of industrialists, urban workers and also large farmers. All these categories gain from squeezing agriculture, provided some of the resources are allocated to the large farmers, which then can produce cheap raw materials and food for the urban areas.

Lipton (1977, pp. 158–9) finds that the LDCs now experience a much larger urban – rural output per person disparity than the industrialized countries did during the previous century. The LDCs urban – rural income quotients range between 2.5 and 7.5, while those of the industrialized countries in the nineteenth century ranged between 1.5 and 2.5 Lipton is very pessimistic about the likelihood of a reduction of this gap.

One problem which has been discussed is whether there should be checks on rural – urban migration. However, with regard to income distribution this would imply a deterioration. Bigsten (1980) has shown that migration reduced the growth of regional inequality considerably. Bacha and Taylor (1978, p. 271) find that migration in Brazil had an equalizing effect. Berry and Urrutia (1976, p. 138) note that mobility has 'undoubtedly been an important factor in the decrease in inequality related to regional differences'. The fear that migration would increase the regional differences attributable to 'positive selectivity' of migrants has not been vindicated in the case of Colombia.

Papanek (1975) finds that even if the poor of Jakarta are really poor, the move from the rural areas did increase their incomes by two-thirds. There the poor urban dwellers are better off than the poor rural dwellers, and restrictions on migration would thus make the situation of the poor even worse.

Another study, which is of interest in this context, had been made in Mexico. Young *et al.* (1979, p. 683) have performed a principal factor analysis of regional differences in rural poverty. They find that poverty is attributable to lack of differentiation, peripheral location and an involved and rigid social organization. Obviously, regional structure is an important determinant of the incidence of rural poverty and thus also of how the overall income distribution changes over time.

Regional inequality has a tendency to increase or, at least, to remain serious in the early stages of development. To be able to counteract the tendencies towards regional imbalances in the early stages of development, an active regional policy is necessary.

Countries with a well-developed rural infrastructure, which has made it possible for non-agricultural production activities to develop alongside agriculture in the rural areas, have experienced improvements in the distribution of income. One example of this is Taiwan, where 'after 1968 rural by-employment had become the dominant form of rural labour reallocation and source of rural income' (Fei, Ranis, and Kuo, 1978, p. 34). Chinn finds that 'non-farm sources of income allowed households with small holdings to close the income gap between themselves and larger farms by allocating more of their labour to non-farm activities. Thus, the expansion of non-farm opportunities had the effect of reducing relative inequality in the rural areas.' (1979, p. 299).

Improved integration of the economy and a more even spatial

distribution of economic activity are, thus, important factors contributing to the equalization of incomes.

5.4.7 Wage determination and employment

There are two competing paradigms with regard to wage determination. The traditional conception of the labour market is one where wages are determined by supply and demand. There is, however, a competing paradigm which sometimes is referred to as the job competition model. According to this people compete for jobs with given characteristics and given incomes and are placed into these jobs according to, say, their educational characteristics and there is therefore very little wage competition. If supply is greater than demand at a certain level, those at the end of the labour queue are bumped downwards to the next lower level of the hierarchy, and so on. If the labour market follows this pattern, expansion of education will not lead to equalization.

There are some labour markets where there really is wage competition, e.g. Hong Kong's market for unskilled or semi-skilled labour; but even within this economy there are segments of the labour market that do not compete with each other. Still, the labour market is generally competitive. Establishments are small and labour-intensive. Workers are predominantly unskilled, or semi-skilled, and there is little collective bargaining and little government intervention in the labour market. The economy is very flexible, with high labour mobility and continual establishment of new industries. This has led to a considerable uniformity in the movement of wage-rates among different industries (Hsia and Chau, 1978a, pp. 14, 17). Wages are thus basically determined by the workings of supply and demand, and the emergence of a labour shortage has therefore had a profound effect on the income distribution. The Gini coefficient fell from 0.49 to 0.41 between 1966 and 1971.

The lower 60% get about 30% of the income while the top 20% get about 50%. The high incomes are earned within finance, import and export trade, professional and government services. For these sectors there are barriers to entry. To a large extent, the income differences are thus caused by sectoral imbalances.

The main conclusion that can be drawn from the study is that a tight labour market is a very efficient means of achieving an improved distribution of income. Increasing the demand for unskilled labour may therefore be the major means of trying to bring down inequality.

In Collier and Bigsten (1981) evidence is presented which shows that there is a considerable flexibility in the Kenyan labour market. In the late 1960s and in the 1970s there was a decline in real wages and a change in the structure of relative earnings. The labour market can therefore not be characterized as rigid. Still, during this period the wages of skilled manpower remained fairly stable in the face of rapidly increasing supply. However, this need not be explained as a market imperfection. The employers are increasingly making use of screening by educational grade which offsets the downward pressure exerted on wages by the increasing supply.

The most important factor explaining the positive trend in income distribution in Pakistan during the 1960s was the character of growth in the agricultural sector. The removal of government controls and regulations helped turn the internal terms of trade in favour of the agricultural sector (Guisinger and Hicks, 1978, p. 128). Another important factor was the fact that the increased output did not come about through increased mechanization, but through increased use of labour. This meant that the real wages in the agricultural sector increased which, in turn, pushed up wages in the formal sector.

The main conclusion that can be drawn from Guisinger and Hicks's study of Pakistan, as well as from that of Hong Kong, is that the most important force improving distribution is an increasing demand for unskilled labour.

Countries, such as Taiwan, that have managed to end their labour surplus condition, that is, reached what Fei and Ranis have called the commercialization point, have experienced an improved income distribution. To get to the commercialization point as soon as possible is thus of fundamental importance for a sustained, long-run improvement in income distribution. High growth can thus be considered central to the goal of long-run equalization.

An increasing demand for unskilled labour is probably the most important single factor to have contributed to improvements in income distribution in the countries considered here. It has already been shown that access to non-agricultural rural employment has a very favourable effect on income distribution. Also informal employment can be an important complement to other employment opportunities. The existence of monopsony on local labour markets as a result of, for example, the dominance of one employer or land-owner tends to decrease the share of labour.

There is not much evidence in the material on the effects of trade unions on the development of income distribution. They may be expected to increase the incomes of their members at the expense of the rest of the community, that is employers and non-union members, even if the bargaining power of trade unions in many Third World countries is limited. One cannot a priori say in what direction this will change the size distribution.

Analysis of the wage-fixing institutions of Brazil shows that the government was able to hold back increases of real wages for labour. This was done by keeping the minimum wage low and by allowing firms to pass on wage increases in the form of higher prices. There was thus a wage squeeze after 1964. This meant that the share of profits did increase. It is also found that there are two non-competing groups in the labour market, labourers and managers. The latter are paid considerable increases, and thus get a share of the surplus that is left after workers have been paid their share (Bacha and Taylor, 1978, p. 272).

Bacha and Taylor (pp. 274–5) also argue that

> the relative levels of wages parallel the structure of command and influence within organizations, with market processes guaranteeing rough comparability of remunerations across management units. The average wage differential between 'managers' and 'workers' widens as gross profits increase and is influenced by the level of payments received by upper level government technocrats. If the market at the top end of the wage spectrum tightens, vacancies are more likely to be filled by accelerated on-the-job training and downgrading of ascriptive job characteristics, than wiped out by wage adjustments.

This pattern at the top and the wage-squeeze at the bottom of the scale seem to have contributed to the growth in inequality. Higher profits were actually filtered down the organizational hierarchy.

This explanation dovetails, according to Bacha and Taylor, with a neo-Keynesian explanation in terms of growing income concentration with growth. According to this hypothesis savings tend to adjust to the current value of investment through increased private savings from profits. Thus, Bacha and Taylor explain the growth in inequality by the wage-squeeze, wage-spreading and this neo-Keynesian explanation (see also Taylor *et al.* 1980).

The effects of industrialization on employment have been much discussed. The evidence is surveyed by Morawetz (1974) and Bruton (1974), but also some papers in Stewart (1975) and Bruton (1977) and the study by Hsia and Chau (1978a, 1978b) referred to above are of interest in this context. As was pointed out above in the discussion on economic structure, the effect on income distribution of industrial growth in poor countries may be negative. However, it is necessary in the long run to end the labour surplus condition, and there is a great deal of evidence indicating that this is a major turning point also with regard to income distribution.

Making labour scarce is the best method of ensuring higher wages in a market economy. In a planned economy there is more scope for policy-makers. Cuba, for example, has consciously tried to decrease wage differences. However, in the 1963–64 wage scales the lowest wage was only 1/13 of the highest one (Mesa-Lago and Hernandez, 1976, p. 81). In 1966, more emphasis was put on moral incentives, but after 1970 there was a return to the scales. How large the differences are at present is difficult to ascertain; it is therefore also difficult to say anything about the development of income distribution since the early 1960s.

5.4.8 Ownership of assets

The size of the capital stock and the amount of land available to the economy relative to the availability of labour is a major determinant of the functional distribution of income.

The pattern of ownership of assets and its change over time has its major effect on the evolution of size distribution. Particularly in the poorest LDCs the distribution of land is crucial. The countries that have succeeded in combining growth with a relatively equal income distribution have been characterized by a fairly even distribution of land among rural families. This has made it possible for large segments of the rural population to share in the increased agricultural incomes. The countries that have had a less satisfactory development of income distribution often have an uneven distribution of land to start with. Increasing landlessness is a factor which seriously aggravates the distribution problem. The most discussed success cases among the mixed economies are South Korea and Taiwan, but Japan in earlier stages may also be included here.

The successful rural development of South Korea is attributable to three major factors, according to Lee (1979; see also Rao, 1978, p. 384). First, the egalitarian conditions created by early land reforms (to some extent undertaken by foreigners – Japanese and American). Essentially these allowed tenants to obtain ownership. Second, disequilibrating tendencies were efficiently checked. A major factor was the three hectare land ceiling, which worked well. Third, the extremely rapid growth of the non-agricultural sector relieved the population pressure in the rural areas.

In Japan, the creation of irrigation institutions, together with a fairly equal distribution of land, ensured that the benefits of productivity increases were spread to large segments of the population (Francks, 1979). Like South Korea, Japan had an agricultural sector with a low land/man ratio and labour intensive paddy production, where small units using family labour were efficient and competitive (Lee, 1979).

In the introduction to the large International Labour Organization study on rural Asia (1977, see also Griffin and Khan, 1978) the editors emphasize the uneven distribution of wealth (land in particular), the concentration of the surplus and the fragmented allocation mechanisms as important factors perpetuating poverty in rural Asia. The most important policy conclusion that emerges from the study is that land must be redistributed if the poorer rural strata are to get a reasonable share of the growing production.

Such a redistribution has, for example, taken place in China, and the consequences are discussed in one chapter of ILO (1977). The chapter on China is not based on the same amount of empirical data as the rest, but the tentative (and plausible) conclusion is that the extent of poverty is decidedly smaller and the degree of inequality is also less than in other countries on a similar per capita income level. (See also Macrae, 1977, on how the production result is distributed).

Griffin and Ghose (1979, p. 367) note that 'except in countries which have had a radical redistribution of land, the degree of inequality in rural Asia has not diminished significantly and in most countries it has increased'. There is also evidence in some regions of increasing absolute poverty, although the data supporting this are less solid. Griffin (1981, p. 10) argues that the principal component in an attack on poverty has to be a redistribution of wealth.

For Latin America, there is quite a lot of evidence concerning Mexico. Nguyen and Martinez-Saldivar (1979) find that the Mexican land reform has done fairly well with regard to productivity and employment objectives, but that it has been somewhat disappointing in its effect on income distribution. The average income on land reform farms is low in comparison with those in the private sector (but, of course, these people might have been even poorer without the reform). More complementary resources must be made available to the land reform farmers to help them increase production. This would not imply any efficiency loss, since the marginal returns to inputs are higher in this sector than in the private sector.

It has been argued by many that when it comes to land reforms we often do not face the classical conflict between growth and distribution. Yotopoulos and Nugent (1976, p. 103) conclude in a study of Indian agriculture that small farms are more efficient than large farms. Similarly, Cline (1972b) points out that the agricultural economies of scale argument warrants little weight in the context of the developing countries. Finally, Singh (1979, p. 19) notes that

there is ample evidence to show that small farmers generally have higher yields per acre, and often higher overall productivity, have higher cropping intensities, more area proportionately under irrigation, and use their resources more efficiently. Although data are scarce their production appears to have grown just as rapidly as that of the larger farmers. Furthermore, there is growing evidence that when small farmers have had access to new technologies, and where these technologies have been profitable and within their means, they have been equally responsive and eager to adopt them.

Land reform may therefore be an appropriate first step in a policy aiming at combining growth with a more equal distribution (see also Lipton, 1977, pp. 97−8). There may be one problem in the long run, though. Even if output goes up, the surplus may go down when the large farms have been subdivided. Smallholders may increase their consumption. If the surplus previously was used for investment purposes, this will constitute a drag on growth. Still, in the short run poverty will be reduced.

Moreover, even if a land reform does not imply any sacrifice in economic terms, as far as politics is concerned it is often the most difficult type of reform to carry out. Land-owners are a strong political force in most LDCs.

There are other physical assets than land, and these are normally even more unequally distributed. How this distribution evolves over time has to do with the savings rates in various socioeconomic categories. Since these tend to be higher among the rich than among the poor, there is not likely to be any automatic equalization in the distribution of these assets. (see for example Williamson, 1968; Cline, 1971, 1972a; Prebisch, 1971; Snyder, 1974; Lluch, Powell and Williams, 1977). Since the size of the physical capital stock grows over time the income from these assets will also grow. Rao (1978), for example, fears that inequality may start to increase in South Korea as a result of the increasing importance of urban wealth, which is very unequally distributed.

The savings behaviour also means that there may be a conflict between redistribution and the desire for a high savings rate. There are, however, ways of increasing the national rate of saving that do not rely on an unequal income distribution, for example through public saving, by improving the institutions in which people can save, and by increasing interest rates (see e.g. Chinn, 1977). Ranis (1977) points out that there are cases where growth and distribution seem to be complements rather than trade-offs.

Apart from the level of incomes the differences in savings rates among categories of people is also affected by the access to savings institutions and, to some extent, by the availability of investment opportunities. Banks are normally much better organized in urban areas than in the rural areas, where most of the poor people reside. Access to loans is also very much biased against the small farmers. In Colombia, the financial sector has mainly benefited the large-scale farmers (Berry and Urrutia, 1976, p. 174), and this is certainly not a unique case. Moreover, since the interest rates have been kept at an artificially low level in most of these countries, the banking system has tended to redistribute money from savers to borrowers, which, in many cases, means from the poor to the rich. Even if the rich save more than the poor, their dominance on the lending side is even larger.

It is not clear from the material whether capitalist development with a large share of multinational corporations gives a more uneven income distribution than capitalist development based mainly on domestic capital.

5.4.9 Social stratification

The next characteristic considered is social stratification. There may be many explanations to this apart from strictly economic ones. Ethnic affiliation often is an important factor. One may here consider minority groups such as the Indians in East Africa, the Chinese in South-East Asia, or white settlers in former colonies, which all are economically much better off than the majority of the population. Other groups, such as the Indians in Latin America, are discriminated against. The economic differences between ethnic groups often are difficult to eliminate.

Where stratification is pronounced, privileges tend to remain with the elite groups. This has a large effect on the size distribution of income. Entrepreneurs tend to be recruited from the same circles all the time, and there is limited mobility and flexibility in the economy. A number of opportunities are not open for, or may not even be known to large strata of the population. A rigid social structure tends to inhibit growth, since it distorts resource allocation and stifles initiative.

Myrdal points out (1968, p. 579) that social stratification, in itself, is an aspect of inequality, at the same time as it in Asia 'impedes the rise of social, regional, and occupational mobility and encourages the persistence of multi-dimensional segmentation of social and economic life, which is a major obstacle to economic growth'. Similar ideas are advanced in Gunter (1964), Baster and Scott (1969), Baster (1970) and Nafzinger (1977).

Elliott found in his study of stratification that

the privileged groups owe their privileges to their ability to secure superior access to productive assets – land, credit, education – or employment in the formal sector. This superior access is not randomly distributed: it depends on the interplay of political, social, economic and ecological forces that combine not only to give specific groups preferential opportunities but also to reinforce that pattern and, all things being equal, make it decreasingly open and malleable.   (1975, p. 313)

Poor families (particularly agricultural ones) also tend to have more children than well-educated and wealthy ones. It is argued by Fishlow (1972) that the educational level of parents influences the productivity of schooling. Both for reasons of poverty and because of the large number of children, poor families spend less on the education of each child than the rich. Thus, the family institution tends to propagate inequality. Moreover, the assets of the rich are bequeathed to their offspring, who therefore get a better start with regard to access to both physical and human capital. Inequality is therefore transferred from generation to generation.

The stratification is a major determinant of how the pattern of inequality is carried over to the next generation. If the social stratification remains severe, one must also expect political power to be very unequally distributed. It is then difficult to pursue a policy aimed at reducing inequalities.

5.4.10 Fiscal policy
As has already been pointed out the aim of economic policies often is to change one or several of the above characteristics. In the respective sections we have already touched upon many policy aspects relating to the various factors. Still, it may be worthwhile to discuss directly a few types of economic policy that are of great importance to income distribution. First, we will take a look at some aspects of fiscal policy.

Almost any type of policy that implies increasing unemployment will, at least in the short run, have a strong negative effect on income distribution since the incidence of unemployment normally is regressive. For example, a very strict stabilization policy may have this effect. On the other hand, a rapid inflation normally transfers incomes to those with property, i.e. the rich. A slow-down of inflation may therefore have beneficial effects on income distribution in the long run.

Several studies have been made about the incidence of the government budget, among which we can mention Foxley *et al.* (1979) on Chile in the late 1960s and Meerman (1979) on Malaysia. These studies show that the government, in countries on this level of development at least, can really contribute to an equalization in standards of living. Meerman (1979, p. 324) finds that the share of the poorest in income increases by as much as 29% after budgetary effects have been taken into account. Foxley *et al.* (1979, p. 200) find that the 30% poorest families only received 7.6% of the original income, but they got as much as 15−18% of government expenditures. This increased their income share to 10.5−11.8%. This represents a considerable improvement. In these relatively developed countries the government activities thus can contribute to an equalization in the level of consumption. To what extent this also helps reducing inequality in pre-tax incomes is less clear. It seems reasonable to assume that the fact that poor people get access to education and health services, for example, which they otherwise would not, ought to contribute something to the reduction of the pre-tax income gap.

A number of studies have analysed interdependence between the pattern of demand and income distribution. Interesting in this context are the papers by Paukert, Skolka and Maton (1974) and Skolka and Garzuel (1976) which within a consistency model test the effects of different income distribution patterns on, for example, employment. Other important studies are Morley and Williamson (1974), Figueroa (1975) and Ballentine and Soligo (1978).

Figueroa notes that the consumption bundle of the rich is different from that of the poor and then goes on to estimate the derived demand for labour in manufacturing in Peru under different assumptions. He finds that an income redistribution towards the poor would increase employment in industry, which would further improve the income distribution. Figueroa's analysis, however, is partial, and he does not trace the second-round effects.

The study of Ballentine and Soligo, on the other hand, is based on a closed input-output model of the Colombian economy by which they can trace the full effects of the consumption − earnings chain on income distribution. They find that a tax-subsidy scheme that transfers income from the rich to the poor and thus changes the pattern of consumption has the effect that factor earnings of the rich increase more than those of the poor. Thus, the distribution of earnings shifts towards the rich contrary to expectations. They have therefore not found any evidence to support the thesis that the poor consume a bundle of goods that generates more earnings for the poor.

Thirsk (1979) has suggested that the small secondary effects of income redistribution found in many studies may be a result of aggregation bias. Thirsk has extended the model used by Ballentine and Soligo and partitioned each sector into one with small firms and one with large firms. Then he tests, with this partially closed input-output model of Colombia, the hypothesis that poor people spend their money on goods from small firms in each sector, while rich people spend their money on goods from large firms. In this case such an assumption yields an ultimate income increase for the poor of two to three dollars for each redistributed dollar.

Also James (1980) suggests that the disappointing results that have been obtained in studies of the effect of income redistribution are a result of aggregation bias. The aggregation of products into broad categories implies that it is impossible to capture the effects of shifts within the categories to goods produced with different factor combinations. James tests the extent of aggregation bias in the sugar industry in India, where there are two distinct types of products. One is produced with labour-intensive methods, while the other is produced by capital-intensive methods. The former is purchased by the low-income earners, while the refined variety is purchased by the better-off.

James finds that, at least with regard to the rural areas, there is a considerable aggregation bias. The employment effect of redistribution is considerably larger in the disaggregated analysis than in the aggregated variant. Employment increased twice as much in the disaggregated analysis. The same kind of conclusion is reached by House (1981) in a study of Kenyan furniture-making.

Thus, the differences in results may naturally reflect the specific economic characteristics of the respective countries. One must be cautious about drawing conclusions about employment expansion before this has been empirically investigated. The aggregation problem is obviously serious in this context, and the secondary effects of redistributions may plausibly be assumed to be larger than what some studies have suggested.

However, none of these studies analyse the effects of the redistribution on investments and economic growth, which in the long run may be more important determinants of income distribution. It has been pointed out already that a more equal income distribution may yield less savings.

For many countries it has been shown that the development of the domestic terms of trade is a major determinant of the evolution of income distribution. This can be influenced by policy-makers to some extent. For example, King and Weldon (1977) find that the government control of rice prices had a highly negative effect on rural incomes in Java during the 1960s. This means that it also had a negative effect on income distribution. This important issue will be discussed further in Chapter 6.

5.4.11 *Educational policy*

There is ample evidence that the degree of schooling and on-the-job training are very important determinants of the income that a person may earn (see e.g. Fishlow, 1972; Bhagwati, 1973b; Hoerr, 1973; Hinchliffe, 1975; Jallade, 1976; Psacharopoulos, 1977; Harbison,

1977; Richards, 1977; and Rodgers, 1978), but it has been difficult to show that more expenditure on education in a country gives a more equal income distribution.

Several studies show that the private returns to schooling are high. Psacharopoulos (1977) finds, for example, that in a Moroccan sample of 1600 people, differences in schooling and experience explain about 70% of the relative earning dispersion (see also Hoerr, 1973). But it is not clear if this is because of increases in productivity, or because each labourer is given a place in the job-structure ladder in accordance with his formal merits. It may well be that it is mainly the job structure that matters, that is that there is job competition rather than wage competition. Here the large size of the government sector in Third World countries contributes to the rigidity of the wage structure (Richards, 1977). Also Lal (1976) is sceptical about the positive effects of education on income distribution. He believes that this argument amounts to placing the cart before the horse, and argues that it is better to increase the demand for labour. That this actually is a fairly effective policy has been pointed out above.

Berry and Urrutia (1976, p. 199) strongly believe in the equalizing effect of an expansion of primary education. In the early stages of development, the demand for skilled labour tends to increase more rapidly than the demand for unskilled labour, while the supply of skilled labour increases only slowly. Skilled manpower therefore earn high scarcity rents which can be eroded by a rapid expansion of education.

However, Carnoy *et al.* (1979) report on empirical studies of the effects of education on earnings distribution in Brazil, Peru, and Mexico. All three case studies come to the conclusion that the effect of changes in schooling on the distribution is very small in comparison with changes relating to the demand side of the labour market. They conclude that income distribution policies based on the equalization of supply-side characteristics is bound to fail. 'Rather, government incomes policy effecting the reward of different levels of schooling, different work sectors, different types of occupations, and different regions of the country may be a much more important factor in understanding changes in income distribution' (Carnoy *et al.*, 1979, p. 98). Thus, even if educational policy can play a part in a policy package aimed at equalization, it seems to have a relatively small effect on income distribution by itself.

Rodgers (1978) has made simulations with the Bachue model for the Philippines. From these experiments he draws the conclusion that only slight declines in inequality can be obtained after an extended period with a human capital approach to development. With regard to

Brazil, Bacha and Taylor (1978, p. 272) found that the increases in skill at least did not contribute to increased inequality during the 1960s. The supply of skilled labour increased very much, and they argue that 'with plausible elasticities of substitution and a competitive labour market, the rewards for skills must have fallen'. Thus, more education may reduce skilled – unskilled wage differentials, and benefit rural areas more than urban, because of the promotion of out-migration and terms of trade effects. Education may also facilitate a skill- and labour-intensive development strategy of South Korean type with beneficial distributional consequences.

Bhagwati (1973b) argues that education benefits the upper classes disproportionately because (i) the opportunity cost of labour is higher for the poor; (ii) the benefits of education are lower; and (iii) the opportunity cost of capital is higher. Similar arguments are presented by Jallade (1976) and Harbison (1977). There is therefore a tendency for inequality to be carried over from one generation to the next. Still, the inequalities within the new generation may be less than in the old one because of increases in education.

5.4.12 Trade policy

An import-substitution policy has been followed in most LDCs. The major contributions to the debate on the effects of trade policy on income distribution are the large OECD study summarized in Little, Scitovsky and Scott (1970) and the NBER study summarized in Krueger (1978) and Bhagwati (1978). The main conclusion from these studies is that import-substitution industrialization has contributed to a deterioration of income distribution. It has tended to favour industry in contrast to agriculture. The domestic terms of trade of the latter have fallen, and thus the incomes of the people employed in the sector have become lower than what they otherwise would have been.* There has also been a bias in favour of capital which has contributed to increasing inequality. Bhagwati (1973a) writes that 'the exchange control regime has made mockery of income distributional objectives by creating profits and privileges'.

The policy has also created a structural look (Baer, 1972). The productive structure which resulted from the import-substitution policy reflects the demand profile that existed at the time when the process was started. This demand profile was based on a distribution

---

*In India, however, terms of trade have favoured agriculture. Between 1960/61 and 1974/75 the barter terms of trade moved 1.4% a year in favour of agriculture, relative to industry (Bharadwaj, 1979, p. 271).

of income which, in most cases, was quite unequal. Thus, if one is to be able to use the productive capacity well, the distribution of income must remain unequal.

Market imperfections also contribute to inequality in LDCs. One major cause of the market fragmentation is the trade policy of these countries. This creates monopolies, which make it possible to reap monopoly rents.

Berry and Urrutia point to the role of the import-substitution policy in Colombia, which up to the mid-1950s tended to increase the payments to the scarce capital factor and generate monopoly profits and thus worsen the income distribution. Trade policy has mainly benefited the large industrialists (Berry and Urrutia, 1976, p. 229). The policies pursued in Colombia were the usual ones of subsidized interest rates, overvalued exchange rates, and ceilings on savings rates. These policies diminished the demand for labour and therefore had a negative effect on the labour share in income.

One of the best analysed examples of a successful change in trade policy is the case of South Korea. The two main policies that were initiated in the mid-1960s were an interest rate reform, which meant a doubling of the interest rates, and a 50% devaluation. The combined effect of these two changes led to an impressive increase in exports combined with a rapid increase in non-farm employment (see Adelman and Robinson, 1978). This rapid growth was combined with rapid increases of the incomes of the poor. The real income of the 20% poorest more than doubled between 1964 and 1970. Thus, this export-oriented development strategy based on the comparative advantages of the country led to a more labour-intensive production pattern. As has already been pointed out, strategies that increase demand for unskilled or semi-skilled labour tend to improve income distribution.

5.5 Concluding remarks

The problems of inequality and poverty in the Third World remain grave in spite of considerable increases in total production since the 1950s. There are, however, a few countries that have managed to decrease poverty considerably, which shows that it can be done, but the majority of the poor in the Third World have experienced only marginal improvements.

Faced with rapidly increasing oil prices and sluggish growth in the DCs, one can hardly be optimistic about the likelihood of substantial improvements for the poor during the coming decade. Large segments of people in Third World countries have actually experienced substantial reductions in real incomes in the last few years. Still, in this chapter I have tried to identify the factors that are important with regard to income distribution. When devising a development strategy the knowledge about the determinants of income distribution that has by now accumulated should be taken into account. It is income distribution which together with growth determines the future incomes of the poor.

In a recent book Sen (1981) analyses a number of serious famines. He introduces the concept of entitlement. An entitlement mapping may, for example, transform an endowment vector of commodities into an alternative availability vector of commodities. Whether someone is starving is then dependent on whether he can command a bundle of commodities with a sufficient amount of food. It is shown very clearly by Sen that entitlement failures can appear both when there is a food availability collapse and when it is not. That food is available is not enough to avoid starvation.

Certain groups may still starve because of endowment losses or entitlement failures. In an analysis of these issues one needs to take ownership rights, contractual obligations and other legal relations into consideration.

One problem upon which I have only touched briefly in this chapter is the question of political power, and it may well be the crucial factor. Drastic changes in a direction that favours the poor can not be expected, unless they obtain a certain amount of political clout. Unfortunately, economic poverty is often combined with other forms of deprivation, for example, lack of political influence.* It is, therefore, not easy to be optimistic.

The research surveyed in this chapter is of both a cross-sectional and a time-series type. The former may provide some suggestions as to what factors determine the evolution of income distribution in the long run, but it seems unlikely that much more can be gained from pursuing this line of analysis. What is needed is better analyses of the experiences of individual countries. The country studies surveyed here usually tries to piece together evidence of household budget surveys, labour market surveys, national accounts, etc. The difficulties faced in guaranteeing consistency for individual years are often great, and the problem of making comparisons between different years are even greater. Still, the data situation is improving and there is considerable scope for improvements also in the use of historical material. Consistency checks within a social accounting matrix framework may be one alternative.

---

*Also on this point there are exceptions. In Malaysia the Chinese are dominating economically, while the Malayans constitute the majority in parliament and the government. The latter use this position to redistribute income towards the Malayans.

However, once the empirical picture has been drawn, one needs to take the more difficult step of explaining the pattern of development. Most of the general country studies discussed here have used fairly *ad hoc* methods. To some extent this is inevitable, but efforts should be made to go further in the attempts to do the analysis within some consistency framework or model. Even if socio-political factors are very important in this field, it seems to me that more methodological and theoretical stringency is required, if we are to proceed beyond the present level of understanding. In Chapter 6 analyses of this type will be discussed.

References

Adelman, I. and Morris, C.T. (1971), *An Anatomy of Income Distribution in Developing Nations – A Summary of Findings*, mimeo, International Bank for Reconstruction and Development.

Adelman, I. and Morris, C.T. (1973), *Economic Growth and Social Equity in Developing Countries*, Stanford University Press, Stanford.

Adelman, I. and Robinson, S. (1978), *Income Distribution Policy in Developing Countries. A Case Study of Korea*, Oxford University Press, Oxford.

Ahluwalia, M.S. (1976a), 'Income distribution and development: some stylized facts', *American Economic Review*, Vol. 66.

Ahluwalia, M.S. (1976b), 'Inequality, poverty, and development', *Journal of Development Economics*, Vol. 3.

Ahluwalia, M.S. (1978), 'Rural poverty and agricultural performance in India', *Journal of Development Studies*, Vol. 14.

Ahluwalia, M.S., Carter, N.G. and Chenery, H.B. (1979), 'Growth and poverty in developing countries', *Journal of Development Studies*, Vol. 16.

Ahluwalia, M.S. and Duloy, J.H. (1980), comment to 'Who benefits from economic development', *American Economic Review*, Vol. 70.

Anand, S. (1977), 'Aspects of Poverty in Malaysia', *Review of Income and Wealth*, series 23.

Bacha, E.L. and Taylor, L. (1978), 'Brazilian Income Distribution in the 1960s: Facts, Models, Results and the Controversy', *Journal of Development Studies*, Vol. 14.

Baer, W. (1972), 'Import Substitution and Industrialization in Latin America. Experiences and Interpretations', *Latin American Research Review*, spring.

Baer, W. (1976), 'Technology, Employment and Development: Empirical Findings', *World Development*, Vol. 4.

Ballentine, J.G. and Soligo, R. (1978), 'Consumption and Earnings Patterns and Income Distribution', *Economic Development and Cultural Change*, Vol. 26.

Baster, N. (1970), *Distribution of Income and Economic Growth*, United Nations Research Institute for Social Development, Geneva.

Baster, N. Scott., W. (1969), *Levels of Living and Economic Growth*, *A Comparative Study of Six Countries 1950–1965*, United Nations Research Institute for Social Development, Geneva.

Berry, A. (1978), 'Income and Consumption Distribution Trends in the Philippines, 1950–1970', *Review of Income and Wealth*, series 24.

Berry, A. and Urrutia, M. (1976), *Income Distribution in Columbia*, Yale University Press, New Haven.

Bhagwati, J. (1973a), *India in the International Economy*, Lal Bahadur Shastri Memorial Lectures, Institute of Public Enterprise, Hyderabad.

Bhagwati, J. (1973b), 'Education, Class Structure and Income Inequality', *World Development*, Vol. 1.

Bhagwati, J. (1978) *Foreign Trade Regimes and Economic Development: Anatomy and Consequences of Exchange Control Regimes*, Ballinger, Cambridge, Mass.

Bhalla, A.S. (ed.) (1975), *Technology and Employment in Industry*, ILO Geneva.

Bharadwaj, K. (1979), 'Towards a macroeconomic framework for a developing economy: the Indian case', *The Manchester School*, Vol. 47.

Bigsten, A. (1975), 'Ekonomi och utvecklingsstrategi i Kina', *Sosialökonomen*, Vol. 29.

Bigsten, A. (1980), *Regional Inequality and Development. A Case Study of Kenya*, Gower Press, Farnborough.

Bruton, H. (1974), 'Economic development and labor use: a review', in Edwards (ed.).

Bruton, H.J. (1977), 'Industrialization policy and income distribution', in Frank and Webb (eds.).

Carnoy, M. *et al.* (1979), *Can Educational Policy Equalize Income Distribution in Latin America?* Saxon House, Harmondsworth.

Chapman, J.G. (1978), 'Are earnings more equal under socialism: the Soviet case with some United States comparisons', in Moroney (ed.).

Chenery, H. *et al.* (1974), *Redistribution with Growth*, Oxford University Press, London.

Chenery, H. and Syrquin, M. (1975), *Patterns of Development, 1950–1970*, Oxford University Press, London.

Chinn, D.L. (1977), 'Distributional equality and economic growth: the case of Taiwan', *Economic Development and Cultural Change*, Vol. 26.

Chinn, D.L. (1979), 'Rural poverty and the structure of farm household income in developing countries: evidence from Taiwan', *Economic Development and Cultural Change*, Vol. 27.

Chow, S.C. and Papanek, G.F. (1981), '*Laissez-faire*, growth and equity – Hong Kong', *Economic Journal*, Vol. 91.

Cline, W.R. (1971), 'The potential effect of income redistribution on economic growth in four Latin American countries', *Development Digest*, Vol. 9.

Cline, W.R. (1972a), *Potential Effects of Income Redistribution on Economic Growth: Latin American Cases*, Praeger, New York.

Cline, W.R. (1972b), 'Interrelationships between agricultural strategy and rural income distribution', *Food Research Institute Studies in Agricultural Economics, Trade and Development*, Vol. 11.

Cline, W.R. (1975), 'Distribution and development: a survey of literature', *Journal of Development Economics*, Vol. 1.

Collier, P. (1981), *Oil and Inequality in Rural Nigeria*, WEP-Working Paper, ILO, Geneva.

Collier, P. and Bigsten, A. (1981), 'A Model of Educational Expansion and Wage Adjustment in Kenya', *Oxford Bulletin of Economics and Statistics*, Vol. 43.

Cromwell, J. (1977), 'The size distribution of income: an international comparison', *Review of Income and Wealth*, series 23.

Dandekar, V.M. and Rath, N. (1971), *Poverty in India*, Indian School of Political Economy, Bombay.

Dernberger, R.F. (ed.) (1980), *China's Development Experience in Comparative Perspective*, Harvard University Press, Cambridge, Mass.

Edwards, E.O. (1974), *Employment in Developing Nations*, Columbia University Press, New York.

Elliott, C. (1975), *Patterns of Poverty in the Third World. A Study of Social and Economic Stratification*, Praeger, New York.

Fei, J.C.H., Ranis, G., Kuo, S.W.Y. (1978), 'Growth and the family distribution of income by factor components', *Quarterly Journal of Economics*, Vol. 92.

Fields, G.S. (1977), 'Who benefits from economic development? – a re-examination of Brazilian growth in the 1960s', *American Economic Review*, Vol. 67.

Fields, G.S. (1980), reply to comments to 'Who benefits from economic development?', *American Economic Review*, Vol. 70.

Figueroa, A. (1975), 'Income distribution, demand structure and employment', in Stewart (ed.).

Fishlow, A. (1972), 'Brazilian size distribution of income', *American Economic Review*, Vol. 62.

Fishlow, A. (1980), comment to 'Who benefits from economic development?', *American Economic Review*, Vol. 70.

Foxley, A. (ed.) (1976), *Income Distribution in Latin America*, Cambridge University Press, Cambridge.

Foxley, A., Aninat, E., Arellano, J.P. (1979), *Redistributive Effects of Government Programmes*, Pergamon Press, Oxford.

Francks, P. (1979), 'The development of new techniques in agriculture: the case of mechanization of irrigation in the Saga plain area of Japan', *World Development*, Vol. 7.

Frank, C.R. Jr. and Webb, R.C. (eds.) (1977), *Income Distribution and Growth in the Less-Developed Countries*, the Brookings Institution, Washington, DC.

Gerhart, J. (1975), *The Diffusion of Hybrid Maize in Western Kenya*, Princeton University, PhD thesis.

Gilbert, A. and Goodman, D.E. (1976a), 'Regional income disparities and economic development: a critique', in Gilbert and Goodman (eds.).

Gilbert, A. and Goodman, D.E. (eds.). (1976b), *Development Planning and Spatial Structure*, Wiley, New York.

Grassman, S. and Lundberg, E. (eds.) (1981), *The World Economic Order: Past and Prospects*, Macmillan, London.

Griffin, K. (1974), *The Political Economy of Agrarian Change. An Essay on the Green Revolution*, Harvard University Press, Cambridge, Mass.

Griffin, K. (1981), *Land Concentration and Rural Poverty*, 2nd edn., Macmillan, London.

Griffin, K. and Ghose, A.K. (1979), 'Growth and Impoverishment in the Rural Areas of Asia', *World Development*, Vol. 7.

Griffin, K. and Khan, A.R. (1978), 'Poverty in the Third World: Ugly Facts and Fancy Models', *World Development*, Vol. 6.

Guisinger, S. and Hicks, N.L. (1978), 'Long-term trends in income distribution in Pakistan', *World Development*, Vol. 6.

Gunter, H. (1964), 'Changes in occupational wage differentials', *International Labour Review*, Vol. 89.

Hamilton, C. and Söderström, H.T. (1981), 'Technology and international trade: a Heckscher – Ohlin approach', in Grassman and Lundberg (eds.).

Harbison, F.H. (1977), 'The education – income connection', in Frank and Webb (eds.).

Higgins, B. (1975), 'Review of Adelman and Morris: Economic growth and social equity in developing countries', *Economic Development and Cultural Change*, Vol. 24.

Hincliffe, K. (1975), 'Education, individual earnings and earnings distribution', in Stewart (ed.).

Hoerr, O.D. (1973), 'Education, Income and Equity in Malaysia', *Economic Development and Cultural Change*, Vol. 21.

House, W.J. (1981), 'Redistribution, consumer demand and employment in Kenyan furniture-making', *Journal of Development Studies*, Vol. 17.

Hsia, R. and Chau, L. (1978a), *Industrialization, Employment and Income Distribution. A Case Study of Hong-Kong*, Croom Helm, London.

Hsia, R. and Chau, L. (1978b), 'Industrialization and income distribution in Hong-Kong', *International Labour Review*, Vol. 117.

ILO (1972), *Employment Incomes and Equality. A Strategy for Increasing Productive Employment in Kenya*, Geneva.

ILO (1977), *Poverty and Landlessness in Rural Asia*, WEP Study, Geneva.

Jallade, J – P. (1976), 'Education finance and income distribution', *World Development*, Vol. 4.

James, J. (1980), 'The employment effects of an income redistribution. A test for aggregation bias in the Indian sugar processing industry', *Journal of Development Economics*, Vol. 7.

Karvis, B. (1960), 'International differences in the distribution of income', *Review of Economics and Statistics*, Vol. 42.

King, D.Y. and Weldon, P.D. (1977), 'Income distribution and levels of living in Java, 1963–1970', *Economic Development and Cultural Change*, Vol. 25.

Krelle, W. and Shorrocks, A.F. (eds.) (1978), *Personal Income Distribution*, North-Holland, Amsterdam.

Krueger, A.O. (1978), *Liberalization Attempts and Consequences*, Ballinger, Cambridge, Mass.

Kuznets, S. (1955), 'Economic growth and income inequality', *American Economic Review*, Vol. 45.

Kuznets, S. (1963), 'Quantitative aspects of the economic growth of nations VIII: distribution of income by size', *Economic Development and Cultural Change*, Vol. 11.

Lal, D. (1976), 'Distribution and development: a review article', *World Development*, Vol. 4.

Lardy, N.R. (1978), *Economic Growth and Distribution in China*, Cambridge University Press, New York and London.

Lee, E. (1977), 'Development and income distribution: a case study of Sri Lanka and Malaysia', *World Development*, Vol. 5.

Lee, E. (1979), 'Egalitarian peasant farming and rural development: the case of South Korea', *World Development*, Vol. 7.

Lipton, M. (1977), *Why Poor People Stay Poor. Urban Bias in World Development*, Temple Smith, London.

Lipton, M. (1978), 'Inter-farm, interregional and farm – non-farm income distribution: the impact of the new varieties', *World Development* Vol. 6.

Little, I.M.D. (1976), 'Review of Adelman and Morris: Economic growth and social equity in developing countries', *Journal of Development Economics*, Vol. 3.

Little, I.M.D., Scitovsky, T. and Scott, M. (1970), *Industry and Trade in Some Developing Countries*, Oxford University Press, London.

Lluch, C., Powell, A.A. and Williams, R.A. (1977), *Patterns in Household Demand and Saving*, Oxford University Press, New York.

Loehr, W. and Powelson, J.P. (eds.) (1977), *Economic Development, Poverty and Income Distribution*, Westview Press, Boulder, Col.

Lydall, H. (1977), *Income Distribution During the Process of Development*, WEP Working Paper, Income Distribution and Employment Programme, Geneva.

MacEwan, A. (1981), *Revolution and Economic Development in Cuba*, Macmillan, London.

Macrae, J. (1977), 'Production, distribution and economic organization: income distribution and resource allocation at the team level in rural China', *Journal of Development Economics*, Vol. 4.

Meerman, J. (1979), *Public Expenditure in Malaysia. Who Benefits and Why*, Oxford University Press, New York.

Mesa-Lago, C. and Hernandez, R.E. (1976), 'Workers' income in socialist Cuba', in Foxley (ed.).

Michal, J. (1978), 'Size distribution of household incomes and earnings in developed socialist countries: with a proposed marginal-utility weighted Gini coefficient', in Krelle and Shorrocks (eds.).

Minhas, B. (1970), 'Rural poverty, land distribution and development strategy: facts', *Indian Economic Review*, Vol. 3.

Morawetz, D. (1974), 'Employment implications of industrialization in developing countries', *Economic Journal*, Vol. 84.

Morley, S.A. and Williamson, J.G. (1974), 'Demand, distribution, and employment: the case of Brazil', *Economic Development and Cultural Change*, Vol. 23.

Moroney, J.R. (ed.) (1978), *Income Inequality*, Lexington Books, Lexington, Mass.

Myrdal, G. (1968), *Asian Drama*, Pantheon, New York.

Nafzinger, E.W. (1977), 'Entrepreneurship, social mobility, and income redistribution in south India', *American Economic Review*, Vol. 67.

Nayyar, R. (1979), 'Rural poverty in Bihar 1961–62 to 1970–71', *Journal of Development Studies*, Vol. 15.

Nguyen, D.T. and Martinez-Saldivar, M.L.M. (1979), 'The effects of land reform on agricultural production, employment and income distribution: a statistical study of Mexican states, 1959–69', *Economic Journal*, Vol. 89.

Oshima, H. (1962), 'The international comparison of size distribution of family income with special reference to Asia', *Review of Economics and Statistics*, Vol. 44.

Papanek, G.F. (1975), 'The poor of Jakarta', *Economic Development and Cultural Change*, Vol. 24.

Paukert, F. (1973), 'Income distribution at different levels of development. A survey of evidence', *International Labour Review*, Vol. 108.

Paukert, F., Skolka, J. and Maton, J. (1974), *Redistribution of Income, Patterns of Consumption and Employment. A Case Study of the Philippines*, WEP-Working Paper, Income Distribution and Employment Programme, ILO, Geneva.

Perkins, D.H. (1980), 'The central features of China's economic development', in Dernberger (ed.).

Prebisch, R. (1971), 'Income distribution in Latin America: structural requirements for development', *Development Digest*, Vol. 9.

Psacharopoulos, G. (1977), 'Schooling, experience and earnings: the case of an LDC',

Journal of Development Economics, Vol. 4.

Pyatt, G. and Srinivasan, T.N. (1980), comment to 'Who benefits from economic development', *American Economic Review*, Vol. 70.

Rajaraman, I. (1975), 'Poverty, inequality, and economic growth: rural Punjab 1960/61–1970/71', *Journal of Development Studies*, Vol. 11.

Ranis, G. (1977), 'Growth and Distribution: Trade-offs or Complements?', in Loehr and Powelson (eds.).

Ranis, G. (1978), 'Equity with growth in Taiwan: how "special" is the "special case"?', *World Development*, Vol. 6.

Rao, D.G. (1978), 'Economic growth and equity in the Republic of Korea', *World Development*, Vol. 6.

Richards, P. (1977), *Education and Income Distribution in Asia: A Preliminary Analysis*, WEP-Working Paper, Income Distribution and Employment Programme, ILO, Geneva.

Rodgers, G.B. (1975), 'Nutritionally based wage determination in the low-income labour market', *Oxford Economic Papers*, Vol. 27.

Rodgers, G.B. (1978), *An Analysis of Education, Employment and Income Distribution Using an Economic-Demographic Model of the Philippines*, WEP-Working Paper, Population and Employment Programme, ILO, Geneva.

Seers, D. (1974), 'Redistribution with growth: some country experiences. Cuba,' in Chenery *et al.*

Sen, A. (1975), *Employment, Technology and Development*, Clarendon Press, Oxford.

Sen. A. (1981), *Poverty and Famines. An Essay on Entitlements and Deprivation*, Clarendon Press, Oxford.

Singh, J. (1979), *Small Farmers and the Landless in South Asia*, World Bank Staff Working Paper no. 320.

Skolka, J. and Garzuel, M. (1976), *Changes in Income Distribution, Employment and Structure of the Economy: A Case Study of Iran*, WEP-Working Paper, Income Distribution and Employment Programme, ILO, Geneva.

Snyder, D. (1974), 'Economic studies of household saving behaviour in developing countries', *Journal of Development Studies*, Vol. 10.

Stewart, F. (1974), 'Technology and employment in LDCs', *World Development*, Vol. 2.

Stewart, F. (ed.) (1975), *Employment, Income Distribution and Development*, Frank Cass, London.

Stewart, F. (1978), 'Inequality, technology and payments systems', *World Development*, Vol. 6.

Swamy, S. (1967), 'Structural change and the distribution of income by size: the case of India', *The Review of Income and Wealth*, series B.

Taylor, L., Bacha, E.L., Cardoso, E.A. and Lysy, F.J. (1980), *Models of Growth and Distribution for Brazil*, Oxford University Press, New York.

Thirsk, W.R. (1979), 'Aggregation bias and the sensitivity of income distribution of changes in the composition of demand: the case of Colombia', *Journal of Development Studies*, Vol. 16.

Tokman, V.E. (1975), 'Income distribution, technology and employment in developing countries: an application to Ecuador', *Journal of Development Economics*, Vol. 2.

Tuckman, B.H. (1976), 'The Green Revolution and the distribution of agricultural income in Mexico', *World Development*, Vol. 4.

Urrutia, M. (1976), 'Income distribution in Columbia', *International Labour Review*, Vol. 113.

van der Hoeven, R. (1977), *Zambia's Income Distribution During the Early Seventies*, WEP-Working Paper, Income Distribution and Employment, ILO, Geneva.

van Ginneken, W. (1980), *Socio-Economic Groups and Income Distribution in Mexico*, Croom Helm, London.

Wehr, P. (1977), 'Intermediate technology and income distribution in developing nations' in Loehr and Powelson (eds.).

Wiles, P. (1974), *Distribution and Income: East and West*, North-Holland, Amsterdam.

Wiles, P. (1978), 'Our shaky data base', in Krelle and Shorrocks (eds.).

Williamson, J.G. (1965), 'Regional inequality and the process of national development: a description of patterns', *Economic Development and Cultural Change*, Vol. 13.

Williamson, J.G. (1968), 'Personal savings in developing nations: an international cross-section from Asia', *Economic Record*, Vol. 44.

Yotopoulos, P.A. and Nugent, J.B. (1976), *Economics of Development, Empirical Investigations*, Harper and Row, New York.

Young, F.W., Freebaim, D.K. and Snipper, R. (1979), 'The structural context of rural poverty in Mexico: a cross-state comparison', *Economic Development and Cultural Change*, Vol. 27.

6 Model Analyses of Income Distribution in LDCs

6.1 Introduction

In Chapter 5 I attempted to present in a systematic fashion the knowledge about the evolution of income distribution in LDCs, which we have by now acquired from analyses of statistical material. In this chapter I shall try to do the same thing with the knowledge of income distribution determination in LDCs, which we have gained from the major model analyses of that issue.

A major methodological problem in this context is the extent to which the results of the analyses are predetermined or biased by the choice of model specification. There has, in recent years, been an interesting debate about what the appropriate closure rules are for a model of a LDC. Another methodological issue that is important is whether there really is a need to use as large models as those discussed in this chapter. There is a risk that you lose track of the underlying theory in these large models. Obviously, one should always try to use as simple a model as possible.

6.2 On the usefulness of general equilibrium models for income distribution analysis

As was pointed out in Chapter 2, one can distinguish three different approaches to the analysis of income distribution. At one extreme we have the wholly micro-oriented, individualistic approaches such as the human capital approach. In those, the economic structure is taken as given, and what one is trying to do is to establish a relationship between the size distribution of income and individual characteristics. At the other extreme we have the wholly macro-oriented approaches which are concerned with the functional distribution of income (for example neo-Keynesian type of analyses; Kaldor, 1956). In these models, the causality runs from investment to savings to income distribution. Between these two extreme alternatives is the economy-wide general equilibrium model. The basis for this type of approach is the belief that the sectoral structure of production, employment and prices have a decisive effect on income distribution, that product and factor markets are important transmission mechanisms of policy changes, and that there are important indirect effects which makes a general equilibrium type of approach essential. That the sectoral structure is of importance in LDCs was emphasized in Chapter 3, so this kind of approach should give us useful and realistic insights.

In Chapter 5 it was shown that there is a very broad spectrum of factors which influence income distribution. Most of the studies discussed there belong to the individualistic category, even if some of them also touch upon macro issues as well. Even if many of the studies surveyed did try to take several factors into account and often managed to tell quite convincing stories about the income determination process, the interactions among factors could not be adequately represented or analysed, since the studies did not have a general equilibrium framework. The major advantage of the models discussed in this chapter is their ability to take this kind of interactions into account. The models discussed in this chapter are therefore clearly better suited for the analysis of the effect of policy changes. In most cases the incidence of policy changes is too complex to be dealt with adequately within a partial equilibrium framework.

Compared with the *ad hoc* studies discussed in Chapter 5, the model analyses give a better understanding of the interactions between parts of the whole, while the partial studies may give a superior representation of individual aspects of the process. However, it may be pointed out that the model-builder needs a much wider data base. Since the data base is notoriously weak in LDCs, model-building may in many cases be infeasible or, alternatively, it has in many parts to be based on guesswork and strong a priori assumptions. When this is the case, the usefulness of the large general equilibrium model is, of course, diminished. Extensive sensitivity analyses are vital. Caution is in any case always called for in the evaluation of the results.

Thus, because of the limitations imposed on model-builders, particularly in LDCs, the models discussed in this chapter are no substitute for detailed micro studies of partial aspects of the income distribution determination process, but a complement in the search for an explanation of income distribution. Their superiority is most marked when it comes to evaluating the effects of policy and economic strategy changes, since trade-offs and indirect effects are very important in that context. The practical policy-maker, as well as the scholar, is, however, wise to try to learn both from the micro studies and the economy-wide equilibrium models. The day when all relevant aspects can be incorporated in one model will never come.

These models mainly describe the economic mechanisms influencing income distribution, while social and political factors often are difficult to incorporate. This is naturally a problem which all model-builders are well aware of. For example, Adelman and Robinson (1978) discuss this at the end of their book on South Korea, where they point out some problems with regard to the income distribution strategies proposed. First, it is difficult to predict the political response to measures such as land reform and nationalization. Capital flight and other types of opposition may occur. Secondly, the government system may be too corrupt or inefficient to cope with a large increase in tax collection and expenditure. Finally, there may be inertia in the social structure which hinders the implementation and efficient functioning of the new policies proposed.

Obviously, the results from model experiments must be comple-mented by other information by the policy-makers. Still, it is certainly very useful and educational to get some idea about the magnitudes and directions of the effects one will get with different policies. Even if there are some aspects that have to be treated as exogenous and some repercussions that can not be taken into account, it is useful to have analyses performed within a consistent framework, which makes it possible to avoid at least certain contradictions.

6.3 Model descriptions
The discussion in this chapter is based on three major model analyses of income distribution performed so far in LDCs. The models are the economic – demographic Bachue model of the Philippines in Rodgers, Hopkins and Wéry (1978), the economy-wide computable general equilibrium models of South Korea in Adelman and Robinson (1978) and of Brazil in Taylor *et al.* (1980). In this section I shall very briefly describe the structure of the respective models. In section 6.5, I shall compare the analytical results concerning income distribution which have been derived.

First, we shall look at the Bachue model of the Philippines. Even if it is a very large model, it cannot incorporate all important aspects of the development process. The main emphasis of this model is on the interrelationships among population, employment, and income dis-tribution. These aspects have been modelled in considerable detail, while quite a number of other elements have been treated as exogenous.

The model is a dynamic, recursive one. In the model, growth is treated as a disequilibrium process, which continually adjusts towards equilibria, which themselves change over time. Households are the units of analysis at the micro level. The micro units are integrated in a macro model with relationships between demographic, output, employment and income variables. The model distinguishes 150 basic

demographic categories as well as eight rural and nine urban producing sectors. There are 40 different profit and wage receiving
categories.

The model is broken down into three sub-systems – an economic, a
labour market and income distribution, and a demographic system.
The major effort has been devoted to the two latter sub-systems, for
many aspects of the economic sub-system are fairly rudimentary.

The economic sub-system is composed of a demand-based multi-
sectoral model, which generates sectoral outputs within an overall,
exogenously set, output constraint. Total investment is mainly a
demand component in the basic model. Total investments are exogenously determined independently of domestic savings. The gap
between domestic savings and investments is assumed to be filled by
foreign capital inflow. The size of this inflow does not affect the
solution.

The only price that is endogenous in the model is the terms of trade
between agriculture and non-agriculture. Two reasons are given for
making this price endogenous. First, the great importance of that
price in the determination of both rural and urban well-being.
Secondly, the potential constraint on output because of the finite
availability of land.

The labour market and income distribution sub-system is in the
model segmented between the categories employed – self employed,
skilled – unskilled, urban – rural, and modern – traditional. The
dualist assumption is made that the traditional sector has an absorp-
tive character, that is if you cannot get a job in the modern sector you
can always go back to work in the traditional one. Unemployment
then is regarded as a social phenomenon rather than as something
being caused mainly by an imbalance between the supply and demand
for labour.

In the first step in the analysis labour supply is determined by an
allocation of time model within the constraints of the economic
structure. The supply is determined by a linear model of labour force
participation rates, which are functions of demographic and
economic variables.

After labour supply has been estimated, unemployment is
determined. It is argued that those that are openly unemployed are
people who have an alternative source of support and thus are able to
queue for more desirable jobs. It is pointed out that the majority of
the unemployed are young and not heads of households. In the model
unemployment is explained behaviourally, and is assumed to decrease
when the modern – traditional wage-differential decreases, since such
a reduction means that the return to waiting becomes less.

After unemployment has been estimated the remainder of the labour force is distributed into five urban and four rural categories. The value added of each sector is distributed among non-wage income, educated workers' income, and non-educated workers' income. The share of non-wage income is assumed to fall over time according to an exogenously determined trend based on experiences from other countries.

The size of the category self-employed and profit-earners is first determined. This category is simply assumed to grow at the same rate as population. Next urban unskilled employment in modern and traditional sectors are determined simultaneously. With an exogenously determined wage-differential between the two types of unskilled employment, the employment levels can be calculated from a set of simultaneous equations. Then skilled urban employment is calculated. Here one uses labour demand functions, in this case inverted Cobb – Douglas production functions. Modern rural employment is determined in a similar fashion to the urban case. Finally, traditional rural employment is residually determined.

Intersectoral labour migration occurs in the model to make up for the rigidity of the system of labour demand functions. It is a function of wage-differentials. Migration is estimated on the basis of the wages that would have prevailed in a given period without migration. Wages are then re-estimated after migration.

The labour market calculation of income is finally transformed to a household income distribution. Households are categorized according to the activity of the head. One first gets average income by labour market category of the household head. Then, the variation within each category is taken into account, since it constitutes as much as 50% of the variation. Finally, one can put these distributions together to get the overall income distribution and calculate inequality measures such as the Gini coefficient.

The demographic sub-system is based on household decision models. It determines the marriage rates, fertility, migration, mortality, and education.

The Philippinean Bachue model is thus worked out in great detail with regard to the labour market and income distribution, while the basic economic model is a simple, demand-driven, fixed-price, intersectoral model. There are no price adjustments except in the agricultural – industrial terms of trade, but the model captures the effects of structural change on income distribution.

The model of South Korea by Adelman and Robinson is more ambitious in its specification of the basic economic model. It is a computable general equilibrium model within the neoclassical tradition, but it also includes disequilibrium features. It consists of two parts, a *static*, within-period adjustment model which is linked to a *dynamic*, intertemporal adjustment model. The model simulates the operation of factor and product markets with profit-maximizing firms and utility-maximizing individuals. It solves prices endogenously, and the solution is based on achieving a measure of consistency among the results of the optimizing behaviour of economic agents.

Within each period, the degree of adjustment is constrained by the existing capital stock, the immobility of the self-employed, the rigidities of the wage structure, and restrictions imposed on the economy by the government. Between periods, there is some flexibility because of capital accumulation, population growth, migration, change in the number of self-employed, and changes in the structure and size of production. The constraints imposed on the model imply that it cannot achieve a full Walrasian equilibrium by shifting factors around.

The behaviour of the model may be described as one of a lurching equilibrium. It continually tries to adjust to inter-temporal disequilibria. In each period, the economy adjusts to equate demand and supply, but this is done without full equilibrium in the factor market and within the institutional constraints. The latter result from imperfect mobility of funds, credit rationing, and export targets set by the government. The solution is therefore not Pareto efficient. Over time, the model should move towards an inter-temporally efficient equilibrium path, but because of the differences in productivity growth, educational level of the labour force, etc., the economy may never reach such an equilibrium.

The model goes from factor payments and employment to household income. The savings and expenditure decisions of the different household categories together make up demand.

The authors have modelled foreign trade in great detail. The character of the external relations of a sector determines the types of market behaviour specified for that sector in the model. For nontraded or protected goods there is insulated market-clearing, while for traded goods the market-clearing price is dependent on tariffs and subsidies and the world market price.

Because the authors are trying to analyse the distribution of income, the model must, by necessity, be highly disaggregated. They use a 29 sector disaggregation, but as they found out that there were large productivity differences within these sectors as well, they disaggregated each sector by an additional four size categories; this implies that it was possible for them to capture economies of scale dynamically by altering the size composition of a sector between periods.

The model is not a forecasting model. Exogenous shocks and short-term cyclical variations are disregarded. The authors have tried to construct a realistic, structural model, which is so wide in scope that it can be used to simulate the effects of variations in a large number of policy parameters.

The solution procedure used in the model tries to simulate market behaviour, a kind of tatonnement process. A number of excess demand functions are reduced to zero. By choosing such a solution procedure, it is possible to use a wide variety of specifications of how market actors behave and how the markets work.

An important part of the model is the simulation of the workings of the credit market. Producers demand loanable funds on the basis of expected sales and expected prices. Credit is rationed according to some policy rule. The output of this stage is an allocation of loanable funds among firms and sectors, and thus an injection of credit into the economy.

As a result of their expectations about output prices and wages, the firms demand fixed capital to minimize the cost of producing the expected output. The demand for working capital is a function of expected sales and the interest rate. To what extent the firms can obtain the desired amount of funds depends on the amount of retained earnings within the firm and the workings of the credit market. Once the allocation of loanable funds has been made, the firms are assumed to carry out their investment plans in nominal terms during the period, regardless of whether expectations are fulfilled or not.

In most general equilibrium models, it is assumed that relative prices and real variables are homogeneous of degree zero in all prices, wages, and money. In this model, however, this is not the case: the authors incorporate the role of inflation. Nominal money supply is partly endogenously determined, since sectors can hoard or dishoard money. The desire of recipients of factor incomes to hold money balances is assumed to be a function of their income and the price level. Inflation is the equilibrating factor between supply and demand for money. The real variables in the system are affected by the inflation.

The income side of the model is, of course, modelled in detail. The authors differentiate among six different skill categories in the labour market in addition to agricultural workers. The model solves for over 500 separate wages by skill, sector, and firm size; in addition, the incomes of the self-employed, capitalists, different groups of farmers and agricultural labour, and government workers have to be calculated. This calculation gives average incomes by 15 different occupational groups. Distribution within these is then represented by a two-parameter, log-normal distribution. These group distributions together constitute the overall distribution. Subsequently the Korean tax structure and average collection ratios are imposed on this distribution, with the effects of various transfers taken into account; this gives the disposable income by individual.

Fifteen different socioeconomic groups are identified by the occupation of the head of the household. With information about occupational distribution, average number of workers by household category, and total number of workers in each category (determined within the model), it is possible to derive the number of households in each category and their average incomes. As before, it is assumed that the distribution of income within each household category is log-normal. This then, finally, gives the income distribution by household.

The South Korean model is a very ambitious attempt at realistic modelling with the help of the neoclassical tool-kit. The Brazilian model also uses the same kit quite extensively, for example, to model the various factor markets (see Taylor *et al.*, 1980, Chapter 7). An interesting aspect of the Brazilian study is that Taylor and his colleagues experiment with different closure rules. They show that the analytical results may be affected quite a lot by the choice of closure rules, that is the way in which the model achieves macroeconomic equilibrium between supply and demand. A comparison between a neoclassical closure and a neo-Keynesian closure of an aggregated version of the model is performed. They first set up the accounting identities which are the same in the two model specifications. Then they add to this basic structure the assumptions that are needed to make the solution determinate, that is close the model.

The basic neoclassical assumption is that full employment of factors is maintained by freely varying prices of factors of production. The real returns are determined by the marginal productivity of factors, so, with full employment, income flows depend very much on the supply side of the model. In the neoclassical variant of the model, the aggregate price level is assumed to be fixed, so that money wage changes also represent real wage changes by an equal amount. This assumption can be justified on the ground that the output of a sector can be used either at home or abroad, so that the domestic price will be equal to the constant world price. From incomes personal savings are determined by behavioural parameters, and then investment is assumed to adjust to the availability of savings. Productivity and savings are crucial factors in the neoclassical explanation of growth and income distribution.

The neo-Keynesian story is somewhat different. Here real investment is determined by factors such as expectations, non-market considerations or possibly the interest rate. This is sometimes referred to as the 'animal spirit'. The supply of real savings is therefore not the determinant of investment and income distribution. Instead, factor payments and employment are assumed to adjust in such a manner that savings come to equal investment demand. For example, if real investment demand increases, the income distribution will have to shift towards groups with a higher savings propensity to make the necessary finance come forth.

Taylor and his colleagues describes how the adjustment process may work with a neo-Keynesian specification:

> Consider an economy in which labour and capital can substitute freely along a well-behaved production function and in which raw material imports are also required to support production. The cost of imports and the money-wage are assumed to be fixed, and some labour is unemployed. If investment demand rises, output will go up as more workers find jobs. If exports are fixed in the short run, the balance of payments deficit will become larger, since a higher production level requires more raw material imports. The rate of profit (marginal product of capital) will increase since there are decreasing returns to the existing stock of capital in the short run. The real wage, however, will fall, since higher profits will be passed along in a higher price of output and the money-wage is fixed.
>
> Now look at what occurs in terms of saving and investment. Real investment demand has gone up, and the current value of investment has gone up even more because of the price increases. The extra saving comes from increases in real profits that are partly hoarded and from the increased balance of payments deficit, or 'foreign saving'. But real-wages have fallen, and the real-wage bill could have gone either up or down, depending on the elasticity of substitution. The income distribution has shifted to favour national profit recipients and foreigners over workers. Forced saving at the expense of labour has occurred.   (1980, pp. 7—8)

To sum up: with a neoclassical closure investment demand varies to equate available saving, which is equal to the sum of the government surplus, the foreign deficit, and domestic saving from labour and capital incomes. The factor incomes are determined from the supply side as explained above.

With the alternative neo-Keynesian closure, investment is exogenously determined (or at least determined independently of savings). The assumptions that there is full employment of factors and the returns are determined by marginal productivity at full employment are excluded from the model, which allows factor returns to adjust in such a way that savings comes to equal investment. The price is determined as the sum of the costs of labour, capital, and raw material imports. Changes in costs are passed on in the model, and therefore an increase in the nominal wage will result in a smaller increase in the real wage. This means that the extent of substitution is limited in the neo-Keynesian model, and the resource allocation is therefore less affected by changes in nominal wages. The overall consumption propensity will change when income distribution changes, since agents have different consumption propensities. Output must therefore adjust to restore the savings – investment balance if some kind of disturbance has occurred.

In their test of the macro model with different closure rules, Taylor *et al.* find that the neo-Keynesian specification manages to replicate the actual Brazilian development pattern better than the neoclassical specification (1980, Chapter 4, Appendix B). Particularly the growth rate of consumption and savings and thus also GNP shows a better fit in the neo-Keynesian version of the model.

Still, maybe the authors go a bit too far in asserting the superiority of the neo-Keynesian version of the model compared with the neoclassical one. They solve the model in two steps. First, they calculate the growth of a number of exogenous variables and use these to estimate the growth rates of the endogenous variables in a differential version of the model. In a second stage they then start from the level estimates generated from this model and iterate towards a fully consistent set of macroeconomic accounts for some subsequent year. The important stage here is the first one, where more of demand is exogenously determined in the neo-Keynesian version of the model than in the neoclassical version. Specifically the growth rate of investments is determined from data on the actual development. Since this is the case, it is not surprising that the neo-Keynesian version of the model manages to replicate the growth pattern better than the neoclassical one, where investment demand is endogenously determined. The more data on actual development you put into the model, the more its development pattern should resemble actual development. The development of demand over an extended period will obviously always show a parallel development with production. This does not, however, prove that demand is the causal factor or that the level of investment determines the savings level. The same parallel development would occur if the causality went the other way.

To be able to draw general conclusions about the usefulness of the respective model specifications for prediction one should compare their accuracy in predicting the development over a period of time without any prior knowledge about and use of data for the period in question. Over a long period of time, it is possible that the growth rate of investment is better predicted by the availability of savings than some estimate of 'the animal spirit'.

Still, in the case of the development of Brazil during the 1960s, the neo-Keynesian version most closely replicates the actual variables, and it is therefore used by the authors as the base for their construction of the multi-sectoral model for analysis of income distribution. It should be remembered, however, that to solve the model over time, the authors (Taylor *et al.*, 1980, p. 204) have had to 'specify its exogenous variables for all years in which it is to be solved'.

The full model of Brazil contains 25 sectors, whose capital stocks are assumed to be fixed in each sector. There are six different types of labour, which can move among sectors. Overall real wages are endogenously determined, but since there are persistent inequalities among sectors for equally skilled labour, these differences have been built into the model in the form of proportional wage differentials between sectors. Distributional shifts within the labour force are therefore brought about by labour movements among sectors. Since, unlike labour, capital cannot move between sectors, there is a separate rate of profit in each sector. There are also separate proprietors in each sector. Both the profit rate and the output price are linked to wages and import prices through cost functions.

Value added is produced according to production functions, where labour and capital are combined. In the model there are separable sub-functions for labour and capital. There are 11 capital goods in the model (10 domestic and 1 imported), which enter in fixed proportions as an aggregate in each sector. The six types of labour can be substituted for one another fairly easily, that is, the elasticity of substitution is assumed to be high.

There are four consumer classes in the model, all having different savings propensities. The demand of each class for the outputs of the 25 sectors plus imports is derived from utility maximization. The demand works through the input-output system, and together with other demands and the supply side of the model it constitutes the full general equilibrium system.

There are in the model some hundred labour income flows, which are determined together with profits and the renumeration of unincorporated independent proprietors such as peasants and shopkeepers. All these incomes flows together give the size distribution of income.

When trying to understand how the model works one can separate the adjustment process into two stages. The first one is the macroeconomic adjustment where saving is equated with investment (or, equivalently, supply with demand). This is brought about by changes in the value of saving and investment, which are attributable to changes in both relative prices and the absolute price level relative to payments fixed in nominal terms. Fixed rates are the exchange rate, certain government taxes and transfers, and the remuneration of some proprietors and entrepreneurs. The most important of the latter are small owner operators in agriculture and services. Deflation does benefit the recipients of fixed incomes. Falling prices also reduces the value of a given real investment vector, and this leads to changes in savings.

Apart from this macro adjustment there are numerous micro adjustments in the model, which can affect the income distribution in complex ways. This will be discussed further below.

6.4 On the choice of closure rules

Before looking at the results of the various studies in detail, we shall dwell a bit on the importance of the specification of the model (see e.g. Taylor, 1980, and Dervis *et al.*, 1982). One can distinguish three basic types of multi-sectoral models, namely a fixed-price model, a model with flexible prices and a neoclassical closure, and a model with flexible prices and a neo-Keynesian closure. Neither of the models considered here is a pure case, but one might say that each of them tends towards one of these variants. The Bachue model is mainly a fixed-price model, even if the agricultural – industrial terms of trade are endogenously determined. The Adelman – Robinson model is the most neoclassical of the models, although also this model contains macro elements of a Keynesian nature. The Taylor model is leaning more in the neo-Keynesian direction, but it also contains many neoclassical traits. Therefore, the models cannot be used for a clear-cut comparison of the three different types of specification. Still, the fact that they are specified differently should be kept in mind when evaluating the results of the policy analyses.

We can, for example, compare the effects of a fall in foreign capital inflow in the two types of flexible price models. (In the Bachue model there is no explicit mechanism to react to such a change.) The result of the reduction of the inflow of foreign capital is an imbalance between savings and investment. In the neoclassical model relative prices, for example the foreign exchange rate, will adjust to restore the balance. Investment will decline since it adjusts to the decreased availability of savings. The relative price of capital goods will decline. Wages and profits and thus income distribution will be changed by these changes in relative prices.

In a neo-Keynesian model the level of real investment is fixed, so something else will have to adjust in response to the original imbalance. If we assume that savings out of profits are higher than savings out of wages, the equilibrium can be restored by an increase in the share of profits in the GNP. The increase has to be so large that domestic savings increase sufficiently to replace the decline in foreign savings. This shift in the functional income distribution is brought about by a fall in real wages, which can be realized through an increase in the price level with given nominal wages. Taylor and his colleagues rely on such an inflation mechanism to bring about equilibrium. The effect of the initial disturbance on the functional income distribution may be larger with the neo-Keynesian closure, since the real wages have to adjust directly to bring about equilibrium. With the neo-classical closure, the effects are more indirect through changes in commodity and factor prices, brought about by changes in the structure of production among sectors with varying factor intensities and factor mobility.

There are two aspects of the issue of model closure that need to be discussed. Let us examplify with the foreign exchange problem. First, it could be argued that the neo-Keynesian and neoclassical variants of the model represent different views of the flexibility and the scope for adjustments in a LDC. The purely neo-Keynesian view is that the economy is very inflexible and that the possibilities for adjustment to trade problems are very limited. The purely neoclassical position is that import-substitution is possible if relative prices are appropriately adjusted, among other things through a devaluation of the currency. The differences may also reflect a difference in the time perspective of the analysis. The neo-Keynesian specification assumes an essentially short-term adjustment mechanism, while the neoclassical variant considers adjustments over a longer period of time. This fact may to some extent justify the assumption of flexibility, since the economy undoubtedly can adjust considerably if only the time period considered is sufficiently long.

The second important aspect is that the choice of specification also may be a reflection of the kind of issues on which one wants to focus. The choice of a neoclassical specification can be justified if one is interested in analysing the microeconomic determinants of income distribution. If that is the case, one should attempt to specify closure rules that are as harmless as possible in their effect on income distribution. One should probably also be more interested in the long run than the short run. In a neo-Keynesian model, the effects of adjustments of real wages relative to profits tend to swamp all other effects working through adjustments within the multi-sectoral framework.

An alternative closure rule has been used by, for example, Johansen (1974) who lets the government play an active role in generating the savings required to realize a given investment target. In this case, there is not necessarily a need for any change in the functional income distribution. This type of closure is therefore also fairly harmless.

In both the Adelman – Robinson and the Taylor models, the aggregate price level is endogenous. In the former model, the price level is determined by a quantity theory demand for money function, while the latter adjusts according to the neo-Keynesian rules described above. The Adelman – Robinson model leaves greater scope for relative price adjustments than does the Taylor model, since it does not assume that nominal wages are fixed.

Still, when one compares the three models discussed in this chapter, one finds that the overall income distribution is fairly stable in all of them. This finding thus seems to hold irrespective of the choice of closure rules and irrespective of whether the prices are endogenous or not. However, the models also show that the relative incomes of specific groups can be very differently affected by different policy changes. To analyse this issue one must have a multi-sectoral framework and different income recipient categories. Macro models are not sufficient to deal with this issue.

In the next section we shall consider the major results of the model studies presented in this section.

6.5 Analytical results

The analytical technique used in the studies cited here is simulation modelling. The models constructed provide a coherent framework for the analysis of different policy options. It should be emphasized that they provide conditional forecasts, and that the value of single runs is limited. It is by comparing the results of different runs that one can get interesting insights into the effects of policy variations on income distribution. The models thus have their major use in the analysis of the impact of various policy changes on income distribution.

First, we shall consider the major results in the models, particularly with regard to the effect of broad strategies on income distribution. After this, we shall look in more detail at some policy issues, which are of special importance to income distribution in LDCs.

Adelman and Robinson (1978) first perform a number of comparative static experiments which are very instructive. These show very clearly that measures aimed at improving income distribution must be analysed within a general equilibrium framework. It turns out that certain policies which, a priori, seem to benefit the poor have an adverse effect on their incomes. It is also shown that the size distribution of income is one of the most stable features of the South Korean economy. It is thus very difficult to change it by economic policy. It is possible to affect the income distribution by socio-economic groups to a considerable extent, but the overall size distribution still changes very little. To be able to get substantial results, there is a need for a concerted effort. When a set of policies is implemented, it is obviously even more difficult to predict the overall effect on income distribution of the policies than for individual policies, and the need for a general equilibrium approach is still greater.

The urban-oriented policies tested relate to human resources, employment, technology, nationalization, and a combination of these. It turns out that to devise policies that primarily benefit the poorest groups is more difficult in the urban than the rural economy. This is because the urban poor are more dispersed among sectors and types of employment. When there is any effect at all, the benefits tend to go to the middle class instead of the poorest deciles. Moreover, in the long run, the benefits of urban anti-poverty measures seem to be transmitted to the rural areas, mainly through changes in the terms of trade. In general, urban policies are much less effective than their rural counterparts. The authors characterize the urban economy as a rubber toy; no matter how it is squeezed, it returns to its original shape.

Still, there are some possibilities of combining rural and urban packages so that a good overall effect on income distribution is obtained. Some more limited policies are tested, but the most interesting policy experiments are the two policy packages that imply comprehensive strategies of poverty eradication. One is called 'reform capitalism' and the other 'market socialism'. The main difference is that in the market socialism package land reform and nationalization of industry is included. The reform capitalism strategy is one of labour-intensive, export-oriented growth, while the market socialism strategy implies a mild degree of import-substitution. In both programmes, rural cooperatives are included, but only in the reform capitalism alternative is this assumed to imply increased productivity! Both packages include consumption subsidies to the poor, a massive educational programme, reduced population growth, and public works.

One might, of course, question the labelling of these alternative strategies as well as the specification of them. The reform capitalism package includes what a government ought to do, if it were aiming at de-pauperization, while the socialist package includes those programmes which socialist oriented countries usually have pursued. As far as I can see, it would be perfectly possible for a socialist government to pursue a strategy similar to the one labelled reform capitalism. To include a measure of import substitution in the socialist package naturally tends to work against this alternative, as it tends to restrict the supply of urban goods and turn the terms of trade against agriculture.

It is necessary to remember the differences in specification of the strategies when comparing their results. By exogenously specifying that productivity growth is slower in the socialist package, one naturally reaches the conclusion that, in the long run, everyone is worse off with this than with reform capitalism. This is not the result of any analysis, and cannot form the basis for a choice between the two packages. It only shows that, in the long run, growth may be better than distribution, provided the latter has negative effects on the growth rate.

Still, over the nine-year period covered by the simulations, the socialist strategy does very well. The degree of income equalization is larger than in any other package. Over this period, only the three top deciles come out worse than they do in the basic run. However, in terms of absolute levels of income, the capitalist package does better for all deciles, even the poorest ones.

The big problem with reform capitalism, which the authors rightly point out, is that it is highly unlikely that a non-socialist government would adopt such a far-reaching policy. It would go against the established interests; the poorer deciles which would benefit from such a policy very seldom have any political leverage. Therefore, to be able to introduce a strategy aimed at poverty eradication, the government will have to have a very solid support. The active participation of the poor in the political process is probably a *sine qua non* for the implementation of such a strategy.

The authors identify two potentially useful strategies for equitable growth. One is an intensification of the strategy that South Korea is already pursuing; that is, export-led, labour- and skill-intensive growth. Important preconditions for such a strategy are (i) that a large proportion of the labour force must consist of well-educated and skilled workers; and (ii) that there is some way of controlling the development of agricultural terms of trade.

The second potentially efficient strategy is one of emphasizing rural development. Here, there are also two preconditions: (i) there must be a relatively equitable distribution of land tenure arrangements; and (ii) as in the previous case, control of the development of agricultural terms of trade. It should be pointed out that the major reason for falling terms of trade in the model in response to increased supply is the assumption of domestic market-clearing. If this assumption were relaxed, the issue of urban – rural terms of trade might be less problematic. Obviously, exports of agricultural products are feasible.

One general conclusion that can be drawn is that to improve income distribution significantly a broadly based approach must be followed. A whole spectrum of policies aimed at different socioeconomic target groups are required. In the economy, there are many adjustment mechanisms which try to 'correct' the disturbance that a single policy would imply. As has been observed many times, you cannot beat the market; at least it is difficult and requires considerable skill and a variety of measures. As mentioned, it also requires political power and determination and this may be the most pervasive constraint in a typically underdeveloped economy.

Also in the analysis of the Bachue model, it is found that single policy changes have only very small effects on the size distribution of income. Concerted efforts are called for, if one really has the ambition of changing the income distribution.

Five different strategies are tested within the Bachue model for the Philippines. The industrialization strategy is characterized by urban, modern sector oriented growth. The strategy leads to an increased urban bias and aggravated labour market dualism. However, if it leads to increased aggregate growth these negative consequences are weakened by the higher growth rates, which makes it possible to maintain modern sector employment and reduce unemployment. But if growth does not increase, poverty as well as inequality increases. It need also be pointed out that the increased investment level is assumed to be brought about by the state. If it were left to the private sector to increase investments through the reinvestments of profits, the distributional consequences would be considerably worse.

The rural development strategy is composed of faster development of the rural infrastructure, more rural education, land reform, rural wage subsidies, expansion of rural small-scale industry, a changing demand pattern in favour of primary production, and cooperative marketing.

The implementation of this strategy increases the share of primary production in total output from 19% in the year 2000 in the base run to 27%. Rural wage differences decrease somewhat, agricultural terms of trade improve a little, and this together with the land reform leads to more equality in the rural areas. The strategy has a negative effect on the urban economy. Its traditional sector is forced to absorb more labour and inequality increases. To sum up the outcome of this experiment, one can conclude that it is fairly successful. Incomes are equalized between urban and rural areas and rural incomes are increased. Food demands are satisfied and food prices do not rise too much, at the same time as the need to import food is reduced. In terms of overall income distribution, there is an improvement (a lower Gini coefficient). The strategy is superior to the industrialization strategy in this respect. However, as has already been pointed out, aggregate growth is exogenously set to be the same in both cases, and it is therefore not possible to draw definite conclusions as to which strategy should be chosen, since the level of production may also be affected.

The egalitarian strategy can be characterized as a basic needs strategy aimed at enabling the poorest 20% to satisfy their basic needs. This strategy includes wage subsidies, public works, rural education, income transfers to low income groups, extensive modern sector nationalization, increased migration, increased labour intensity in the modern sector, land reform, small-scale industry promotion and a shift in demand towards labour-intensive sectors.

This strategy is successful in decreasing inequality. It decreases in the urban areas, in the rural areas, and between these two areas. The bottom rural deciles particularly gain. However, while rural incomes increase considerably, the urban poor are left behind. One problem with the strategy is that both the government budget deficit and the external deficit are becoming very large. One might therefore have some doubts about the feasibility of the strategy in the long run. Moreover, as the authors themselves point out, it is difficult to predict the effects of drastic changes in the organization of production and in the incentive structure. There are obviously large difficulties in analysing these large changes in policy within a model which basically assumes that the structure remains the same.

The fourth strategy is a quantification of the recommendations made by the ILO mission to the Philippines. This strategy presupposes a different trade pattern, and it emphasizes the development of rural industries. It leads to a reduction of the income shares of the high and middle urban income-earners to the benefit of the urban poor and the rural dwellers. Its main result is the elimination of unskilled unemployment by the mid-1990s and the reduction in the level of skilled wages relative to the base run. The Gini coefficient is reduced, but less than in the previous strategy. It need also be pointed out that a considerable part of this effect is because of transfer payments, without which the effect on inequality would be limited.

The last strategy is a population strategy, which is really no complete strategy. Anyway, if it is possible to reduce fertility without reducing output growth, there will be a positive effect on this in the long run as a consequence of reduced pressure on the labour market.

The overall conclusions that can be drawn from the analyses is that income distribution is very resistant to policy changes, although the relative position of different socioeconomic groups may change. To obtain any significant effect one has to devise packages of mutually supporting policies aimed at changing the structure of the economy.

The links between urban and rural areas are found to be of great importance. The two types of linkages emphasized here are migration and agricultural terms of trade. Both these factors have a very large effect on rural incomes particularly, and as the rural areas contain most of the poor, this becomes very important for the development of inequality.

It is also found that the incomes of the rural poor are the most sensitive ones; that is, there is a great variation in them between different simulations. This may of course to some extent be because the agricultural terms of trade are explicitly taken into account, while other prices are not.

The most successful strategy in terms of income equalization is the egalitarian strategy, followed by the ILO mission strategy and the rural development strategy.

Both the Philippine and South Korean studies suggest that the size distribution of income is very stable. However, the relative position of various socioeconomic groups is more sensitive to the choice of policy. The composition of the poor and the rich groups can therefore be affected.

The findings of the Brazilian study to some extent stand in contrast to the pessimistic view that size distribution is very resistant to change. Public policy here seems to matter more. The differences may result from differences between the countries or to differences in model specifications. South Korea, for example, was more egalitarian to start with than Brazil, and there were therefore less scope for further improvements in the income distribution. The Adelman – Robinson model is also more micro oriented than the Taylor model, in which the functional income distribution changes more directly.

In the Brazilian study, there are no tests of broad policy packages as in the other two studies, but it is said that it should be possible to achieve significant improvements by a broadly based strategy, since already single policy interventions have a considerable effect on income distribution. The discussion of the results of the Brazilian study must therefore be restricted to single policy changes. This has the advantage that it is easier to identify the effects of a specific change, but on the other hand, it does not show what can actually be achieved with a broad based approach.

A major point that Taylor and his colleagues (1980) and Taylor and Lysy (1979) try to make is that the type of closure rules adopted may strongly affect the results of the model analysis. The importance of explicit or implicit assumptions about closure of the model was discussed already by Sen (1963) in an article where he tries to pinpoint the fundamental differences between neoclassical and neo-Keynesian income distribution models.

The two models differ in an important way in the manner of which wage changes affect the solution (see Taylor and Lysy, 1979, pp. 26–7). If money-wage changes do not affect the price level, for example because of trade arbitrage, they also imply a shift in real wages, which leads to substitution and considerable changes in the resource allocation. However, if instead the overall price level moves closely in response to changes in nominal wages, there will be little change in real wages. The substitution between labour and capital will therefore be slight. Most of the changes in production and income distribution will then come from the demand side as a result of real income shifts brought about by price and wage changes relative to income flows fixed in nominal terms. The effects of wage changes on the functional income distribution in such a model are slight, and even the sign is unpredictable.

If the neo-Keynesian description of the price setting procedure is realistic, the income distribution is likely to be fairly stable in response to changes in wages. Both the Taylor and the Adelman – Robinson models have a combination of income types fixed in nominal terms and prices and wages, which can vary in nominal terms. In both models, the overall degree of inequality changes very little. There are, however, micro processes which in a complex way bring about changes between sectors and groups.

In the Brazilian model, Taylor and his colleagues test the effect of reduced labour substitutability. This makes it more difficult to replace a worker of a certain skill with one of another. The flexibility of the economy is reduced, and prices are increased. In the specific case of Brazil, this turns out to have beneficial effects on the functional income distribution. Since there is a rapid increase in the number of highly skilled labour, and since these now less easily can replace other skills, the relative wages of skilled labour is reduced.

The authors also test the effects of less supply flexibility, that is, lower capital – labour elasticities of substitution, in the 'labour surplus' sectors agriculture, commerce, and services. Also this change makes the economy less flexible. It means that supply is reduced and with more or less given demand there is inflation. The capital – labour elasticities are higher in the labour surplus sectors relative to industry, the wage is less, and labour – labour elasticities are higher. Therefore, labour is being drawn from industry into these low-productivity sectors. Reduced flexibility in this case therefore means that both equity and growth objectives become more difficult to achieve.

Taylor and his colleagues also test the effects of a reduced investment demand. They find that in their model, the immediate effect is equalizing, since the economy is under less pressure to produce savings. The profit share therefore can fall. This is a consequence of the neo-Keynesian specification. In the long run, however, because the elasticity of substitution is less than one in the sectors where most of the profits are generated, the share of profits rises. The functional income distribution then shifts in favour of capital. Eventually, there is also inflationary pressure, which as always in this model worsens income distribution. This is because major poor groups have incomes fixed in nominal terms.

Taylor *et al.* also test the effect of a reduction in government spending on goods and services. Such a reduction implies that government savings increase, which leads to a shortfall in aggregate demand. This has the effect that corporate earnings must fall to bring savings back into line with total investment demand. The profit share thus falls and the functional income distribution moves in favour of labour. There is also deflation which means that the real incomes of proprietors increase. Since these are poor in Brazil, this also improves income distribution. There is initially an increase in unemployment, and lower wages are required to bring the economy back to full employment. Still even after this, the income distribution is equalized in comparison with the initial situation, since profits remain low because they have been replaced to some degree as a source of savings by the government and foreigners.

Taylor *et al.* disregard the fact that different expenditures have different distributional consequences. For example, it is shown in the Bachue model that public works in the rural areas reduce inequality. They raise food prices and agricultural incomes, at the same time as they help in reducing the urban employment problem through reductions in migration.

In the Brazilian model, reduced government employment has an equalizing effect on income distribution for the same reasons as reduced spending. Reduced government transfers also lead to deflation, which as usual means that the share of capital and labour decreases while proprietors gain, and income distribution improves.

Reductions in the wage tax, which is paid by industrial sectors in Brazil, lower government savings and with fixed investment demand there is inflation. The GNP-share of proprietors falls and income distribution deteriorates. It turns out that even the drastic shift in labour costs of industry had a fairly small effect on employment, because the cost of capital moved in the same direction as the cost of labour. Relative costs changed little. Why was this? First, capital is mainly produced by the same industrial sectors. Production costs of capital have therefore been reduced. Secondly, the fixity of capital stock and the inelasticity of demand meant that capital and labour had to be combined in more or less the same proportions as before to produce a given output. Thus, profits on fixed capital might have to fall, but overall income distribution deteriorates.

Reductions in profit taxes are even more inflationary and thus income distribution deteriorates even more. On the other hand, in combining a profit tax increase and a wage decrease one can achieve substantial improvements in income distribution, at least if the net effect is deflationary.

In the Bachue model, the introduction of minimum wages increases the wages of unskilled workers, but it also reduces modern sector employment. This also implies that traditional sector wages fall, and overall inequality is increased. Wage subsidies, on the other hand, increase employment and are thus a more successful policy. It leads to a slight reduction in inequality.

In the Brazilian model, with its neo-Keynesian specification, an increase in the minimum wages increases the share of labour and therefore improves the situation for some of the poorer groups. The cost is a slightly higher rate of inflation, which hurts the proprietors. The effect on the growth rate is not necessarily negative. It is thus possible to eat into the profits through an increase in the minimum wages but still eventually get a higher growth rate.

It may be of interest to consider what the models have to say about the trade-off between growth and distribution. Within the Bachue model it is impossible to perform any explicit analysis of the trade-off. The authors therefore make a few simulations with slightly different model structures, where the growth rate to some extent is determined within the model. The alternatives tried are to let it be determined by demand growth directly, be constrained by the balance of payments, or be determined by investment through an aggregate production function. It is found that these different structures in certain cases lead to results different from the basic version of the model. Since it is difficult to say a priori which approach is the most appropriate one, a case can be made for accepting the choice of an exogenous growth rate for the simulation experiments.

The authors point out that very little is known about the determinants of long-run growth. Obviously, a mixture of factors interact. However, when looking at the results of the various simulation experiments, one must keep in mind that the model assumes constant growth, at the same time as changes are introduced, which one would assume to have a certain effect on the growth rate.

In the other two models, there is more scope for analysis of the trade-off, since the growth rate of the capital stock is endogenously determined. Obviously, a more rapidly growing capital stock leads to a higher growth rate of production than a more slowly growing one. With savings propensities higher for the wealthier classes, higher growth should be associated with higher inequality.

It is shown in the Adelman – Robinson study that over a period of a decade faster growth makes a lot of difference. They compare a slow growth strategy aimed at equalization with another one with less equalization but higher growth. After a decade, everybody is better off in absolute terms in the high growth alternative, although the distribution is less equal.

In the Brazilian model, there is a very obvious link between a high rate of profit and a high rate of growth in production. The link to size distribution is less obvious. However, the direction of causality assumed in the neo-Keynesian model is from investments to savings rather than the other way round. Therefore, the demand side is very important, and if demand is curtailed by, for example, lower labour incomes, the growth rate may go down. Thus, even if growth and inequality go together, the causation is not from inequality to growth but the opposite. It is therefore not clear in this analysis that the growth rate can be increased through a primary increase in inequality in favour of high saving groups.

A very important factor with regard to the development of income distribution is the agricultural – industrial terms of trade. When these improve for agriculture, income distribution improves. Thus, the development of agriculture relative to the rest of the economy should be in focus when one sets out to devise strategies for equality.

In the Bachue model, growth paths are generated under a few different assumptions. In the reference run, it is assumed that the growth rate is 7%. Labour productivity growth in agriculture is restricted to 3% per year. With this formulation, the terms of trade of agriculture increase by 50% over the simulation period, which implies that the share of agriculture in output remains practically constant at current prices. Overall inequality declines slowly. Unemployment declines, and there is also a sharp decline in the proportion of the population engaged in agriculture. Rural traditional wages increase from 46% of the traditional urban wages in 1965 to 77% in the year 2000. The share of the modern sector labour force increases from 17 to 28% over the same period. Both educated – non-educated and urban – rural differences decline. The latter, of course, to a considerable extent (although not wholly) is a consequence of the development of the terms of trade of agriculture. The development of those terms of trade, in turn, is to a high degree determined by the assumptions about trade in food products. With a restrictive assumption about food imports, the terms of trade are bound to go up. It should here be pointed out that the trade estimates are very uncertain.

Other alternatives with different growth rates and different assumptions about trade of food are also tested. In an experiment, where labour productivity is allowed to grow by 4% instead of 3, the effects on rural incomes are very negative. This, of course, must in part be because of the assumption that the increased production cannot find an export market, and that may be questioned. In any case, it illustrates that the demand side must also be taken into account when one devises development strategies.

In Adelman and Robinson's model, policies aimed at increasing agricultural productivity lead, ceteris paribus, to a deterioration of the terms of trade of the sector and lower rural incomes. Such a policy can therefore not be pursued in isolation, but must be combined with a policy that guarantees that the price of the output of the agricultural sector is upheld. The larger the agricultural sector is relative to the total economy and the further monetization of the sector has gone, the more important this effect is.

After the comparative static experiments have been made, the authors perform a variety of dynamic experiments with different policy packages. In the chapter on rural policies they test the effects of land reform, various measures to increase agricultural productivity, employment policy, investment in human resources, and a few combined packages (overall rural development strategy). The most striking conclusion from these tests is the dominating importance of the agricultural terms of trade for the agricultural sector and thus the poorest groups in the economy. If the economy is self-sufficient in food production, the farmers are actually hurt by increased agricultural output, unless prices are stabilized in some way. It is also shown that eventually all rural strategies help urban groups through a trickle-up process: through cheaper food or increased demand for urban output.

However, a broadly based, overall rural policy package (particularly one that includes land reform) may have a considerable effect on income distribution. Such a package should include not only policies aimed at agricultural production and terms of trade, but also measures aimed at creating other types of employment in rural areas (either through public works or industry).

There is no such explicit discussion of the agricultural – industrial terms of trade in the Brazilian study. However, the small farmers in Brazil are in the proprietors category, and are therefore assumed to receive fixed nominal incomes. They therefore gain when there is a deflation and lose when there is inflation.

One type of policy that is discussed in all models is expansion of education. In the Bachue model of the Philippines, the effects of educational policy are widespread but not very large. The distribution of income seems to be rather insensitive also to large changes in educational policy. However, fast educational growth turns out to have more egalitarian effects than slow. Expansion of secondary education seems to be more egalitarian then expansion of primary education. Here, however, it must be kept in mind that no effects on productivity are assumed (growth is exogenous). The best result in terms of equality is obtained with a broadly based educational policy.

Adelman and Robinson also find that there are beneficial effects from upgrading the labour force. For South Korea, this means increased supply of skilled labour and it helps to reduce poverty. It is also a necessary ingredient in the labour and skill-intensive, export-oriented development strategy, which is found to have beneficial effects on the income distribution.

Taylor *et al.* find that upgrading of the labour force has positive distributional consequences. It increases aggregate supply and reduces the price level. In their model, this increases the share of the proprietors and other receivers of fixed nominal incomes. Because this group is relatively poor, income distribution improves.

It is shown that, in Brazil, expansion of primary and secondary education has better distributional consequences than a comparable expansion (in terms of its effect on GNP) of university education. It is also shown that there is a higher return to money invested in primary education than in university education at the same time as it has more beneficial income distribution consequences. In this case, there is therefore no conflict between growth and equality.

There are some attempts at investigating the effects of changes in the demographic variables, particularly in the Bachue model. Among the demographic variables tested there are, for example, measures to decrease fertility. It turns out that the effects on per capita incomes and inequality up to the year 2000 are very limited. The case for family planning thus is less strong than what is often believed. It would have to be argued on the basis of micro arguments rather than macro arguments.

Migration, on the other hand, turns out to be an extremely important equilibrating mechanism. It helps reducing disparities and contributes to the trickle-down process. When migration is restricted, the income distribution deteriorates sharply.

The results of the Adelman – Robinson model is that migration is next to the urban – rural terms of trade in importance for the anti-poverty programme. Reduced migration increases the pressure on the poorer areas. Also in this model, all population policies are insignificant over the period of analysis.

In both the Philippine and the South Korean models an appropriate trade strategy is shown to have significant and positive effects on the incomes of the poor. The major effect on income distribution is not direct through changes in urban wages and employment. It is instead the indirect effects on the rural economy in the form of migration and terms of trade changes which matters. A labour-intensive export-promotion strategy can help to improve the agricultural terms of trade and thereby income distribution.

The effects of a devaluation in the Brazilian model is deflationary, contrary to what one would normally assume. This is because it leads to increased foreign savings (that is a deficit in the balance of payments) and thus less effective demand. Exports are not stimulated in the short run and imports are price inelastic. Eventually, corporate earnings are lowered enough to bring about a full employment equilibrium. The deflation, as usual in this model, improves income distribution.

Taylor and his colleagues also test the effects of increased exports. They find that exports of high-technology goods would have a very small influence on Brazilian employment, especially of the less skilled workers. Expansion of food and other agricultural exports would, on the other hand, have very beneficial distribution effects. The export promotion policies pursued by the Brazilian authorities have been of the first type.

6.6 Income distribution analysis in a one-sector model

The models discussed in this chapter are all of a very large scale, and it is sometimes difficult to look through their complex structure and see the underlying economic theory. Taylor and Lysy (1979) use a one-sector version of large-scale simulation models to compare qualitative aspects of different formulations. Also in their book on Brazil, Taylor and his colleagues (1980) use a simplified macro economic model to discuss the choice of closure rules to be used in the full-scale multi-sectoral model.

Here we shall look at a simple graphical analysis of growth and distribution within a one-sector neoclassical model presented by Bruno (1979). Hopefully, the discussion of that model will give some understanding of the basic theoretical relationships between production, savings, and the functional distribution of income in the large-scale models. The discussion should also give a feeling for the limitations imposed on the analysis by the underlying functional income distribution theory, as well as by the model building technique.

The further step from the functional income distribution to the size distribution will not be discussed here, and also the important social and political dimensions of the problem will be left out. The discussion here therefore only concerns the essential economic and theoretical basis of the more complex model analyses.

The discussion is most relevant to the models of Adelman and Robinson and Taylor *et al.*, since they have flexible prices. They both have a multi-sectoral framework and emphasize the determination of functional shares of capital and labour, which are determined from marginal productivity considerations. Also the composition of final demand and savings is important in the models.

Bruno (1979) specifies a simple closed one-sector economy with constant returns to scale. The economy produces output (Y) with the help of labour (L) and capital (K). Output per unit of labour, ($y = Y/L$), is an increasing function of the capital – labour ratio, ($k = K/L$), and can be written as y (k). Income is divided between labour (wL) and capital (rK). We thus have

$$Y = wL + rK \tag{6.1}$$

which after divison by L can be written

$$y(k) = w + rk \tag{6.1a}$$

For a given technique (k) this equation expresses a relation between r and w, which can be represented in Figure 6.1 by a straight line (BC) with the slope $-k$. The intercept OC measures output per unit of labour (y) and OB measures the output – capital ratio (y/k). The point Q at (r_0, w_0) gives QB/CQ $= w_0/r_0k = (w_0L/r_0K)$, that is the relative shares of labour and capital.

Assume that Y is divided between consumption (C) and savings (S), and that there are different rates of saving for capital and labour incomes (s_r, s_w). This gives the classical savings function

$$S = s_w wL + s_r rK \tag{6.2}$$

The savings – investment equilibrium condition can then be written:

$$i/k = \frac{I/L}{K/L} = \frac{I}{K} = \frac{S}{K} = \frac{s_w wL + s_r rK}{K} = \frac{s_w \cdot w}{K/L} + s_r r$$

$$= \frac{s_w w}{k} + s_r \cdot r \tag{6.2a}$$

where i is investment per unit of labour, (I/L). For given k and i equation (6.2a) is represented by the straight line DA. Here OD $= i/s_w$ and OA $= i/ks_r$ and the slope is $- ks_r/s_w$.

The slope of DA is greater in absolute value than the slope of CB as long as $s_r > s_w$, which is a very reasonable assumption. If the workers do not save anything at all, the line DA becomes vertical and $I/K = s_r r$, that is the rate of growth of the capital stock becomes proportional to the rate of return.

Now we have two equations but four unknowns, w, r, k, and i. We must fix two of these four to determine the other two uniquely. As the model is specified so far, it is not necessarily neoclassical on the production side. It may also be noted that the number of sectors can be increased. The income distribution rules will continue to apply as long as there are two factors and two corresponding savings groups. We can here easily see that if k is fixed and i increases, the rate of return must increase as well as the share of profits in output to restore

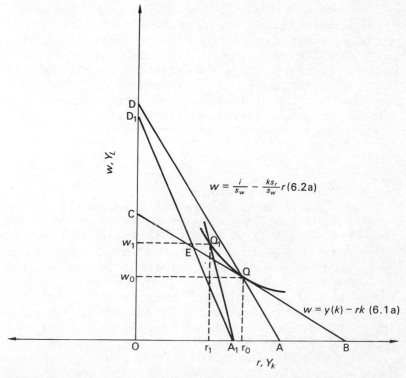

Figure 6.1   Output in a one-sector economy with constant returns to scale

equilibrium. DA must shift outwards or to put it differently: If investment demand per worker (I/L) increases, at the same time that production per worker (Y/L) remains constant, the consumption demand per worker (C/Y) must be reduced to retain the equilibrium $Y = C + I$. The reduction of (C/Y) requires a redistribution of income. This is the central feature of the Taylor model discussed in the previous section.

After specifying these general rules, Bruno goes on to make the model more neoclassical. A well-behaved production framework has a Factor-Price Frontier (FPF). This is a technological concept which measures the maximum marginal productivity of one factor among all available techniques, given the marginal productivity of the other.

If we now also introduce the marginal products of capital and labour (Y_K, Y_L) on the two axes of our figure, we can draw the downward sloping FPF $g(Y_L, Y_K) = 0$. This is the FPF of the production function $y(k)$, where k is allowed to vary. Since Y_K is a decreasing and Y_L an increasing function of k, Y_L will also be a decreasing function of Y_K. As long as we have only one sector, the FPF will always be convex. It has the property that at any point it indicates the k that is chosen if a certain pair of marginal products is given. For example, at Q in Figure 6.1, $w = Y_L$ and $r = Y_K$, since the BC line is a tangent to the factor price frontier. Here the neoclassical competitive assumption provides part of the closure. When this assumption is made, we need only to fix one of our four unknowns to make the system fully determinate.

Bruno compares three different closure systems.

6.6.1 Neoclassical full employment

If $\bar{K}$, and $\bar{L}$, are given, then also $k = \bar{k}$, is determined by the tangent at Q. If there is perfect competition in the factor markets this determines the real wage (w_0) and the profit rate (r_0) and the relative factor shares (QB/CB). For a given k and alternative i equation (6.2a) gives a number of parallel lines. The one through Q determines i under full employment, and thus the system is fully determined.

Now, let us see what happens in the next period if k increase as a result of investment i, and assume that there is no technical progress so that the FPF remains fixed. The new equilibrium may then be at Q_1, with $w_1 > w_0$ and $r_1 < r_0$. The relative factor share of labour (w/rk) will rise or fall depending on whether the elasticity of substitution between labour and capital is less than or greater than one. A new level of i can now be determined and this in turn gives a new k for the following period.

6.6.2 Classical unemployment

Here, we assume that the real wage is given and at subsistence level w_0. This then determines the profit rate r_0 as well as the competitive capital – labour ratio k_0 (= slope of CB). Given the amount of capital $\bar{K}$ only $\bar{K}/k_0$ workers will be employed. This may be less than $\bar{L}$, the labour force, and if so there is classical unemployment. As the capital stock increases, more workers will be employed, but w and k will remain constant. The end of the labour surplus condition, the turning point, will occur when $K = \bar{L}k_0$. This is the end of the labour surplus phase discussed by Lewis (1954) and Fei and Ranis (1964). After this phase has ended, traditional marginal productivity conditions may come to determine incomes also in the agricultural sector.

6.6.3 Keynesian unemployment

In the first two cases, the system is completely supply-determined. Output adjusts to factor quantities and prices. Here, we shall instead consider the case when the capital stock ($\bar{K}$) is given in the short run and the demand for investment (I) is exogenously determined. Suppose that with given $\bar{L}$ and $\bar{k}$ (by the slope at Q) the investment line is A_1D_1. Thus I_1 is less than I given by AD.

In this case, the A_1D_1 line cuts BC at E, which gives the demand given functional shares under full employment. However, point E is not a competitive production equilibrium. With the real wage at E the employers would want to employ less labour and earn a higher profit rate. If we want the solution both to represent the demand determined investment level and fulfil the neoclassical marginal productivity conditions, we may get an equilibrium at Q_1 at the FPF. The line A_1D_1 rotates to A_1Q_1, since point A_1 stays fixed because $OA_1 = I_0/\bar{K}s_r$ stays fixed. The capital – labour ratio increases to say k_1 (= slope of A_1Q_1), which means that employment is reduced from full employment at $\bar{L}$, to $\bar{K}/k_1 < \bar{L}$. This is called Keynesian unemployment.

At Q_1 both the profit rate and the wage-rate are higher than at E, but there is not full employment. This can be restored if investment increases from I_1 to $\bar{I}$. The competitive equilibrium point would move from Q_1 to Q on the FPF. The labour share will increase if the elasticity of substitution is greater than one, otherwise it will decline. The labour share will decline if an investment increase makes the equilibrium move from E to Q with BC fixed, even if we do not make any competitive assumptions.

The framework used here can be extended somewhat to make it

more similar to the large-scale models discussed above. One can allow the economy to trade. Assume imports (M) is a fixed proportion (m) of gross output (X). Then $M = mX$ and value-added $V = (1 - m)X$ is produced by L and K in a neoclassical fashion. Exports (E) then becomes part of the demand and the foreign balance $B = M - E$ must be incorporated in the system. One may also introduce taxes and multiply the savings rates with the net-of-taxes factors $(1 - t_w)$ and $(1 - t_r)$. Equation (6.2a) can then be rewritten as

$$I/K - B/K + F/K = (s_w(1 - t_w)/k) w + s_r(1 - t_r)r \qquad (6.2b)$$

where F is the net government deficit. One needs also to introduce a distinction in the model between output prices and GNP prices, but we shall disregard that problem here.

We can now, for example, see from equation (6.2b) that an increase in the foreign deficit B reduces the need for domestic savings to retain a given equilibrium. We can also see that, if the government deficit F increases, so must savings from labour and capital incomes increase to compensate for this, if the equilibrium is to be restored. We can further note that if tax rates are increased and at the same time the budget deficit is reduced by the same amount, the equilibrium is not disturbed. In this equilibrium formula government savings can therefore replace private savings.

The discussion around this model has only concerned variables in real terms. In both the Taylor model and the Adelman – Robinson model, the price level is endogenously determined. To get an understanding of how the inclusion of nominal variables affect the system, one must see how the nominal variables affect the real ones. The other effects are captured by the system as outlined above. As one example one may assume that nominal wages fall and that this reduces the price level, while, at the same time, the government expeditures remain fixed in real terms. This is equivalent to an increase in the left-hand side of equation (6.2), and then the A_1D_1 curve is shifted to the right. The share of labour falls.

Bell (1979) introduces a subsistence sector into the model outlined here and analyses the complications that this gives rise to. These will not be further pursued here, since the basic points of illustration have been possible to make within the framework of the simple one-sector model.

The models in the previous part of this chapter are of a comparative static nature and do not explicitly analyse the process of adjustment. Many equilibrium features are therefore left out of the picture, although they may have important effects on income distribution.

However, the present state of the model-building technique does not make model analyses of these problems possible.

6.7 Major conclusions

The purpose of this chapter has been to show what has been learnt from model studies about the determinants of income distribution in LDCs and particularly about what can be achieved in terms of equalization by economic policy. By using economy-wide models, one can also take indirect effects into account, and it is in this respect that the studies discussed in this chapter are superior to those dealt with in Chapter 5.

A general conclusion that can be drawn from all three models discussed here is that the overall size distribution of income is very stable. It is difficult to change it by single policy interventions. However, the relative position of individual groups can be very significantly affected by such policies. The largest effects on distribution seem to be achieved within the more neo-Keynesian Brazilian model. This may be an indication that the type of model specification chosen really does influence the outcome of the analysis. Alternatively, it may be because Brazil starts out with a more unequal distribution than the other ones. It is very difficult to differentiate between these two explanations.

All models are of a general equilibrium character, but they differ in the extent to which rigidities are introduced. The model attributable to Adelman and Robinson shows the greatest degree of flexibility. In this model, the overall size distribution is very stable. Most interventions are compensated to a high degree by market adjustments. Most of all, it is therefore the forces of supply and demand which matter, not government intervention. To get a significant effect on the size distribution of income, a concerted effort aimed at a whole spectrum of conditions is needed. In the two other models, which lean more in the structuralist direction, there is somewhat greater scope for improvements, but also here the size distribution is very stable. The conclusion about the stability of the size distribution of income therefore seems to stand independently of the model specification chosen. Profound policy changes are called for if any significant improvements in income distribution are to be achieved from government interventions.

In the Brazilian model, the authors test whether income distribution policy is or is not facilitated by more rigidities in the model. It turns out that depending on the type of rigidities the effect can be either way. However, less of flexibility means that the resource allocation becomes less efficient, and the growth rate will be lower than what it would be in a more flexible economy. Flexibility is therefore beneficial to long-term poverty alleviation.

The relationship between growth and income distribution is of considerable interest in this context. High savings rates tend to accompany high growth rates, but whether it is the high savings rate which causes the high investment rate and thus the high growth rate, or vice versa, is a matter of debate.

The model studies indicate that it is easier to devise, in theory, general policies aimed at improving the lot of the rural poor than that of the urban poor. The latter are more dispersed among sectors and types of employment, and policies aimed at improving their position tend to trickle up to the middle class. The major effect on rural poverty is achieved by measures aimed at improving rural – urban terms of trade. Also migration out of the rural areas relieves the pressure on the rural labour market and improves the incomes of those remaining in the rural areas. Thus the urban – rural linkages are of major importance for poverty alleviation in the rural areas. An equal distribution of land is an important precondition for a successful income distribution policy in the rural areas. Development of the rural infrastructure is also helpful in this context, because it increases rural productivity as well as giving incomes to the rural inhabitants.

An emphasis on industrialization through an import-substitution policy has a very strong urban bias, since it has to be pursued at the expense of agriculture. Therefore, it has a detrimental effect on income distribution. If it has a positive effect on the overall growth rate, the effect on the absolute incomes of the poor may in the very long run be positive, but whether this really is possible in the countries concerned here is very doubtful. A trade strategy that takes the comparative advantages into account can have a significant effect on poverty, since this normally means that labour-intensive production will expand. This increases the demand for labour, increases the agricultural terms of trade and thus improves income distribution.

It is also shown in the models that educational expansion is equalizing, because it reduces the scarcity rents that can be earned by scarce skilled labour categories. However, the overall effect on inequality is limited. The educational policy can therefore only be a component of a broadly based income distribution policy. Another aspect of this issue, which also should be taken into account, is that an expansion of labour supply ahead of demand may well have a positive effect on distribution, but such an expansion has a cost and may well retard growth, if the resources to finance the expansion are drawn from more profitable investment opportunities. An analysis of this trade-off is, however, hard to perform.

It is also possible to analyse the effects of a change in the price level on income distribution within two of the models. It is by the differential effect on receivers of fixed nominal incomes and variable nominal incomes that the effect on the overall income distribution comes about. In the Brazilian model, at least, it is the poor who suffer from the inflation, since they cannot compensate themselves fully with higher prices and incomes.

References

Adelman, I. and Robinson, S. (1978) *Income Distribution Policies in Developing Countries. A Case Study of South Korea*, Oxford University Press, Oxford.

Bell, C. (1979), 'The behavior of a dual economy under different closing rules', *Journal of Development Economics*, Vol. 6.

Bruno, M. (1979) 'Income distribution and the neoclassical paradigm: introduction to a symposium; *Journal of Development Economics*, Vol. 6.

Dervis, K., de Melo, J. and Robinson, S. (1982), *General Equilibrium Models for Development Policy*, Cambridge University Press.

Fei, J.C.H. and Ranis, G. (1964), *Development of the Labor Surplus Economy*, Irwin, Homewood, Ill.

Johansen, L. (1974), *A Multi-Sectoral Study of Economic Growth*, 2nd edn., North-Holland, Amsterdam.

Kaldor, N. (1956). 'Alternative theories of income distribution', *Review of Economic Studies*, Vol. 23.

Lewis, W.A. (1954) 'Economic development with unlimited supplies of labour', *Manchester School of Economic and Social Studies*, Vol. 22.

Rodgers, G.B., Hopkins, M.J.D. and Wery, R. (1978), *Population, Employment and Inequality: Bachue-Philippines*, Saxon House, Westmead.

Sen, A. (1963), 'Neoclassical and neo-Keynesian theories of distribution', *Economic Record*, Vol. 39.

Taylor, L. (1980), *Macro Models for Developing Countries*, McGraw-Hill, New York.

Taylor, L., Bacha, E.L. Cardoso, E.A. and Lysy, F.J. (1980), *Models of Growth and Distribution for Brazil*, Oxford University Press, New York.

Taylor, L. and Lysy, F.J. (1979), 'Vanishing income redistributions: Keynesian clues about model surprises in the short run', *Journal of Development Studies*, Vol. 6.

7 Income Distribution Policy in East and Central Africa

7.1 Introduction

During the 1950s and the early 1960s the development problem was considered to be a question of economic growth. If the economy was only growing at a sufficiently rapid rate the problems of poverty and inequality would eventually be alleviated by the natural course of change. During the 1960s it became increasingly clear that large segments of the population in LDCs often benefited very little from the quite considerable increases in aggregate output. During the 1970s there has therefore been a search for development strategies, where income distribution and direct poverty alleviation are integral parts. This issue has been touched upon in every chapter of the book, but it may be worthwhile to try to summarize the main points in the discussion of development strategies during the 1970s, before we go on to look at how the strategy discussion has manifested itself in the actual development policies pursued in three African countries, namely Kenya, Tanzania, and Zambia.

The two major new broad strategies presented during the 1970s were the Redistribution with Growth strategy and the Basic Needs strategy. These will be presented in section 7.2. Then in section 7.3 we will take a look at how the development strategies pursued in Kenya, Tanzania, and Zambia have evolved during the period since independence. In section 7.4 we will do a more detailed comparison of the distribution policies of the respective countries in specific policy areas. Those are agricultural policies, industrialization and trade policies, prices and incomes policies, and fiscal policy. It needs to be pointed out that it is not possible to compare in any detail the extent of inequality and poverty in the respective countries. That would require an extensive research effort. However, some data that are of interest to the discussion of the various policies will be given.

Finally, in section 7.5 I attempt to summarize and compare the experiences of Kenya, Tanzania, and Zambia. I also try to draw some general conclusions about income distribution policy on the basis of those experiences.

Naturally, it would have been desirable to take a look at a larger sample than just the three countries mentioned. However, they are sufficiently dissimilar to cover quite a lot of the variation at least in sub-Saharan Africa. Kenya is a capitalist economy with few natural resources (except land). Tanzania is a country with a socialist ideology striving for self-reliance. Zambia, finally, is a country which, ideologically, might be placed somewhere between the other two and which is heavily dependent on its copper export.

The income distribution policies of some other countries of the Third World were discussed in Chapters 5 and 6. The evidence presented there concerns mainly Latin America and Asia. There is therefore some merit in taking a more detailed look at a few African countries, since they are more neglected in the literature.

7.2 Equity oriented development strategies
A basic characteristic of the development efforts of most LDCs during the 1950s and 1960s was the attempt to bring about an industrialization through a policy of import-substitution. They tried to bring about a structural change that implied relatively more industry and less agriculture.

This development path had been suggested by many (see, for example, W.A. Lewis, 1954). In his model the essence of development (see Chapter 3) was the expansion of the modern sector to let it absorb the surplus labour of the traditional sector. This perception of the development process was underlying the strategies of most LDCs. They supported the modern sector through protection and various forms of subsidies to make profitable production possible. It was hoped that the absorption of labour from agriculture would lead to higher incomes in the agricultural sector.

During the 1960s the per capita incomes in LDCs actually grew faster than during any period in history. The growth was concentrated in the modern sector. Since production per worker there increased rapidly, the demand for labour did not expand as rapidly as Lewis had predicted. A contributing factor was that modern sector wages were not bound to the level of subsistence incomes in agriculture. Instead they increased quite considerably, at the same time as the use of capital was subsidized. This stimulated the use of capital intensive methods of production.

The effect of the import-substitution policy was to shift income distribution against agriculture (as already discussed in Chapter 5), where most of the poor are to be found. Since the wages of those who managed to get a modern sector job were quite high, while the incomes of those who remained in the traditional sector stagnated, the income inequalities tended to increase.

Around 1970 the ILO undertook a series of country studies of the employment problems in LDCs. It was discovered that the development path so far followed by the LDCs in most cases could not solve their employment problems within the foreseeable future. There also started a discussion of the relationship among employment, income distribution, and growth. In 1973 there was a large conference at the Institute of Development Studies in Sussex on this theme, where one concluded that there were development problems which could not be attacked with the traditional planning models. The outcome of the conference was a book called *Redistribution with Growth* (Chenery *et al.*, 1974) where a new planning strategy for the LDCs was sketched. I will here outline some major aspects of the strategy.

All the proposals in the volume are such that they in principle should be possible for non-socialist LDCs to accept. It is therefore not a socialist strategy that is outlined, even if the redistribution of land and capital plays an essential role.

It was argued that the starting point for the new strategy should be the identification of certain target groups of poor, which are relatively homogeneous with regard to the effects on them of relevant economic policies. The four groups of poor which are picked out are (i) small farmers; (ii) landless and farmers with so little land that it does not provide for their subsistence needs; (iii) the urban unemployed; and (iv) the urban working poor. Most of the poor are thus assumed to have some sort of work, albeit very unproductive.

It is argued in the book that one can group the LDCs according to three dimensions, that is the degree of urbanization, access to land, and the degree of concentration of the land ownership. The course of action is then dependent on which category the country belongs to.

A general policy problem that was identified is that even if the actions are aimed at helping the poorest, there is considerable leakage to wealthier groups. It was therefore suggested that one should consider creating special institutions which are working only for the interests of the poor.

For the groups in the rural areas the most important factors were said to be access to land, knowledge, and credit. With regard to the cities there is a wider spectrum of measures to choose from, among other things this is because of the more extensive interdependence which exists between the informal urban sector and the rest of the economy. Here one advocated a production strategy and a transfer strategy. The first one is aimed at increasing the employment opportunities and the productivity in existing jobs. This can be done through a correction of biases in factor prices and through support of small scale producers. The transfer strategy includes among other things better access to public goods and housing for the poor.

It was also suggested that a new welfare indicator should replace GDP. In the weighted measure proposed you start by dividing the households into a number of equally large income groups. Growth is then defined as the average proportional income increase for these groups. An income increase of $1 in a group with an annual income of $100 is thus of the same weight as $100 is to a household in the $10 000 annual income group.

The use of such a weighted measure of growth would adjust the growth rate of countries with an inequitable pattern of development downwards, while countries pursuing income equalization will show a higher rate of growth. It would lead to the choice of another set of policies if applied.

The authors point out that since it is very unlikely that there will be large-scale income transfers in LDCs, for both political and administrative reasons, one must attempt to devise the development policy in such a way that it gives incomes to those who shall use the income in the end. Therefore what is needed is a structure of growth such that the situation of the target groups is improved.

The authors are fairly optimistic about the prospects of devising policies that have an acceptable distribution profile without sacrifices in terms of growth. However, as has been pointed out already in previous chapters, there are obviously several situations where there is a trade-off between growth and distribution. Then the choice of strategy will be affected by the time preferences of the decision-makers and the choice of welfare indicator.

In Chapter 5 it was shown that the problems of poverty and inequality are still very severe in most LDCs, and in places the problems are even increasing. In any case the rate of improvement for the poorest is very slow. ILO (1976) therefore argued that it is not sufficient to rely on the trickle-down mechanism to solve the problem of poverty, since the poor would have to wait a very long time before they experience any substantial improvements. ILO therefore outlined its basic needs strategy, where the aim is to increase directly the standard of living of the poorest groups. The indicator of success in this approach therefore is the change in the degree of satisfaction of certain basic needs in the population. The ideas presented by the ILO can be regarded as extension of the analysis put forward in *Redistribution with Growth*.

The main ingredigents of the strategy can be summarized (ILO, 1976, p. 68) in six points:

1. Productive employment for the poor.
2. Increased investments in traditional agriculture and the informal sector and the elimination of the obstacles for the development of these sectors. Resources should be distributed more equitably between the modern sector and the rest of the economy.
3. The entire population should be given access to basic consumption goods and the increased public expenditures should be financed by a progressive tax.
4. The differences among households in consumption of basic goods and services should be decreased.
5. Exports should be increased to finance imports to meet basic needs without too much dependence on aid.
6. Creation of institutions that make it possible for the poor majority to take an active part in the development efforts.

The ultimate aim of the ILO strategy is to guarantee that all people in the world have reached a certain minimum standard by the turn of the century. The great inequalities that exist make it imperative to put priority on measures that are directly aimed at improving the lot of the poorest. The most important ingredient in the strategy is to try to create productive employment for all.

There must be a change in economic policy, primarily nationally but also internationally, if the poor are to get a reasonable living standard within the foreseeable future. The governments should define the lowest acceptable standard of living. Among basic needs are, on the one hand, certain private consumption goods such as food, shelter, and clothes, and, on the other, certain essential services such as health services, education, water and sanitation, and transport.

The basic needs should be defined as minimum level for these (and possible other) factors. When this has been done one can either determine the level of basic needs satisfaction for each good separately or try to calculate some basic needs income; that is, an income that is sufficient to buy the basic needs bundle.

When the levels have been specified one can compare these with the existing pattern of consumption to find out how large the shortfall is and what the incidence among different socioeconomic groups is. On the basis of this information one should try to outline a policy of distribution. Obviously a large degree of structural change and redistribution will be required. Given the large inequalities that exist at present, the extent to which one can meet the basic needs to a high degree depends on the degree of equality that can be achieved. Measures discussed include changes in relative prices, direct transfers of resources to the poor for consumption and investment, and distribution of the stock of assets and land in favour of the poor. The emphasis thus is on a change in the structure of incomes and growth and on a change in the pattern of ownership. Growth of total production normally makes it easier to increase the standard of the poor, as redistribution then does not have to be so painful for the rich. The political opposition to redistribution might thus be somewhat less stiff.

To be able to reach the goals set up by ILO a radical policy change is obviously called for. ILO argues that it will be necessary to increase the rate of growth of GNP at the same time as there is a large change in the distribution of income among different socioeconomic groups. It is doubtful if one can really accomplish both these things. One would expect a certain cost in terms of growth if radical redistribution is pursued.

The main line of argument through the entire ILO report is that one should make it possible for the poor to earn themselves through productive employment what they need for subsistence. The alternative of redistributing resources through public transfers and taxation is often not feasible.

It is argued that there would be more employment creation if some of the biases in the price system could be removed. Less biased prices would increase the growth rate through a more efficient allocation of resources, and it would also lead to the use of more labour intensive methods of production. Thus, an improvement of the price system is a part of a policy aimed at creating employment for the poor.

Public services, primarily education and health services, satisfy important basic needs. Basic education is both consumption and investment. In its first role it directly satisfies a basic need and in its second it increases the possibility of satisfying other needs. Health services can contribute to the increase of the productivity of the labour force, but to be in good health is also a basic need. The health service must in the new strategy to a greater degree be directed to the people in the urban slums and in the rural areas, who now are undersupplied. The concentration of health services on the urban rich is enormous. In the ILO report one also points to other public sectors which should be emphasized, for example, low income housing, water supply and sanitation.

A consequence of a basic needs strategy is that a greater emphasis, than has been placed in the past, be put on the traditional rural sector and the informal urban sector. The evaluation of future policies should be made according to their effects on the poor groups. A land reform combined with complementary services to the poor farmers would be a central component in a basic needs strategy in the rural areas. These actions should be combined with public works, which could give direct employment to the poorest groups in the rural areas and contribute to the construction of a rural infrastructure.

The urban situation is more complex. The slow rate of growth of urban industrial employment combined with a rapid rate of urban population growth has created employment problems in the cities. Many people have to earn a living in non-productive services or other informal employment if they are not openly unemployed. Open unemployment is primarily an urban phenomenon. There may be a certain increase in the demand for labour from the modern sector as a result of the changes discussed above, but one should also support the informal sector. The need for public services is large in the slums, but it may be difficult to earmark resources only for the poor. We noted in Chapter 6 that there is a problem of trickle-up in the urban areas. However, it should be possible to initiate policies aimed at improving housing, water supply and sanitation which are of such a character that the poor are reached.

To conclude this section on equity-oriented strategies we can take a look at a categorization of policies aimed at poverty alleviation. Selowsky (1981) distinguishes among three types of policies. The first type includes the elimination of distortions that inhibit trickle-down. Their goal should be to increase the employment content of growth. The second type of policy concerns investment policies aimed at increasing human and physical capital endowments of the poor. In this category we include only those policies that are beneficial both for growth and poverty alleviation. Thus, neither of these two types of policies imply any trade-off between growth and poverty alleviation. The third type of policies are pure basic needs policies; that is policies that improve indicators such as health status, life expectancy, literacy, etc. The reason for separating these policies from the first two is that they may imply a lower rate of GDP growth.

The two major types of distortions that have negatively affected employment growth are first, those that have distorted the composition of output such as trade policies or domestic price policies and second those that have increased the relative price of labour above that corresponding to the relative abundance of labour in the economy.

Under the second heading Selowsky groups investments in the poor which are also profitable also from an aggregate viewpoint. Which investments that are profitable will vary from country to country depending on characteristics of the poor. First, of course, there is investment in human capital such as education, on-the-job training, child nutrition, etc. Second, there are measures that increase the physical assets of the poor in the rural areas. How these policies should be designed is very much dependent on the distribution of land. If land is very unequally distributed it is difficult to devise policies that mainly benefit the poor.

The third type of policies are basic needs services which were discussed above; that is, policies on education, health, water, housing, etc. These may be desirable from a basic needs perspective, even if they imply a lower GDP growth rate.

Thus, there are policies which both improve the situation of the poor and contribute to growth in total output. For policies, which are more purely basic needs oriented there is a trade-off, but the nature of this trade-off is not yet very clear. It is an empirical question, which has to be settled for each individual country.

7.3 Government strategy concerning the distribution of income and public services

In this section we will consider the development strategies pursued in Kenya, Tanzania, and Zambia since they have become independent. We are particularly concerned with the way in which they have dealt with the problems of income distribution and poverty.

7.3.1 Development strategy in Kenya

Kenya became independent in 1963. The major policy emphasis during the period immediately after independence was on 'Africanization'. The civil service was naturally the prime target, but efforts were also devoted to the Africanization of agriculture, industry, and services. The replacement of a vast number of expatriates in leading positions in these areas by Africans implied a reduction of racial inequalities. Still, the economic structure of the country did not change much, so the decreasing inter-racial differences did not imply any significant change in overall inequality.

It was, nevertheless, emphasized in official policy documents that a more equal income distribution was one of the main government aims. In the frequently quoted Sessional Paper no. 10 of 1965, 'African socialism and its application to planning in Kenya', the official policy objectives were stated as (i) a continued expansion of the economy; (ii) a wider sharing of the benefits of expansion; (iii) a national integration of the economy; and (iv) an attack on extreme imbalances and disparities. It was, however, emphasized that policies for a more equal distribution of income must not retard economic growth.

The major strategy followed by Kenya has been the policy of import-substitution. The rate of protection for industry has remained high, even if there have been some signs of a move away from the policy in the last few years.

The policies from the first plan period (1966—70) that are of most interest here, apart from the import-substitution policy, are the agricultural and land policies. The redistribution of land had beneficial effects on the distribution of income.

In the Second Development Plan (1970—74) there was a change of emphasis in the development strategy. Rural development played a much more prominent role than in the first plan. This was a reflection of the insight that some segments of the economy had been benefiting disproportionately from the industrialization strategy. It was necessary to channel more resources directly to the rural areas to combat the tendency towards an increasing urban – rural imbalance. The primary means mentioned in the plan was the generation of adequately paid employment opportunities in the rural areas. However, even if there were a change in emphasis, the most important concern continued to be industrialization and the aggregate rate of economic growth.

In 1972, the very influential ILO report on employment and earnings in Kenya was published. The ILO mission found that there were three fundamental imbalances that needed to be corrected (ILO, 1972, pp. 13—14). They were:

1. The imbalance between the rate of population growth and the nature of technology.
2. The imbalance between the centre and the periphery, i.e. essentially the imbalance between Nairobi and the rest of the country, between the rural and the urban areas in general, and among provinces and districts.
3. The imbalance between the formal and informal sectors.

The imbalance between different regions was thus pointed out by the Mission as one fundamental aspect of the general problem of inequality in Kenya, and in the report it is also pointed out (ILO, 1972, p. 301) that

differential access on a regional basis to such advantages as roads, education and development projects is closely related to (family) economic disparity, and is thus a major force behind migration, both from the country to the towns and from one rural area to another. Particularly serious is the way in which regional imbalances interact with tribal fears and forces, partly as a cause and partly as a result. The report of the National Assembly's Select Committee on Unemployment showed tribalism to be an aspect of regional and ethnic inequality with serious effects on social and economic progress: where tribalism exists, many of the recommendations made in this report (for example, equitable distribution of development efforts geographically, equitable distribution of incomes, decentralization of industry, efficiency in Civil Service) cannot be implemented.

In the Kenyan government's reply to the report of the ILO mission the central theme of the report is accepted, i.e. that

> Kenya's employment and unemployment problems are deeply embedded in the country's social and economic fabric and that these problems can be significantly alleviated only by fundamental changes in the pattern of development and in the structure of key institutions.

As far as regional inequality is concerned there was a declared readiness to do something about it. The same sessional paper (paras. 242–243) stated that

> the Government is aware of the fact of regional inequalities in the distribution of welfare, services and amenities. . . . The Government accepts that geographic quotas are probably necessary for a variety of services, activities and programmes. . . . Current planning practices and procedures will be examined with a view to introducing geographic quotas for a variety of services and amenities and for expenditures during the next Plan period.

The Third Development Plan (1974–78) was influenced by the ILO mission and by the discussions of the type that was reflected in *Redistribution with Growth*. Once again it was emphasized that the distributional consequences of the development up until that time had been unsatisfactory. In the Development Plan 1974–78 there was considerable emphasis on employment and equity objectives, and it stated (p. 148) that improved income distribution and greater employment were to be the primary objectives of the plan, and that the generation of productive employment opportunities was one of the basic means to achieve the aim of a more equitable distribution of income and a reduction in the incidence of poverty.

Killick concludes from his review of the plan and other policy documents (Killick, 1976, p. 30) that the response of the Kenyan government to the ILO mission may be characterized as a dilution; in other words, it expresses agreement in principle, but is unwilling to commit itself to specific actions.

The report from the follow-up ILO mission (Ghai *et al.*, 1979, p. 160) contains a comprehensive summary of the extent to which the recommendations of the ILO mission of 1972 have been implemented. It concludes that

> while it is true that many of the ILO report's recommendations were implemented, implementation has been distinctly selective. Some of the measures taken are perhaps surprising in the extent to which they confront vested interest (e.g. the capital gains tax, taxation of luxury goods, abolition of investment allowance) but on the whole measures implying structural upheaval, such as land ceilings and redistribution, land tax and a freeze on the incomes of the higher paid, have been avoided.

As far as regional policy is concerned, it is possible to identify three phases since Independence. From 1963 to 1967 a phase of centralization; the Administration was concentrated to Nairobi, and industrial efficiency was the only criterion for location. Between 1967 and 1974 there was a swing towards a policy of industrial dispersion. The third phase, from 1974 and onwards, Norcliffe (1977) calls a period of ambiguity: rural development is emphasized, but it is not clear whether the government is willing to pursue an active policy of industrial dispersion or not. Norcliffe (1977, p. 10) states that 'by and large policy seems to have drifted with individual locational decisions being made on an *ad hoc* basis'.

The regional imbalance with regard to industrial location is also important for the distribution of income among smallholders. The Integrated Rural Survey shows clearly that non-agricultural incomes are very important to the smallholders, and a more dispersed industrial structure would make it easier for smallholder households to supplement their farm incomes with some wage earnings.

Soon after the publication of the plan, the country was hit by the international economic crisis, in the form of increasing prices on oil and other imports and a slackening demand for Kenyan exports. This meant that the balance of payments situation deteriorated dramatically, and the country had to resort to strict import controls.

The main theme in the Fourth Development Plan (1979–83) is poverty alleviation and the satisfaction of basic needs. It is interesting to note that you can find the changes in the international discussion on development strategy as described in section 7.2 reflected very clearly in the Kenyan plans. The fields particularly emphasized in the fourth plan are nutrition, water, health, education, and housing. Thus, this plan represents another step towards policies aimed more directly at specific poverty groups. The trend in this direction can be followed all the way through the four development plans. Actually, economic growth is not even stated as a major goal in the fourth plan, but the growth rate is expected to be high. The creation of employment opportunities and measures to increase productivity also play a dominant role in this plan, but they are supplemented by improvements of the expenditure pattern, goals for the provision of basic needs, and institution building relevant for the poverty groups. However, asset redistribution is not really considered as a means of redistributing incomes. No consistent regional policy is presented.

One of the most recent general policy statements is the Election Manifesto of KANU, the ruling party (1979). In this document it is stated that the policies that will be pursued should aim at promoting a widespread ownership of assets, to reduce income differences through progressive taxation, and to provide free or subsidized social services particularly in the areas of health, education, water and housing. It is, however, strongly emphasized that the mixed economy with a large scope for private initiative must be preserved to generate higher total incomes in the future. Thus, there are very definite limits to how far one is willing to interfere with the market economy, and although the plans have changed over time, the basic, underlying ideology is the same. Rapid growth through private initiative (to some extent supported by the Government) and redistribution of the cake to the extent that it does not interfere with the growth of the cake.

It is worth emphasizing again that Kenya's development plans reflect the state of the discussion on development strategy among major international institutions and development economists very well. To some extent this is a reflection of the role of foreign experts in planning. It may also reflect the desire of the government to please foreign donors. The plan is certainly of importance with regard to negotiations with aid agencies. One must therefore be careful about interpreting the intentions of the Government on the basis of the plans only. Yet, there has been a gradual change in emphasis in policy from import-substitution and industrialization, to rural development, employment creation and income distribution, and finally, to a focus on basic needs and poverty alleviation. However, these changes have gone much further in the rhetoric of the plans than in their implementation, and, as has been pointed out, the Government has set definite limits as to what is acceptable in terms of policies that might affect the growth rate. There can therefore not be too much of the type of policy discussed in the previous section. Implicitly, there are, of course, also limits as to what policies are politically feasible in the Kenyan context. Given the social basis of the Government there are obviously certain policy options which have a very small chance of being implemented, even if they might have beneficial effects on income distribution as well as on the growth rate. Further land reforms is a case in point (see Leys, 1979).

Still, there is always some room for manoeuvre, and there has been somewhat more concern for equity issues since President Moi got into office. Thus, even if sweeping reforms are out of the question, there is an increasing concern for policies aimed directly at the poor.

7.3.2 Development strategy in Tanzania

Tanzania gained independence in 1961 after a comparatively smooth process of transition. Tanzania did not have a very large settler community, which could effectively oppose independence.

The colonial policy had mainly been concerned with the

commercialization of agriculture. Economic changes were therefore concentrated on the regions where export crops could be grown, while the people in the peripheral regions were involved in the monetary economy mainly as migrant labour. In Tanzania there was no active policy of discrimination against African farmers like that in Kenya, and racial inequalities were somewhat less pronounced.

Thus, at Independence, Tanzania had neither such an extensive settler agriculture as Kenya, nor as much manufacturing industry. The economic disparities in Tanzania therefore seem to have been slightly less than in Kenya at that time (Ghai, 1964).

Like other African countries Tanzania had to devote the first few years after independence to Africanizing the government machinery. At this time there was a large demand for qualified manpower, and the educational system expanded rapidly. Up until 1967 no drastic changes in policies *vis-à-vis* the economy were introduced. It was allowed to function more or less as before, that is according to normal capitalistic principles. President Nyerere was, however, worried about the increasing inequalities accompanying this development.

Between 1961 and 1967 the real incomes of urban wage-earners increased drastically (about 70%), while the real incomes of the rural population hardly increased at all (about 5%). In the towns, owners of assets increased their wealth, and in the rural areas the 'progressive farmers' (maybe 10, 000 families) increased their incomes substantially.

The Arusha Declaration of 1967 was Nyerere's reaction to this unequal pattern of development. It also reflected the personal philosophy of Nyerere, which obviously has been an important determinant of the choice of development strategy in Tanzania. Nyerere stands for a specific brand of 'African Socialism'. He tries to retain the ties to the traditional African society, which he argues was characterized by solidarity and work for the common good within the extended family or clan. Nyerere wants society to develop in accordance with this perception rather than according to a capitalistic one. He wants people to work together and share the result of production in a fair manner. Nyerere argued that class traditions in the 1960s were not very strong, and that everybody therefore should be able to work together within one party, TANU. Its policy tries to influence the attitudes of people and tries to make them work together in a socialist spirit.

In the Arusha Declaration the socialist society was defined by (i) the lack of exploitation; (ii) popular control of the means of production; and (iii) a socialist attitude among people. People should work together for the common good and control the means of production through the party and the government. The concept of self-reliance was launched, and it was argued that Tanzania should rely on its own resources and pursue an independent development path. The country should not become dependent on foreign finance. Development should start in the rural areas and once development there had advanced, it would produce the surplus capital needed in the rest of the economy. The major policy goals since the Arusha Declaration have been equality, socialism and self-reliance. The income distribution policy envisaged includes a freeze on higher incomes and increases of low urban incomes and rural incomes combined with an expansion of the public services, primarily in the rural areas. Nationalization ensures that much of capital incomes go to the government directly instead of to capital-owners.

There was also a leadership code outlined in the Arusha Declaration. It states that members of the party or the government are not allowed to own shares, be board members in private firms, have more than one salary, or own houses worth more than 100, 000 shillings.

At the same time as the Arusha Declaration was published, Nyerere also published a paper called *Socialism and Rural Development*, in which he presented the concept of 'Ujamaa'. The paper is a critique of the capitalistic tendencies within agriculture and presents an alternative strategy. Nyerere wants peasants to live together in Ujamaa-villages, where they should work together, sell their output together, and invest their surplus together in ways that benefit the entire community. The government is to be the agent of change, which will try to convince the farmers that they should move to villages.

The next important policy paper was published in 1971. It is called 'Mwongozo', the TANU Guidelines. In this paper imperialism is pointed out as the main enemy, and vigilance towards foreign forces is proclaimed. The document also advocates the right of people to criticize authoritarian leaders, even if the leading role of the party is stressed. A lot of criticism and debate in firms and organizations followed the publication of this paper, but in the face of economic difficulties in recent years this has been quieted down. With the creation of the CCM (to replace TANU) in 1977, the supremacy of the party is stressed even more. The emphasis is on discipline rather than the right to oppose.

Initially, planning was mainly concerned with the provision of public services to the people and investments in the communication network. However, production targets have come to play an increasingly important role. Particularly in the Third Development Plan increased production and drastic structural changes is emphasized. However, planning in Tanzania has always been characterized by overly ambitious aims and lack of consistency between goals and available resources. The economic consequences of policies have not been thoroughly analysed (see e.g. Hyden, 1975b).

One of the main aims of TANU (and now CCM) has been to reduce the imbalances between urban and rural areas. This was one of the reasons for the decentralization of planning and policy-making in 1972. Powerful regional planning units have been created in the 25 regions. These hold the power to control the realization of development projects in the respective regions. It seems, however, as if the distribution of authority between these regional authorities and the ministries is far from clear. One problem is that the regional planning units report to the Prime Minister's Office in Dodoma, and the ministries in Dar are thus not always fully informed about what is happening in the country within their own fields of responsibility.

The regional imbalance in the location of production in Tanzania seems to be of practically the same magnitude as that of Kenya. For example, in the late 1970s, the Dar area had about 50% of all employees in industry (Ståhl, 1980, p. 106), which is about the same as for Nairobi in Kenya (Bigsten, 1980). The Third Development Plan indicates a desire to do something about this imbalance, but it does not seem likely that this will be possible within the framework of the new industrialization policy. This is strongly oriented towards the creation of large scale units of production, which probably will be located in the already industrialized areas.

It may also be pointed out that all the people in the country are organized in a hierarchical system down to cells with 10 families at the lowest level. This is part of the policy attempting to mobilize all the people in the process of restructuring society into a socialist one. So far, this policy has not been very successful in terms of production.

7.3.3 Development strategy in Zambia

Zambia became independent in 1964. It relies almost exclusively on copper for its export earnings (92% at the time of independence) as well as for most of its government revenue (71%). It is thus very much a mining economy, which has given the country one of the highest per capita incomes in Africa. Because of this concentration on the mining industry it is also urbanized to an unusually high degree. At Independence about one-fifth of the population already lived in urban areas, and by now this proportion has doubled.

Zambia is a good example of a dual economy. For a long time a modern sector centring around the copper industry has coexisted with a traditional developed agricultural sector. During the colonial period the British used various means to secure the supply of labour for the copper sector. These were similar to those applied in Kenya, i.e. poll and hut taxes, 'active' labour recruiting, and restrictions on African agriculture. This policy aggravated the dichotomy of the economy and the backwardness of the agricultural sector. A large proportion of African males came to be working for wages in the modern sector.

Like in Kenya this system led to large inequalities in incomes and standards of living. The average European income in 1938 was almost 60 times that of the self-employed African cash workers (Fry, 1979, Chapter 1).

In 1963 the ratio between African urban wage-earner income and peasant income was about 5:1, in spite of the fact that the discrimination against African agriculture had decreased by then (Fry, 1979, p. 47). The average earnings of a non-African employee was eight times as large as the average earnings of an African employee. Thus at the time of Independence Zambia showed huge inequalities between races, sectors, and regions.

During the first period after Independence Zambia had to concern itself with the problems of transition; the machinery of government had to be taken over. Before 1964 the Zambian labour market was in disequilibirum. Rural – urban migration was hindered by pass laws etc., and the expected urban wage was much higher, than the rural one. After Independence followed a period of Africanization and expansion of the administration and this naturally meant that a considerable number of Africans got into relatively well-paid jobs. There was also a unification of the wage-scales of expatriates and nationals, and this further increased African modern sector wages. Because the terms of trade also turned against agriculture (from 100 in 1964 to 78.6 in 1973), there was a significant rural – urban migration during the first decade after Independence.

However, already in the first short-run Transitional Development Plan of 1965, there was a concern about the gap between urban and rural areas. The goals given in the plan were (i) monetization of agriculture; (ii) a decrease of the disparities between urban and rural areas; and (iii) self-sufficiency and exports of agricultural products. Thus, there was an official concern for rural development and equity.

In the First Development Plan 1966–70 there was a more extensive discussion of development strategy, in which the goals were given as a reduction in the urban – rural gap, diversification away from the dependence on copper, increasing employment and Zambianization of jobs and expansion of the infrastructure (particularly transport and communications networks, but also education and health facilities). During the 1960s there was a rapid increase in the number of cooperatives, which was part of the strategy for rural development. This reflected the desire of the government to foster collective development. The state also got involved in schemes for state production of cotton, tobacco, beef and milk in the so-called intensive development zones. However, it should be noted that in spite of the official emphasis on agriculture it reached only 8% of the investments during the plan period.

President Kaunda was very active in politics during the late 1960s. He launched his strategy of 'Humanism' and issued a number of policy directives, which resembled those issued in Tanzania during the same period (though usually slightly more moderate). One can broadly identify three phases in Kaunda's approach to policy. The first phase was characterized by the concern with the urban – rural gap and the efficiency of rural development. During the late 1960s this concern for efficiency led to a decrease in the emphasis on communal cooperatives in the rural areas, since a considerable number functioned badly. This particularly concerned production cooperatives. Instead family-based production was supported. A new price and incomes policy was initiated in 1969 to control the growth of urban incomes and stimulate production in rural areas (through higher prices). We shall return to this below.

The second stage in Kaunda's political strategy concerned the foreign domination of the economy, particularly the copper industry. (see particularly his speech at Mulungushi in 1968). The policy launched meant that Zambia wanted a controlling interest (at least 51%) in major enterprises in the country. Thus during the late 1960s and early 1970s there was a rapid increase in para-statal participation in agriculture, commerce, and industry. All mining was formally under local control by 1970, as well as a large part of manufacturing and construction. The firms dominated by para-statals came to constitute about 60% of the manufacturing sector. Also by 1972 trade gradually came under Zambian control. The third area that Kaunda dealt with concerned domestic exploitation, that is, local ownership of assets and means of production. It was decreed that the state should own all land.

During the first plan period GDP increased rapidly, partly because of the favourable development of copper prices. Modern sector employment also increased very much, from 267, 000 to 390, 000. The gap between expatriate and African wages decreased. In 1964 the average expatriate income was nine times the African, while it was down to six in 1970.

The country had a measure of success in the expansion of education and communications. However, the reliance on copper continued, and it was not possible to decrease the urban – rural income gap.

Earnings of employees increased considerably (8% annually in real terms), particularly as a result of the strong bargaining power of the mining unions. These acted as wage leaders for the rest of the modern sector (Knight, 1971). Real incomes of peasants on the other hand remained constant.

The Second Development Plan was initiated in 1972, after the first plan had to be extended for one year. In this plan as well much emphasis was put on the need to eliminate the urban – rural gap, and it was therefore stated that top priority must be given to improvements in agriculture. The need for self-sufficiency in food production was emphasized. In this context it was also emphasized that attention must be given to the subsistence farmers, who, so far, had been little affected by development policies. There was also a shift away from the policy of promoting communal farming cooperatives to services cooperatives. The concern about the dependence on copper exports continued. Diversification of the industry as well as promotion of tourism was therefore supported. It was strongly emphasized in the plan (p. 47) that the country should put increasing (!) emphasis on import-substitution. Naturally, the expansion of both social and economic infrastructure would continue. Increasing concern would also be given to the regional allocation of investments. Also the importance of the incomes policy to control incomes in urban areas was stressed, and it was said that unearned incomes would be better controlled and restricted. On the whole the second plan continued the policies initiated during the first plan period, with special attention paid to rural development, import substitution and infrastructure.

In 1972 the Zambian Leadership Code was published. Here it was argued that Zambia had replaced capitalism with humanism, and that the country now was emphasizing egalitarianism and self-reliance (p. 9). It was decreed that party members should neither be allowed to own houses for renting, nor commercial enterprises. They were allowed to be involved in commercial farming only within the framework of cooperatives. It was thus a parallel to the leadership code of Tanzania.

From an economic point of view the second plan period was much less successful than the first one. One important influence was the struggle in Zimbabwe, but the fall in copper prices was probably more important. In the Economic Report, 1978, it is shown that between 1975 and 1978 both consumption and investments fell. There was an increasing scarcity of goods, and complaints about hoarding, and uncontrollable price increases. The President issued directives to arrange the supply of 12 essential commodities.

The President also called for a streamlining of the para-statals.

These play a very large role in the Zambian economy. INDECO owns a number of holding companies, which control industries in specific sectors. The President emphasized the need to cut down overhead costs and increase efficiency. Thus the problems of Zambia seemed to be similar to those of Tanzania. One really astonishing fact (Economic Report, 1978, p. 26) is that GDP per capita (adjusted for terms of trade changes) fell from 227 Kw in 1973 to 135 Kw in 1978. Even if we disregard the terms of trade losses there is a fall in real per capita incomes of about 5%. Manufacturing production fell in 1975, 1976 and 1977, after having experienced rapid increases up to that time. Employment in the modern sector also started to decline, even if the para-statals and the government tried to retain people. Obviously, Zambia had come into a serious economic crisis at that time.

In a recent budget address the Minister of Finance outlined the main points of the forthcoming Third Development Plan. Those are

1. Emphasis on rural development through increased allocation of investment resources, producer prices based on economic costs, expansion of facilities for credit, marketing and extension services, and specific programmes for small scale and subsistence farmers;
2. Adoption of more labour intensive techniques when possible;
3. Shift of the emphasis in the investment pattern towards productive sectors such as agriculture and industry; and
4. Improvements in the planning machinery.

The government has also emphasized (Economic Report, 1978) that a greater role will be given to rural reconstruction centres and production units at schools, small-scale industry in the rural areas, feeder roads, and the setting up of model villages.

These ambitions do not indicate any break with the earlier development strategy followed. They might possibly indicate a further emphasis on productive investments (particularly with regard to the agricultural sector) and thus relatively less investment in infrastructure.

7.4 Effect of economic policies on income distribution

7.4.1 Agricultural policies

In all the countries considered here the majority of the population is to be found in agriculture. An even larger share of the poor are found in this sector, and it seems fair to say that poverty in East and Central Africa is a rural problem. What is happening to agriculture therefore has a profound effect on poverty and income distribution. We will therefore start our policy review with a comparison of the agricultural policies of the three countries.

The agricultural policies that Kenya has pursued since Independence have in many ways been a continuation of policies initiated by the colonial government during the 1950s. The most drastic change that occurred was the transfer of half of the former White Highlands into African hands. About 47,000 smallholder families have been resettled on mixed farms in the former White Highlands, but of course a number of the large farms were transferred intact to wealthy or influential Africans. This process took place mainly during the 1960s.

Since the 1960s land has become increasingly scarce. Sub-division of plots in the most densely populated areas leaves many families with very small holdings. At the same time there is a process of land concentration, in which wealthy farmers or urbanites are buying up large areas of land. Landlessness is starting to become a serious problem (see particularly Collier and Lal, 1980), which will have vast implications for income distribution.

The distribution of ownership of land is obviously one of the most important determinants of the distribution of income in the rural areas. Capital accumulated in urban areas is also, to a considerable degree, channelled into land purchases. This land is seldom used very intensively. There is evidence that shows that output per hectare is higher on small farms than on large farms and also labour input is higher. Thus, in the present land scare situation there are both efficiency and equity arguments in favour of further land reform. There are some hints in this direction in the most recent Kenyan plan, but there is probably no political will to implement such a policy.

It should also be pointed out that a number of authors have lamented over the extensive government intervention in the system of marketing the agricultural produce of Kenya. There arc numerous marketing boards and statutory authorities. Heyer (1976, p. 314) points out that the degree of control is excessive, for it has led to operational inefficiency and high costs. She also points out that large farmers are favoured over small farmers with regard to, for example, provision of credit and marketing. The highly controlled system is vulnerable to political pressure, which may have a negative effect on both efficiency and equity within the marketing system.

Agriculture in Kenya is still essentially based on independent smallholders, and at least during the first ten years after Independence it expanded rapidly. Since then production has been increasing at a slower rate, but the smallholder economy is in many areas working fairly efficiently.

Now we will take a look at the agricultural policy followed by Tanzania. This has implied much more of a structural upheaval than the Kenyan strategy.

Land in Tanzania is owned by the state, but each individual has the right to use a certain amount of agricultural land under his control. At Independence, there were a number of large commercial farms. A lot of these have been allowed to go on producing like before. In the early 1970s, some coffee plantations were transformed into producer cooperatives, but during the second half of the decade this tendency was reversed and some plantations were handed back to the former owners, who were believed to be able to run them more efficiently. This is one indication that production has not been growing at a satisfactory rate. The production of some cash-crops has actually fallen during the 1970s.

As far as small farmers are concerned the 1970s have been characterized by the 'villageization' campaign. The creation of villages was intended to help realize two aims. First, it would make it easier to satisfy the people's needs for public services. Second, it would make joint efforts in production easier and thus increase production. The voluntary phase of the campaign lasted until 1974, but only a minority of the peasants actually moved together. Thus there was little spontaneous response to the programme. However, in 1974, a country wide campaign to move people into villages started, and during a few years most peasants were actually moved (more or less voluntarily) into villages. Only the farmers in the wealthy north were left untouched by the programme (see Hyden, 1975a).

Obviously, the concentrated pattern of living makes it easier for the government to provide the peasants with public services and to control them. However, with regard to agricultural production the results have not been positive and the problems may well increase in the future. So far, there has been little progress with regard to collective cultivation. Each farmer produces mostly for himself on his own piece of land. Productivity on the communal plots is low.

People have now been concentrated to limited areas of land (usually close to some road). The adjacent land must be used very intensively (use of far away plots is prohibited). This leads to considerable pressure on the nearby land, and ecological degradation may result. On land of low productivity it makes sense to have a dispersed pattern of production, which is the opposite of the present system.

Hyden (1980) has described the 'villageization' programme as an attempt to involve the peasants in the process of national development. So far, African farmers have managed to retain their independence from the government, be it colonial, capitalist, or socialist, because they are not dependent on any other class in society. They can feed themselves and need not produce any surplus for the market. It has therefore been very difficult both for previous governments and the socialist government to extract any surplus to be used in the rest of the economy.

The 'villageization' is the strongest blow, so far, to peasant autonomy. It attempts to close the exit door for the peasants. So far, however, they do not seem completely 'captured'.

The monetary economy has not penetrated very far into the Tanzanian peasant sector. With the exception of a limited number of cash crop producers, income differentials among peasants are determined largely by differences in soil fertility and skills.

The real income of smallholders fell from the late 1960s until 1974. A major factor in this context was the drastic fall in the agricultural sector's domestic terms of trade. They fell by about 20% between 1964 and 1973. In 1974–75, there was a remarkable reversal of this trend, but all the gains of those years were again lost in 1976.

During the 1970s the agricultural sector as a whole experienced a fall in its terms of trade by 23%. However, while food crop prices practically held their own against the rate of inflation, the export crops experienced a severe decline (ILO, 1980D, p. 5).

Thus, although the peasants are not taxed directly, they suffer from the consequences of the import-substitution policy and the overvalued exchange rate, as well as from the price policies of the government (see below). The peasants also suffer from the inefficient and high cost system of marketing their produce. The marketing costs have during recent years absorbed an increasing proportion of producer prices (ILO, 1980D, p. 5). It is therefore difficult to raise these without making the marketing system more efficient. It is now said that the cooperative societies will be revived. They were disbanded in 1976 in favour of state enterprises, but these have turned out to be very bureaucratic and inefficient. It is hoped that the cooperatives will be more efficient in their handling of agricultural commodities.

Tanzania has mainly been concerned with preparing the ground for a future collectivistic system of agricultural production. So far, it is difficult to make any final evaluation of the policy. A preliminary guess may be that it will have a positive effect on income distribution, but that it will be costly in terms of efficiency. Thus, even if inequalities are reduced, poverty may well increase. Set-backs in agricultural production are felt immediately by the agriculturalists, who are also the poor in Tanzania.

Compared with those of Kenya and Tanzania Zambian agriculture is to a very small degree oriented towards the world market. Agricultural products constitute only 2% of Zambian exports. However, in terms of employment agriculture is very dominating also in Zambia. In 1971 there were at least twice as many employed in agriculture as in the modern sector. Most of the poor are to be found in the rural areas in Zambia.

The vast majority of Zambian peasants are oriented towards production for subsistence. Elliot (1980, p. 3) states that only 15–20% of peasant households farm with the intention of selling sizeable proportions of their total output. Van der Hoeven (1977, p. 14) quotes a census of agricultural production showing that as much as 54% of farmers do not market any product. A major problem is that it is mainly the market-oriented group which is affected by rural policies. It has been difficult to reach the pure subsistence farmers and to bring them into the economy. The subsidies, for example on fertilizers, have a tendency to benefit disproportionately the large-scale commercial farmers (Van der Hoeven, 1977, p. 52); they also benefit more from extension services (Elliot, 1980, p. 26). There is a small proportion of agriculturalists (maybe 20,000 families) that can be called prosperous. These usually concentrate on maize production. Still, the country suffers from food deficits. Two major constraints on rural development in Zambia are the lack of skilled manpower and the lack of transportation. As a result of the latter the government has tried to make the various regions self-sufficient in food production.

Elliot (crudely) identifies two opposing views within the government with regard to rural development: the first one, the 'technocratic view', is concerned with efficiency in resource use to maximize total output. The alternative approach, the 'ideological view', is more concerned with income distribution issues. He thinks President Kaunda may be classified as belonging to the latter group, and various forms of cooperatives and state engagements have been favoured. However, no coherent policy seems to have been pursued in this field, and it has not contributed to increased production (Elliot, 1980, p. 12).

The enthusiasm for cooperatives during the 1960s seemed to wane during the 1970s. It was emphasized that only viable cooperatives would be supported. This meant that the number of agricultural cooperatives dropped during the early 1970s, and the emphasis shifted to services cooperatives rather than communal production cooperatives. Dodge (1977, p. 78) concludes from her survey of the agricultural performance during the first decade after Independence that it has been disappointing. The country still has to rely on imports of food; relative incomes of rural areas have not improved; and there has been little diversification away from copper.

We see that the three countries have similar agriculture problems. Tanzania, and to some extent Zambia, have gone further than Kenya in implementing institutional changes in the agricultural sector. These have, however, not been as successful as had been hoped. In the field of agriculture there seems to be a strong efficiency argument for reliance on price incentives and decentralized decision-making. To ensure that such a policy does not lead to unacceptable income differences one needs to consider the distribution of land and the allocation of complementary resources.

7.4.2 Industrialization and trade policy

In a number of countries the domestic terms of trade between agriculture and industry have been shown to have fundamental importance to income distribution (see Chapters 5 and 6). This has obviously also been the case in the three countries considered here.

Domestic terms-of-trade in Kenya moved drastically against agriculture for a decade before the coffee-boom in the mid-1970s. At that time producers of coffee and tea experienced a bonanza, but since then relative agricultural prices have fallen again. Thus, except for this period relative price changes have been unfavourable to agriculture. Since the majority of the poor (say 97%) reside in the rural areas this has been a major, negative factor in the development of income distribution.

The major policy factor behind this development has been, and still is, the import-substitution policy. Its aim has been to promote industrialization by imposing high tariffs and quantitative import restrictions. Hopcraft (1979) gives numerous examples of the functioning of the policy and its consequences. The total effect of the system of protection have been very strong. Imports in several lines of production has been virtually prohibited. Hopcraft writes (p. 19) that 'the basic assumption appears to be that regardless of the international or competitive efficiency of local firms or manufacturing activity, it should be made profitable by the necessary adjustment of local prices'. Thus, the implicit tariffs have for several types of products been extremely high. This has had the result that the agricultural population has been forced to buy expensive products from the inefficient, protected industry. At the same time the incomes of agricultural exporters has been kept at an artificially low level by the overvaluation of the Kenyan shilling, which has been a consequence of the trade policy pursued. Thus, the trade policy is of major importance to income distribution in Kenya.

In Tanzania a large segment of non-agriculture was nationalized after the Arusha Declaration. Most of the large-scale establishments in banking, commerce, and industry were nationalized or the state took over a controlling interest in them. In the late 1960s, a number of para-statals were created to control different industrial sectors (e.g. TEXCO for the textile industry). The pattern of industrialization within this framework has not differed much from that of Kenya. The distributional consequences have been somewhat different, since private capitalists have not been allowed to reap the rents, which the policy of protection creates. On the other hand, a number of the para-statals have been making losses, which thus have had to be paid by the tax-payers.

In response to the inefficiencies in the industrial sector, there has been a partial retreat since 1977 in the attitude towards private industry. It has never been completely eliminated, but since 1977 it has been actively encouraged in some areas.

IBRD (1977) showed that productivity had decreased drastically within the parastatal sector due to low capacity utilization, surplus labour, poor planning, stoppages, etc. Industrial output in 1979 had fallen back, in terms of its share of GDP, to the level of 1967. The government, of course, defends its policy along infant industry lines, i.e. that industrial production is necessary for learning technical and organizational skills.

In the Third Development Plan, large-scale 'industrializing' industries are emphasized. It is argued that industries producing means of production are necessary to realize the goal of self-reliance. Whether this is correct or not may be questionable. Moreover, it hardly seems rational to decide on a process of structural transformation regardless of the cost structure of different alternatives. The choice of an excessively high capital intensity in production will probably have a negative effect on the growth rate over the next decade. Moreover, the distributional consequences will be the same as with the traditionally policy of import-substitution, i.e. the farmers will be the losers. All the arguments about the effect of an overvalued exchange rate are also valid for the Tanzanian case of industrialization.

As far as the goal of self-reliance is concerned, the policy has not been very successful. Morawetz (1980, p. 359) writes, that 'in Tanzania, relatively low priority was placed on the export sector, and little progress was made in diversifying away from traditional export items'. Tanzania is able to pay for a decreasing share of its imports with internally generated resources. The external financing of the development budget is now over 65%, the World Bank being the biggest single budget financier. Thus, Tanzania has become increasingly dependent on external resources, which is ironical, considering that self-reliance has been a major goal in its policy. The large inflow of foreign aid has helped to conceal inefficiencies within the economy.

The copper industry has completely dominated the Zambian industry for a very long time. This meant that Zambia was relatively rich at Independence, but also very sensitive to fluctuations in the price of copper. Because of this there was a desire to move the economy away from copper towards other types of industrial activities. Like most other LDCs at this time, Zambia opted for an import-substitution policy. This has been pursued with increasing vigour since then, and up to the mid-1970s it led to a rapid increase in manufacturing production, 11% per year during the first plan period and 8% per year during the second plan period. Since the mid-1970s, however, manufacturing output has declined, and it seems as if the policy is no longer effective in creating growth of manufacturing production. In Zambia, like in Tanzania, much of the industrialization has taken place within the framework of para-statal organizations, and like in Tanzania, there seem to be considerable problems of inefficiency. The losses of parastatals have to be subsidized by the government budget.

In Zambia, like in other places where this policy has been pursued, the rural population has had to pay the costs of the policy (to the extent that they have any contacts with the modern sector). They have had to face falling domestic terms of trade because of the protection. The economic crisis in the mid-1970s led to financial difficulties for the government decided to reduce subsidies to industrialists (Economic Report, 1976) and compensate them with higher prices. This, of course, also had an effect on the internal terms of trade.

The regional imbalance in Zambia is severe. The modern sector is very much concentrated in the copper-belt and the Central province. In the other regions subsistence production predominates. It is stated in the Second Development Plan that industry will be decentralized, even if it implies higher costs of production. This is considered as part of the policy aimed at decreasing the urban – rural gap. Projects will be screened for locational purposes. The idea is that localization in the rural areas will increase income and employment in them and assist small farmers in the process of commercialization. The Intensive Development Zones and other aspects of agricultural policy are also natural parts of the regional policy of the country. Decentralized industrialisation should also give farmers in the area better chance of alternative employment, but so far not much has been accomplished.

Bhagawan (1979) finds that the regional concentration in industry is as great in 1975 as it was in 1965. Ten towns account for 98% of all enterprises and 81% of employment. Until that time only 15 minor industries had been located in the rural provinces.

We may thus conclude that the experiences in Kenya, Tanzania and Zambia of import-substitution industrialization resemble those of other LDCs. For a certain period it breeds high industrial growth, but there seems to be limits to industrial growth under such a strategy. Eventually one will be forced to seek other ways of fostering growth. Moreover, through its effect on the domestic terms of trade the policy has contributed to an increase in the urban – rural income gap. Thus by now both growth and equity consideration suggests a shift away from the import-substitution policy.

7.4.3 Prices and incomes policy
In all three countries prices and incomes policies have been an important part of the income distribution policy. During the 1970s the Kenyan government has tried to keep the prices low on essential goods, primarily food. This, of course, benefits the poor (as well as the rich) urban dwellers, but hurts the producers of food, that is the farmers and agricultural workers. As has already been pointed out, the vast majority of the poor can be found in the rural areas, and the net effect of this policy on their standard of living is certainly negative.

Trade unions have a long history in Kenya, and the industrial relations machinery has evolved over several decades. Since the 1940s the system of minimum wages has been expanded to cover more and more sectors. Its aim has mainly been to protect the incomes of low-income, urban employees, although some rural workers have been included since 1967.It is difficult to ascertain exactly the effects of minimum wages on income distribution. The minimum wages now mainly seem to follow the market rather than to constitute an important force on their own. However, if the legislation has a wage increasing effect, there must be a cost in terms of employment and possibly also in the urban – rural terms of trade.

Kenya used tripartite agreements (among unions, employers, and government) in 1964, 1970, and 1978 to increase modern sector employment. The agreements in these cases have (with some variations) been of the type in which employers promise to increase employment by, say, 10% in return for a one-year wage freeze. These measures have, in the short run, led to larger formal modern sector employment. The long-run effect, however, is probably insignificant (Stewart, 1979).

Naturally the government can regulate civil service salaries in a fairly detailed manner. There has been a weak tendency towards equalization in public sector salaries, but the gap between highest and lowest income recommended by the Ndegwa Commission in 1971 was 1:38. Since the public sector competes with the private sector for people, it is difficult to depart too far from the private sector wage structure if the aim is to get qualified personnel.

However, the government has also tried to control private sector salaries through an incomes policy. The aim is to create a more fair income distribution. The government issues guidelines and the Industrial Court controls that agreements are in accordance with these. These guidelines have put a ceiling on wage increases. The lower incomes have been allowed to increase more than the higher ones. The controls have been eased or made tighter according to the economic situation of the country. During most of the 1970s the guidelines have not allowed full compensation for price increases. The real incomes of most employees have been falling, but it is far from certain that this is a result of the guidelines. In general the wage increases have been lower than what has been allowed by the guidelines. The falling real incomes may therefore have been market-induced.

There is no control of incomes of employees not covered by the collective agreements, and high income employees have in many cases been able to compensate themselves for inflation. Nor is there any control of rents and profits.

It is difficult to evaluate the overall effects of the prices and incomes policy in Kenya without a thorough analysis. It has probably had some equalizing effects within the group covered and also between this group and the rural economy, but it may also have increased the gap between employees and asset owners.

For a number of years, 1964–73, the centrally determined producers' prices of agricultural products in Tanzania were kept constant. This was done because of concern for urban consumers (who would be affected by the prices of food crops) and because of the government's need to earn a surplus on exports of cash crops. This policy had a detrimental effect on the growth of agricultural production, but it also led to a larger urban – rural income gap. The farmer's purchasing power fell by 20% during the period 1964–73.

Since 1973, the prices have been raised several times, particularly those of food crops. The reason for keeping export crop prices below world market prices is that the government wants to control and distribute as much as possible of the proceeds from exports, but the low prices have also contributed to the poor performance of export crop production. In the Third Plan, the government's response to declining production is not to suggest a substantial increase in prices, but to let the crop authorities run themselves. This is an indication that the government cannot keep prices of agricultural products low while at the same time expecting the farmers to increase marketed output.

Also a large number of industrial prices are controlled by the

National Price Commission. Maximum prices for the sale of consumer goods and services are set for all levels. The import-substituting consumer goods produced behind the high tariff wall are priced according to a cost-plus criterion. This means that the more inefficient a firm is, the higher the profit on each item produced. The net losers are the consumers, particularly the farmers.

There is also rent control. In the early 1970s, all larger houses were nationalized (those worth more than 100 000 shillings) and the level of rents was controlled. It was mainly the Asian community which suffered in this process; since it occurred at the same time as the scope for private industrial activity was drastically reduced, the incomes of the Asians were curtailed. However, they are still the wealthiest group in the country.

The salaries of employees are controlled by the Permanent Tribunal and the Standing Committee on Para-statal Organizations. The tribunal, created in 1967, scrutinizes all agreements even if they are the result of voluntary, collective agreements. It is empowered to change the agreements that do not conform to the official incomes policy, and it can also make awards in cases where no voluntary agreement has been reached. After the nationalizations started in 1967, the Standing Committee has tried to bring the salary structure of the para-statals in line with the government salary structure.

The two bodies set minimum salaries and determine the levels that are acceptable to other employees. The minimum salaries were increased several times up until 1975, but since then they have remained constant and have thus fallen drastically in real terms. For other categories of employees a guideline stated that the annual increase in incomes would be limited to 5% with preferential treatment of the lowest paid categories. This functioned until 1972, but in 1973 the policy of wage restraint broke down in the face of increasing inflation.

The incomes policy is thus one policy instrument used to bring about the more equal distribution of income advocated in the Arusha Declaration. The policy has at least been successful in decreasing differences among wage-earners. The public sector has been leading the way. The highest public sector wage in 1971 was 50 times that of the lowest. By 1976, this gap had been reduced to nine times (after tax, however) (ILO, 1978, p. 14). Thus the income differences within the public sector have been reduced and there has probably also been an overall equalization within the group of employees.

The groups that have benefited are mainly those immediately below the elite, while farmers have been little affected by this policy. The increase in urban unskilled wages has been one of the factors leading to a rapid increase in the urban informal sector employment by attracting people to urban areas and by creating income opportunities also outside the modern sector. The people in the informal sector earn considerably less than the minimum wage.

The gap between urban wage-earners and peasants may have stayed approximately constant since the late 1960s, which is an improvement in comparison with the development during the earlier period. This also implies that the situation of the peasants versus the urban elite, senior civil servants and private executives, has improved, since the latter have experienced a decline in real incomes. However, it may be pointed out that the only group that has received decidedly higher salaries in recent years are the politicians. Salaries and fringe benefits were increased drastically in 1978, and made them one of the best paid groups in Tanzania.

Another problem is that the methods chosen to redistribute incomes determine the growth prospects (see e.g. Morawetz, 1980). He writes that 'the failure to offer incentives to managers and workers in nationalized enterprises in Tanzania has had an important effect on the efficiency with which these enterprises are operated, and the surplus they generate, and, hence, on their contribution to growth and development'.

In the long run it is the growth of productivity which determines the possibilities to increase real incomes. The World Bank (1977) pointed out the problem of falling productivity in their country report on Tanzania. ILO (1978) seemed to take a more optimistic view of the situation, but now obviously also the Tanzanians themselves are worried. In a report (Tanzania, 1980, p. 7) it is noted that production per employee in public corporations fell by 50 per cent between 1972 and 1978! In the same paper it is said that production of crops has been falling (p. 9) and that labour productivity in offices has been falling (p. 12).

Because of these alarming trends there is an increasing concern with productivity and incentives to stimulate higher productivity. The report notes (p. 13) that 'there has been a problem of equitable incomes on one side and giving incentives to hard working workers and peasants on the other'. Because of this 'the system of awarding hard workers be it productive or service sectors should be given high priority' (p. 28)! The paper outlines a system of setting production targets (not just budgetary estimates as earlier), in which workers who surpass the targets are given bonuses, both individually and by firms. As far as salary increases are concerned the authorities in the future will also compare the incomes of peasants with those of the industrial workers when they set the minimum salary. The general salary increases will depend on '(i) the rise in national income through increased production of goods and services'; and '(ii) actual increase in efficiency at work places without jeopardizing the investible surplus or employment' (p. 25). The increases will be at most 60% of (i) and 25% of (ii). With regard to farmers, the present price policy will be continued. When the economy is 'healthy', export taxes may be lowered to give more incomes to the farmers. However, it should be noted that without such an incentive to cash crop production, it may be difficult to restore the economy. It was pointed out above that export-crop growers had to face a drastic drop in their terms of trade during the 1970s. There is also strong evidence that their reaction to this is a reduction in output.

Also in Zambia a wages and incomes policy was initiated in the late 1960s. According to the guidelines issued, wages were not to be allowed to increase by more than 5% per year, provided that this increase was matched by corresponding increases in productivity. However, already in the annual report from the Ministry of Labour for 1973 it was noted that it had been impossible to limit wage increases to 5%. The increases in the costs of living were too drastic. The annual report of 1975 and the Report from the Mwanakatwe Commission once again complained that there had been no comprehensive wages and incomes policy. The industrial relations court had to continue to work in a vacuum, even though it had to decide on whether wage agreements were acceptable or not.

Subsidized housing is a very important fringe benefit to public employees and high level private sector employees. This system means that well-paid employees often pay less for their housing than the low income workers, who have to find some place to live in the squatter areas. The government has not been able to deal with this sensitive issue (van der Hoeven, 1977, pp. 51–2).

There is also a system of price controls, the intent of which is to guarantee fair prices for essential consumer goods. The problem with regard to income distribution is that it often has been easier for industrialists to obtain higher prices (because of identifiable increases in costs) than it has been for farmers. Government policy had four objectives in the pricing of crops (see Dodge, 1977, p. 138): (i) reduction of the urban – rural gap; (ii) increasing national self-sufficiency in food; (iii) increasing cash incomes in rural areas; and (iv) diversification of exports away from copper. The results have been disappointing, and Dodge attributes this to the marketing policy pursued and the contradictory application of the pricing policy. The complete reliance on marketing boards and cooperatives has created a bottleneck in the marketing system, which hinders increasing agricultural production. No clear and consistent criteria have been applied with regard to price policies. Prices have varied from time to time, and the farmers have lost purchasing power because of worsening urban – rural terms of trade. Dodge (1977, pp. 133–4) presents different sets of calculation, which all indicate a decline by at least 20%.

In conclusion it may be said that price and incomes policies can give a contribution to an equity-oriented policy. However, the policies can not be designed without due consideration of the effect on incentives. If this is done one will end up with more poverty, even if inequality may have been reduced.

7.4.4 Fiscal policy

The two sides of fiscal policy are the incomes and the expenditure sides. If the tax structure is progressive, the tax system contributes to an equalization of the distribution of income. As far as Kenya is concerned there is no comprehensive survey of the incidence of taxes but the official rates of taxation are at present undoubtedly quite progressive. The problem seems to lie in the collection of taxes on incomes other than salaries or wages. It can therefore be argued that, at present, it is not primarily the rates which need to be changed, but rather the system of collection which needs to be made more efficient. Expenditures contribute to an equalization, if services are distributed free of charge, or at subsidized rates and if most people really have access to them.

The most important service in this context is education. Since Independence there has been a tremendous expansion of the educational system in Kenya. The enrolment in primary education increased from 870 000 in 1963 to 3 700 000 in 1979. Secondary school enrolment increased from 56 000 to 378 000 during the same period. University enrolment expanded from an insignificant level in 1963 to 6500 in 1979. Thus, the quantitative expansion has been very large, and this sector now swallows over one-quarter of the recurrent expenditures in the budget. It is hardly conceivable that it can increase much above this level.

Naturally, one might expect such an expansion in the supply of educated manpower to have a great effect on the structure of earnings in the country. During the 1960s the relatively few educated Africans could earn a high scarcity rent on their education. Everybody with a secondary education got a well-paid job, often in the rapidly expanding public sector. During the 1970s there have been increasing difficulties for school-leavers to get the jobs to which they have aspired. In

Chapters 2 and 3 we discussed the effect of education. Is it just a criterion according to which individuals are ranked and then allocated jobs with given income levels, or has the increased supply of educated labour tended to reduce the premium on education? Recent evidence seems to suggest that there is a certain flexibility in the Kenyan labour market, and that real earnings adjust in response to the supply and demand conditions in that market (Collier and Bigsten, 1981). If this is the case, increasing education obviously contributes to the equalization of income.

However, the educational system itself is, in many ways, a reflection of existing inequalities in society. This system has in several respects remained intact in post-Independence Kenya, although the segmentation no longer follows racial lines, but socioeconomic ones. Kinyanjui (1979) shows how family background determines the chances of getting access to and qualifying for the better schools, and that the kind of school you enter very much determines your chances of moving on to the next level in the educational system. Thus, the children of the elite go on to higher education and the future top jobs (like in many other countries, it might be pointed out).

Bigsten (1980) provides data on interregional disparities in educational expenditures. They are very large, but there has been some equalization since the mid-1970s as a result of the gradual introduction of (more or less) free primary education.

The imbalance in regional distribution of health services is much worse than that in the distribution of education. Health services are concentrated to the urban areas (primarily Nairobi, where the majority of the physicians of the country are to be found) and the centrally located provinces.

The bias towards the urban areas and Central and Rift Valley provinces is obvious in the total level of recurrent expenditures (Bigsten, 1980, Chapter 12). The Western and Nyanza provinces were lagging very far behind in 1973/74.

In the mid-1960s the National Social Security Fund was started. Modern sector employees and employers contribute jointly to the fund, which pays a pension to the employee upon retirement. There are also some other benefits related to membership in the fund, e.g. health care. Thus, the fund has some importance for employees in the modern sector, even if the sums paid out so far are small.

Another important factor affecting the distribution of income in Kenya is the defects in the administrative machinery. There is, of course, on the one hand outright corruption, which channels considerable sums of money from the government or cooperatives into the pockets of influential individuals, or it may concern the distribution of licences, building plots, jobs, tenders, etc. There are also a lot of activities that may not be legally punishable, but which in any case must be considered unethical. Involvment in the top bureaucracy of the government gives an individual the opportunity to get a share of the private sector gains, which are dependent on government actions. That this is a problem in Kenya is obvious and President Moi has recently launched a campaign against corruption in the government. However, these kinds of practices are deeply embedded in the social structure and are difficult to eradicate. For example, it is more or less considered an obligation to try to arrange jobs for relatives once you are in the bureaucracy. The traditional behaviour, determined by clan loyalties and patron – client relationships, still penetrates the modern sector.

Numerous scandals have been revealed both within the Government and the cooperatives, and these are certainly only the top of the iceberg. That the problem is severe cannot be doubted, although it obviously is very difficult to obtain data on the magnitude of the problem. It is therefore most difficult to say how important it is to overall income distribution.

In the tax system of Tanzania peasants and people earning only the minimum wage do not pay any income tax, although naturally they may pay considerable sums in indirect taxes. Huang (1976) argues that both direct and indirect taxes are highly progressive in Tanzania, and that, relative to its income, the urban sector pays much more than the rural sector. However, it seems as if Huang has used the household budget survey very uncritically. Since the HBS estimates of urban incomes are much too high (see IBRD, 1977, annex IV, appendix G) the progressivity is overstated. It is therefore not quite clear how the Tanzanian tax system ranks in comparison with that of other, similar countries. Still, it seems likely that the Tanzanian tax system is slightly more progressive than the system in similar countries.

To get an idea about the total effect of the budget, estimates of the distribution of expenditures are also required. It is not easy to get an overall picture, but the ILO (1978, p. 167) claims that there has been a net transfer of resources to the rural areas in the 1970s through the fiscal system, which is in accordance with the aims of the Arusha Declaration. However, it should be pointed out that other government policies have had a detrimental effect, e.g. the overvaluation of exchange rate, price controls, export taxes, marketing inefficiences, etc.

Here it needs to be pointed out once again that prices have a very important role as incentives to economic agents. One of the most important effects of the Tanzanian system of price controls has been to create shcrtages of goods in the rural areas, since there is no incentive to transport goods up-country.

The most important public service in Third World countries is education. In 'Education for Self-Reliance' the need to eliminate illiteracy is the main theme. Adult education and primary education have therefore been given top priority, and obviously Tanzania has had some success in its attack on illiteracy, although the goals have not yet been reached. Moreover, in 1977, compulsory education for 7 – 12 years old were introduced. Of course, it has been difficult to keep up the quality of instruction in the face of large increases in the number of pupils during a very short time. Still, education is an unalienable right or basic need, and most children probably do learn to read and write. Whether it leads to a more even distribution of income is uncertain (as was shown in Chapter 5).

It may be doubted whether their education will contribute significantly to agricultural productivity. More vocational training is probably needed for that. There is an awareness of this problem and attempts are made to make primary education self-contained and more oriented towards learning practical skills needed for example in agriculture (Court and Kinyanjui, 1980). So far, the educational system at each level has been geared to guaranteeing success in getting on to the next level. It has thus been academically oriented, while the overwhelming majority of the pupils end up in the agricultural sector.

In the Second Five Year Plan, a strategy for a more decentralized and rural oriented health policy was drawn up. The basic units would be health stations in the villages. This network has been gradually extended during the 1970s, but resources are spread very thinly. So far, these health stations are therefore very inefficient, but the structure is there and it should be possible to improve it in the future.

Also in Tanzania there is a National Provident Fund, to which both employers and employees contribute. From this Fund the worker gets a sum of money when he retires. The amount he receives is related to the level of income he had while in the workforce. Employees also have paid vacation, maternity leave, and access to the health services. However, these benefits accrue only to the wage-employed. In the rural areas the extended family is the only social security network of importance. Naturally, the network of the extended family also reaches across the urban – rural gap. Money is transferred back to the rural areas from the employees in town, although the sums probably are smaller than in Kenya.

The income taxes in Zambia have been very low and thus contributes little to the reduction of inequality. In the 1960s individuals did not have to start paying income tax until the income reached a level which was 13 times the national per capita income (van der Hoeven, 1977, p. 51).

As has already been described, a large part of the investment resources during the first decade of independence was devoted to the expansion of the communication network, education and some other public services; e.g. the achievements in the area of education were quite respectable. Primary school enrolment doubled between 1963 and 1970. The primary objective at present is to implement nine years of universal primary education. A considerable effort in this direction is foreseen under the Third Development Plan. There are also ambitions to make the contents of education more relevant to the immediate needs of the country (see the paper on Education for Development).

The growth of health expenditures has had to be reduced during the period of the same plan, because of the worsening economic situation of the country. The ambition in Zambia, like in other countries of the region, is to shift the emphasis gradually from curative to preventive medicine. Health care is supplied free of charge by the government.

It may also be mentioned that Zambia also has a National Provident Fund of the same type as Kenya and Tanzania. It was started in 1966.

The general conclusion that can be drawn with regard to fiscal policy is that there is some scope for equalization via the tax system, but because of administrative difficulties it is very inefficient with regard to several types of incomes. On the expenditure side the effects are more certain. The spread of for example education has been a major factor in all countries. Public goods provision is therefore a fairly efficient way of equalization of standards of living.

7.4.5 The scope for income distribution policy

In Kenya, the income distribution issue has been discussed ever since Independence, but it has come to play an increasingly central role in documents published in recent years. Whether this has been reflected in the policies actually implemented is more doubtful. It is doubtful whether a government composed mainly of wealthy businessmen and land-owners is really willing to press wholeheartedly for egalitarian reforms. Still, there is some scope for action, and the debate on the issues is fairly free. There is therefore a certain amount of public pressure on the government and some action has been taken. It should also be pointed out that sometimes intervention may produce worse results than non-intervention. That the intentions are good is not sufficient.

In Tanzania a drastic restructuring of the economy has taken place since 1967. The rural population has been moved to villages; industry, services and housing have been extensively nationalized. Prices and incomes policy as well as fiscal policy have been used to support the policy outlined in the Arusha Declaration.

The government policy during the period 1967–74 aimed at restricting the scope for private initiative, which might lead to increased wealth for a small segment of the population. The tendencies that had occurred during the period before 1967 were checked. However, the government has not been equally successful in generating a different type of development. Instead, inefficiency and stagnation in many fields have been the result. Private incentives have been eliminated, while the planning system was not efficient enough to take over the role of allocating resources.

The ILO (1978, p. 111) writes on the issue of efficiency that 'what is required in Tanzania is to strengthen the role of certain coordinating institutions such as the central planning authorities and the Planning Commission'. This may well improve the situation, but given the experiences so far it seems to me that it is fairly optimistic to believe that this is a realistic solution to the problems. A larger scope for market forces and incentives would probably be a more efficient way of attacking the problem, even if it has a certain cost in terms of equity. To stimulate small-scale enterprises within the framework of the Tanzanian planning machinery would definitely be difficult (cf. ILO, 1978, p. 134).

Also the 'villageization' programme emphasized equity at the expense of productivity, and it is really doubtful whether a sufficiently large surplus can be generated within this sector to make the realization of an ambitious industrialization programme possible.

The planning machinery also has problems in delivering the public services that have been promised, e.g. water to the new villages, and this may have a detrimental effect on the active support of government policies.

Another problem that has become increasingly troublesome during the 1970s is increasing corruption (Stahl, 1980). It seems as if Tanzania has the same problems as the other countries in the region. The slow increase of the civil servants' incomes during the 1970s may be one of the reasons behind the apparent increase in corruption, and the increase in politicians' salaries might be an attempt to check this increase. It is probable that corruption among officials has an even greater demoralizing effect in a country such as Tanzania than in other neighbouring countries, since the officials are administrating a policy of equality, moral incentives, and planned change. Just as in other countries, it is difficult to get an exact idea about the magnitude of the effects on income distribution. However, the moral effect may be the more important one in the long run.

At present, the main conclusion that can be drawn about the Tanzanian experience is that it has had some success in its endeavour with regard to the distribution of income and public services, while it is struggling with great problems about growth and economic efficiency. Equity is certainly a major policy objective in Tanzania, and the government has consciously sacrificed some growth for more equity. The Tanzanian experience seems to suggest that there is a trade-off. How to deal with it in the future may be the major policy issue in Tanzania today.

Although Zambia in its plans and public documents had advocated solidarity and equity oriented policies, its income distribution today is one of the most unequal in the region, and it does not seem to have improved since Independence. In van der Hoeven's study (1977) of Zambian income distribution he finds that incomes are more unevenly distributed in urban than in rural areas, that average incomes are higher in urban areas, and that inequality increased during the 1960s as a result of increasing urban incomes coupled with rural stagnation.

It also seems as if transfers from urban to rural areas are of less importance in Zambia than in, for example, Kenya, where they really matter (Van der Hoeven, 1977, p. 17). Van der Hoeven (p. 29) calculated the overall Gini coefficient for Zambia for 1972/73. He found that it was 0.57 for incomes and 0.44 for expenditures.

Zambia has implemented a number of policies resembling those launched in Tanzania. However, it seems as if Zambia has done so rather half-heartedly and without the same consequence as in Tanzania. This moderation has not necessarily been ill-advised, but it seems as if the Zambian leadership does not have a clear strategy. Equity is emphasized and some unsuccessful attempts have been made to improve income distribution, but now Zambia seems to have become trapped in a situation with poor economic growth and a very uneven distribution of income. There is probably little hope of any systematic income distribution policy during the next few years.

7.5 General conclusions on income distribution policy
One chapter does not permit any detailed comparison of the achievements of the three countries. My aim has merely been to describe and briefly discuss the effects on income distribution of their policies. They have very much in common with regard to the problems they face; even in terms of policy they have more similarities than one might expect them to have, considering the differences in their ideological images. Tanzania and Zambia have gone further than Kenya in

terms of direct government intervention in production, but otherwise the respective policy set-ups have many similarities. So far, there has obviously been a considerably discrepancy between rhetoric and results. Policies should be judged by the latter.

First, all three countries went through a similar process of Africanization after independence. During this phase most of the attention had to be devoted to the problem of taking over the machinery of government, and little attention could be devoted to the equity issues.

Since that time the problem of income distribution has become prominent in the policy discussions in the respective countries. Tanzania and, to some extent, Zambia have gone further than Kenya in bringing about institutional changes, which are intended to help realize the goal of a more equitable distribution of income.

In the area of agriculture all these countries have a cooperative movement, but Tanzania has gone further than the others by creating a comprehensive system of rural villages. These are supposed to serve as a basis for a long-run development towards a more collectively organized system of agricultural production. It may be too early to form definite judgements about the outcome of this policy experiment, but the gains in terms of equity certainly seem to have a considerable cost in terms of efficiency. The problems in the Tanzanian agriculture have not entirely been caused by the 'villageization programme', but also by irrational pricing policies and an inefficient, government-run system of marketing.

The Kenyan system of smallholder agricultural production seems to be working most efficiently, although this certainly has its problems as well. Productivity has increased very slowly during most of the 1970s, and there are problems of landlessness and increasing divergences in wealth. Zambia, finally, seems to be stuck with a system that is neither efficient nor equitable.

Thus, none of the countries are pursuing a policy which manages to combine efficiency with an equitable distribution. It seems that at least one general conclusion may be drawn from their experiences. There are definite limits as to what the planning machinery can cope with. If, in this context, private initiatives are stifled and there is extensive interference with the functioning of the price mechanism, problems of allocation of resources are encountered.

Still, as long as a policy improves income distribution, it might still be reasonable. However, policies which have a negative effect on both efficiency and equity goals are impossible to defend. In Kenya, for example, a land reform would probably have beneficial effects on both growth and equity, but it cannot be implemented because of political constraints. The trade policies of all three countries have a negative effect on both equity and short-term allocative efficiency. Whether the long-run gains provide compensation for this is doubtful. Moreover, it has been shown convincingly that trade policy is not the first best policy to correct domestic distortions, which are the basis of the infant industry argument. It is more difficult to measure the gains in terms of goals such as 'self-reliance', but, so far, the policies pursued by Tanzania have had no significant, positive effect on this goal either.

Many of the price policies also fall in the category with negative efficiency and equity effects. They tend to hurt farmers and benefit urban dwellers. However, in the long run urban dwellers may also be hurt by the agricultural stagnation through higher food prices. Some of the income policies, on the other hand, contribute to the equalization of earnings.

The nationalization policy and the organization of huge parastatals to run the economy, particularly by Tanzania, has a considerable influence on income distribution. Capital incomes accrue to the government and not to private capitalists. It seems reasonable to assume that the government spends the money more equitably than a private capitalist would do, although it is not self-evident that the distribution of consumption resulting from the nationalized system is more equitable than that from the alternative system. When all secondary effects of such a system are considered, it is theoretically possible that it would not even lead to a more equitable distribution of income, even if, in the Tanzanian case, it probably has.

A nationalized system places much greater demands on the government, and efficient administration seems to be a scarce resource in all these countries. A highly bureaucratic and rigid economic organization creates inefficiencies of its own and reduces the return on capital .

There is no general answer to the question of which is the optimal trade-off between costs in efficiency and gains in terms of other government goals, but there certainly is a trade-off. The tax system may help to equalize incomes, but generally it seems to contribute only very little. The system is too inefficient to be able substantially to reduce the incomes of the wealthiest categories. The expenditure side of the budget is probably of greater importance to the extent that the public services are widely distributed. However, the distribution of these, be it education or extension services, often reflects the pattern of power and wealth, rather than the pattern of needs. It is generally difficult to pursue equitable policies in inequitable societies.

It is not easy to make a fair comparison between countries which have started with different preconditions. Still, the options open to them have not been that different, and obviously Tanzania and

Zambia have chosen a more interventionistic strategy than Kenya. Tanzania at least seems to have implemented more of pure basic needs policies (type three policies according to section 7.2) than the others. In comparison with Kenya this has reduced the number of very rich individuals, but it is far less certain that it has reduced the number of very poor ones. At present, it seems as if the preconditions for growth and thus the potential for long-run elimination of poverty is greater in Kenya than in the other two countries. However, the fact that the potential exists does not guarantee that it will be realized. The classes benefiting from the present structure of policies may find it in their interest to resist attempts at changes in an equitable direction, and with their increasing wealth and power they may also have the chance of succeeding.

Thus an active income distribution policy must have a political basis. That is the first prerequisite. There must also be a correspondence between the means and the ends. Good intentions are not sufficient. The type of policy implemented must be feasible. So far, the experiences suggest that solutions requiring much of detailed, central administration are inefficient.

Thus planning and administration cannot be substitutes for incentives to economic agents. It is possible to alter the pattern of ownership of the means of production, but once this has been done, prices must be allowed to reflect the real scarcities to a fairly high degree, and firms must be allowed a measure of independence. The informational requirements of a largely planned economy are so great, that these countries are unable to cope with them. The market solves the information problem more efficiently in almost all cases.

It is not easy to classify all the policies pursued in the three categories proposed by Selowsky. Some policies may seem to contribute *ex ante* to both growth and equity, but *ex post* they may contribute to only one or none of these goals. Still, with regard to type one policies we have seen that when it comes to trade policy and prices and incomes policy there are distortions which inhibit trickle-down and have costs in terms of efficiency. With type two policies there is considerable investment in the poor, primarily through education in all countries. Type three policies seem to have been most common in Tanzania. To evaluate them one must weigh gains in terms of the provision of basic needs to poor people against efficiency losses. This will not be attempted here. It is not yet clear how the satisfaction of basic needs in Tanzania really has developed.

To sum: first, there must be a political will and power in support of egalitarian reform, if it is to be successful. Second, equity is not the only objective of government policies. One must balance this objective against others, for example efficiency and long-run economic growth. Third, once this trade-off has been determined, congruence between ends and means must be ensured. Due regard must be given to the administrative, economic and social constraints of the particular economy.

References

Kenya

Anker, R. and Knowles, J. (forthcoming), *Population, Employment, and Inequality: Bachue Kenya*, Gower Press, Farnborough.

Berg-Schlosser, D. (1970), *The distribution of Income and Education in Kenya: Causes and Potential Political Consequences*, Veltforum Verlag, Munich.

Bigsten, A. (1980), *Regional Inequality and Development. A Case Study of Kenya*, Gower Press, Farnborough.

Bigsten, A. and Collier, P. (1980a), *Education, Employment and Wages in Kenya*, Working Paper no. 366, IDS, (Institute for Development Studies), Nairobi.

Bigsten, A. and Collier, P. (1980b), *Education, Innovation, and Incomes in Rural Kenya*, Working Paper no. 369, IDS (Institute Development Studies) Nairobi.

Bigsten, A. and Collier, P. (1980c), *Economic Consequences of Labour Turnover in Kenya*, mimeo, Oxford.

Colebatch, H. (1974), *Local Services and the Governmental Process in Kenya*, PhD thesis, University of Sussex, Brighton.

Collier, P. and Bigsten, A. (1981), 'A model of educational expansion and labour market adjustments applied to Kenya', *Oxford Bulletin of Economics and Statistics*, Vol. 43.

Collier, P. and Lal, D. (1980), *Poverty and Growth in Kenya*, Working Paper no. 389, IBRD (International Bank for Reconstruction and Development).

Collier, P. and Lal, D. (1981), *Coercion, Compassion, Competition*, The World Bank, mimeo.

Crawford, E. and Thorbecke, E. (1978), *Employment, Income Distribution, Poverty Alleviation and Basic Needs in Kenya*, Report of an ILO (International Labour Office) Consulting Mission, Cornell University.

Crawford, E. and Thorbecke, E. (1979), *The Analysis of Food Poverty: An illustration from Kenya*, mimeo, Cornell University.

Fields, G.S. (1975), 'Higher education and income distribution in a less developed country', *Oxford Economic Papers*, Vol. 27, no. 2.

Ghai, D. (1968), 'Incomes policy in Kenya: need criteria, and machinery', *Eastern African Economic Review*, Vol. 1, no. 1.

Ghai, D. (1980), 'Basic needs: from words to action, with illustrations from Kenya', *International Labour Review*, Vol. 119, no. 3.

Ghai, D. and Godfrey, M. (eds) (1979), *Essays on Employment in Kenya*, Kenya Literature Bureau, Nairobi.

Ghai, D., Godfrey, M. and Lisk, F. (1979), *Planning for Basic Needs in Kenya*, ILO (International Labour Office), Geneva.

Ghai, D., Thorbecke, E. and Godfrey, M., *Alleviating Poverty and Meeting Basic Needs in Kenya*, ILO (International Labour Office), mimeo.

Hazlewood, A. (1978), 'Kenya: income distribution and poverty – an unfashionable view', *Journal of Modern African Studies*, Vol. 16, no. 1.

Heyer, J. (1975), 'The origins of regional inequalities in smallholder agriculture in Kenya, 1920–73', *Eastern African Journal of Rural Development*, Vol. 8, no. 1/2.

Heyer, J., Maitha, J.K. and Senga, W.M. (eds) (1976), *Agricultural Development in Kenya*, Oxford University Press, Nairobi.

Heyer, J., (1976) 'The marketing system', in Heyer *et al.*

Hood, M. (1976), 'Income distribution in Kenya, 1963–72', *Journal of Development Studies*, Vol. 12, no. 3.

Hopcraft, P. (1979), *Industrialization, Balance of Payments, and Trade Policy in Kenya: The Effects of Protectionism and Government Intervention on Prices, Exports and Income Distribution*, mimeo, Nairobi.

House, W.J. (1978), *Nairobi's Informal Sector*, Working Paper no. 347, IDS (Institute for Development Studies), Nairobi.

House, W.J. and Killick, T. (1980), *Social Justice and Development Policy in Kenya's Rural Economy*. World Employment Programme, ILO. (International Labour Office).

IBRD (International Bank for Reconstruction and Development) (1975), *Kenya into the Second Decade*, Johns Hopkins University Press, Baltimore.

ILO (International Labour Office) (1972), *Employment, Incomes and Equality: A Strategy for Increasing Productive Employment in Kenya*, Geneva.

ILO (International Labour Office) (1975), *Social Classes and the Government in Kenya: A Comparison Between the ILO Report and the Government's Response*, ILO (International Labour Office), World Employment Programme, Geneva.

KANU, Election Manifesto 1979, Nairobi.

Kaplinsky, R. (1978), *Trends in the Distribution of Income in Kenya, 1966–76* Working Paper no. 336, Institute for Development Studies, University of Nairobi.

Kenya (1965), *African Socialism and its Application to Planning in Kenya*, Sessional Paper no. 10, Nairobi.

Kenya, *First Development Plan 1966–70*, Nairobi.

Kenya (1967), *Kenyanization of Personnel in the Private Sector. A Statement on Government Policy Relating to Employment of Non-Citizens in Kenya*, Nairobi.

Kenya, *Report of the Salaries Review Commission 1967*, Nairobi (Millar-Craig Commission).

Kenya, *Second Development Plan 1970–74*, Nairobi.

Kenya, *Report of the Commission of Inquiry (Public Services Structure and Remuneration Commission) 1970–71*, Nairobi, (Ndegwa Commission).

Kenya (1973), *Sessional Paper on Employment*, no. 10, Nairobi.

Kenya, *Third Development Plan 1974–8*, Nairobi.

Kenya (1975), *Economic Prospects and Policies*, Sessional Paper no. 4, Nairobi.

Kenya, *Fourth Development Plan 1979–83*, Nairobi.

Kenya (1980), *Economic Prospects and Policies*, Sessional Paper no. 4, Nairobi.

Killick, T. (1976), *Strengthening Kenya's Development Strategy: Opportunities and Constraints*, Discussion Paper no. 239, IDS (Institute for Development Studies) Nairobi.

Killick, T. (1979), *By Their Fruit Ye Shall Know Them: Kenya's Fourth Development Plan*, mimeo, Nairobi.

Killick, T. (1981), *Readings on the Kenya Economy*, Heinemann, Nairobi.

Killick, T. and Kinyua, J.K. (1979), *Development Plan Implementation in Kenya*, mimeo, Nairobi.
Kinyanjui, K. (1974), *The Distribution of Educational Resources and Opportunities in Kenya*, Discussion Paper no. 208, IDS (Institute for Development Studies), Nairobi.
Kinyanjui, K. (1979), *The Political Economy of Educational Inequality: A Study of the Roots of Educational Inequality in Colonial and Post-Colonial Kenya*, PhD thesis, Harvard University.
Kmietowicz, T. and Webley, P. (1975), 'Statistical analysis of income distribution in the central province of Kenya', *Eastern Africa Review*, Vol. 7, no. 2.
Leys, C. (1979), 'Development strategy in Kenya Since 1971', *Canadian Journal of African Studies*.
Lijoodi, J.L. and Ruthenberg, H. (1978), 'Income distribution in Kenya's agriculture', *Zeitschrift für auslandische Landwirtschaft*, Vol. 17.
Morrison, C. (1973), *Income Distribution in Kenya*, IBRD (International Bank for Reconstruction and Development), mimeo.
Mott, F. (1980), *The Rural Labour Force in Kenya. An Overview*, mimeo, Nairobi.
Mukui, J.T. (ed.) (1979), *Price and Marketing Controls in Kenya*, Occasional Paper no. 32, IDS (Institute for Development Studies), Nairobi.
Norcliffe, G.B. (1977) *Towards a Locational Policy for Manufacturing Industry in Kenya*, Ministry of Finance and Planning, Nairobi, mimeo.
Nyangira, N. (1975), *Relative Modernization and Public Resource Allocation*, East African Literature Bureau, Nairobi.
Pack, H. (1977), 'Unemployment and income distribution in Kenya', *Economic Development and Cultural Change*, Vol. 26, no. 1.
Rempel, H. and House, W.J. (1978), *The Kenya Employment Problem. An Analysis of the Modern Sector Labour Market*, Oxford University Press, Nairobi.
Sharpley, J. (1979), 'Intersectoral capital flows: evidence from Kenya', *Journal of Development Economics*, Vol. 6, no. 4.
Singer, H. and Reynolds, S. (1973), *Aspects of the Distribution of Income and Wealth in Kenya*, mimeo, UNESCO.
Smith, L. (1978), *Low Income Smallholder Marketing and Consumption Patterns – Analysis and Improvements, Policies and Programmes*, FAO (Food and Agriculture Organization), Marketing Project.
Stewart, F. (1979), 'The tripartite aggrements in Kenya', in Ghai and Godfrey (eds).
Tidrick. G. (1979), *Issues in Agricultural Development*, mimeo, Nairobi.
Westlake, M.I. (1973), 'Tax evasion, tax incidence, and the distribution of income in Kenya', *Eastern African Economic Review*, Vol. 5, no. 2.

Tanzania

Amey, A. (1976), *Urban – Rural Disparities in Tanzania 1960–75*, IBRD (International Bank for Reconstruction and Development).
Bienefeld, M.A. (1975), *The Self-Employed of Urban Tanzania*, ERB Paper Vol. 75, no. 11. Economic Research Bureau, Dar es Salaam.
Bienefeld, M., Godfrey, M. and Lamb, G, (1977), *Basic Needs in Eastern Africa: a preliminary Survey of Kenya, Tanzania and Somalia*, mimeo, IDS (Institute of Development Studies), Brighton.
Chesworth, D. (1967), 'Statutory minimum wage fixing in Tanzania', *International Labour Review*, Vol. 96.

Clark, E. (1975), 'Socialist development in an underdeveloped country: the case of Tanzania', *World Development*, Vol. 3, no. 4.

Clark, W.E. (1978), *Socialist Development and Public Investment in Tanzania*, University of Toronto Press, Toronto.

Collier, P. and Sabot, R. (1976), *Measuring Income Differences Between Rural and Urban Incomes: Some Conceptual Issues*, Research Workshop on Urban Rural Labor Market Interactions, IBRD (International Bank for Reconstruction and Development), Washington.

Constitution of Chama Cha Mapinduzi (CCM) (1977).

Cornell, J. (1974), *The Evolution of Tanzanian Rural Development*, IDS (Institute of Development Studies), Sussex, Communication no. 110.

Damachi, U. *et al.* (eds.) (1976), *Development Policy in Africa and China*, Westview Press, Boulder, Colorado.

Ellis, F. (1980), *Agricultural Pricing Policy in Tanzania 1970–79*, mimeo.

Green, R. (1974), 'Tanzania', in Chenery.

Green, R.H. (1974), *Toward Ujamaa and Kujtegemea: Income Distribution and Absolute Poverty Eradication Aspects of the Tanzanian Transition to Socialism*, IDS Discussion Paper no. 66, (Institute of Development Studies), Sussex.

Green, R.H. (no date) *Tanzanian Political Economy Goals, Strategies and Result*, IDS (Institute of Development Studies), Sussex.

Helleiner, G. (1972),'Socialism and economic development in Tanzania', *Journal of Development Studies*, vol. 8, no. 2.

Huang, Y. (1976), 'Distribution of the tax burden in Tanzania', *Economic Journal*, Vol. 86, no. 1.

Hyden, G. (1975a), 'Ujamaa, villagization and rural development in Tanzania', *ODI Review*, no. 1.

Hyden, G. (1975b), *'We must run while others walk'* – *Policy Making for Socialist Development in the Tanzanian-type of Polities*, ERB Paper 1975, Vol. 1, Dar.

Hyden, G. (1980), *Beyond Ujamaa in Tanzania. Underdevelopment and an Uncaptured Peasantry*, Heinemann, London.

IBRD (International Bank for Reconstruction and Development) (1977), *Tanzania Basic Economic Report*.

IBRD (International Bank for Reconstruction and Development) (1974), *Tanzanian Agricultural and Rural Development Sector Study*, IBRD.

Iliffe, J. (1979), *A Modern History of Tanzania*, Cambridge University Press, Cambridge.

ILO (International Labour Office) (1975), *Report to the Government of Tanzania on the Past, Present and Future Incomes Policy in Tanzania*, Geneva.

ILO (International Labour Office) (1978), *Towards Self-Reliance*, Addis Ababa.

ILO (International Labour Office), *Seminar on JASPA Report on Development, Employment and Equity Issues in Tanzania, 1980*: Report A: Incomes Policy: Scope Record and Area for Action; Report B: Deliberations on Manpower Planning; Report C: Education and Training; Report D: Summary Record of the Discussion on the Rural Economy of Tanzania; Report E: Urban Economy.

Lamb, G. (1977), *Distributive Policies in Tanzania*, Paper presented at the Work Bank Workshop on Distributional Issues in Development Planning, Bellagio.

Lofchie, (1978), 'Agrarian crisis and economic liberalization in Tanzania', *Journal of Modern African Studies*, Vol. 16, no. 3.

Maliyamkono, T.L. (1976), *Educational Reform for Development: a Review of Tanzania Approach*, mimeo, World Bank.

Maro, P.S. and Mlay, W.F.I. (1979), 'Decentralization and the organization of space in

Tanzania', *Africa*, Vol. 49, no. 3.

Morawetz, D. (1980), 'Economic lessons from some small socialist developing countries', *World Development*, Vol. 8, no. 5/6.

Nyerere, J.K. (1967), *Socialism and Rural Development*, Dar.

Nyerere, J.K. (1967), *Education for Self-Reliance*, Dar.

Nyerere, J. (1968), *Ujamaa – Essays on Socialism*, Oxford University Press, Oxford.

Nyerere, J.K. (1972), *Decentralization*, Dar.

Nyerere, J. (1974), *Man and Development*, Oxford University Press, Oxford.

Nyerere, J.K. (1977), *The Arusha Declaration Ten Years After*, Dar.

Nyerere's speeches at the budgetary sessions of the Parliament.

Rice, R.C. (1976), *The Tanzania Price Control System: Theory, Practice and Some Possible Improvements*, Economic Research Bureau, Dar.

Routh, G. (1976), 'Development policy in Tanzania', in Damachi.

Salander, M. (1977), *Resursfördelning och fördelningspolitik i Tanzania*, SIDA.

Ståhl, M. (1980), *Landanalys – Tanzania*, SIDA.

TANU (1967), *The Arusha Declaration*, Dar.

TANU (1971), *Mwongozo – TANU Guidelines*, Dar.

TANU (1976), *The Directive on the Implementation of Education for Self-Reliance*, (*The Musoma Resolutions*).

Tanzania, *First Five Year Plan, 1964–69*, Dar.

Tanzania (1967), *Wages, Incomes, Rural Development, Investment and Price Policy*, Government Paper no. 4, Dar.

Tanzania, *Second Five Year Plan, 1969–74*, Dar.

Tanzania (1975), *The Villages and Ujamaa Villages Act*, Dar.

Tanzania, *Third Five Year Plan, 1976–81*, Dar.

Tanzania (1980), *National Policy on Productivity, Incomes and Wages*, (translated from Swahili), Dar.

Tanzania, Annual Ministerial Budget Statements.

van Ginneken, W. (1976), *Rural and Urban Inequalities in Indonesia, Mexico, Pakistan, Tanzania, and Tunisia*, ILO (International Labour Office), Geneva.

van der Hoeven, R. (1979), *Meeting Basic Needs in a Socialist Framework: the Example of Tanzania*, World Employment Programme, ILO. (International Labour Office).

Zambia

Baldwin, R.E. (1966), *Economic Development and Export Growth: A Study of Northern Rhodesia 1920–60*, University of California Press.

Bates, R.H. (1971), *Unions, Parties and Political Development. A Study of Mineworkers in Zambia*, Yale University Press, New Haven, Conn.

Bhagawan, M.R. (1979), *Zambia – Impact of Industrial Strategy on Regional Imbalance and Social Inequality*, Scandinavian Institute of African Studies, Uppsala.

Blitzer, C.R. (1979), 'Development and Income Distribution in a Dual Economy – Dynamic Simulation Model for Zambia', *Journal of Development Economics* Vol. 6, no. 3.

CIMMYT (1978), *Demonstrations of an Interdisciplinary Approach to Planning Adaptive Agricultural Research Programmes*, Report III, Nairobi.

Dodge, D.J. (1977), *Agricultural Policy and Performance in Zambia*, Institute of International Studies, University of California, Berkeley, Cal.

Elliot, C. (ed.) (1971), *Constraints on the Economic Development of Zambia*, Nairobi.

Elliot, C. (1980), 'Equity and growth – unresolved conflict in Zambian rural development policy', World Employment Programme, ILO (International Labour Office) Geneva.

Fluitman, A.G. (1974), *Employment and Incomes in Lusaka*, mimeo, Lusaka.

Fry, J. (1970), 'The Turner Report: a Zambian view:' *Eastern Africa Economic Review*, Vol. 2.

Fry, J. (1975), 'Rural – Urban Terms of Trade, 1960–73. A Note', *African Social Research*, Vol. 19.

Fry, J. (1979), *Employment and Income Distribution in the African Economy*, Croom Helm, London.

Harvey, C. (1971), 'Control of inflation in a very open economy – Zambia, 1964–69', *Eastern African Economic Review*, Vol. 3, no. 1.

Harvey, R.H. (1973), *Some Determinant of Agricultural Productivity of Rural Households: Report of a Survey in Kalichero District*, Eastern Province, MRD, Chipata.

ILO (International Labour Office) (1969), *Report to The Government of Zambia on Incomes, Wages, and Prices*, (Turner Report), Geneva.

ILO (International Labour Office) (1977), *Narrowing the Gaps: Planning for Basic Needs and Productive Employment in Zambia*, JASPA, Addis Ababa.

Joseph, C.R. (1977), *Report on the Random Pilot Survey of Traditional Farmers in the Central and Northern Provinces of Zambia*, Lusaka.

Kaunda, K.D. (1968), *Humanism in Zambia and a Guide to Its Implementation*, Lusaka.

Kaunda, K.D. (1968), *Zambia's Economic Revolution* (address at Mulungushi, 19 April 1968) Lusaka.

Kaunda, K.D. (1969), *Towards Complete Independence* (address at Matero Hall, Lusaka, 11 August 1969), Lusaka.

Kaunda, K.O. (1974), *Humanism*, Pt II.

Knight, J.B. (1971), 'Wages and Zambia's economic development', in Elliot (ed.).

Maimbo, F. and Fry, J. (1971), 'An investigation into the change in the terms of trade between the rural and urban sectors in Zambia', *African Social Research*, no. 12.

Maimbo, F.J.M. (1975), *An Analysis of the Pattern of Income and Expenditure of a Sample of Farm Families of Chiefdom Hamaundu of the Choma District of the Southern Province of Zambia*, Rural Development Studies Bureau, University of Zambia, Occasional Papers.

Marter, A. and Honeybone, D. (1976), *The Economic Resources of Rural Household and the distribution of Agricultural Development*, UNZA/RDSB, mimeo.

Parsonaga, M.A., *Modern Sector Employment, Earnings and Productivity*, MA thesis, Nuffield College, Oxford.

Rotschild, D. (1974), 'Rural urban inequalities and resource allocation in Zambia', *Journal of Commonwealth Studies*, Vol. 10, no. 3.

Turok, B. (ed.) (1979), *Development in Zambia*, ZED Press, London.

UNIP, *National Policies for the Next Decade, 1974–84*, Lusaka.

University of Nottingham and Zambia, *Agricultural Labour Productivity Investigations*, UNZALPI, Lusaka, 1969–72.

van der Hoeven, R. (1977), *Zambia's Income Distribution During the Early Seventies*, World Employment Programme, ILO (International Labour Office), Geneva.

Zambia (1965), *Transitional Development Plan*, Lusaka.

Zambia (1966–70), *First National Development Plan*.

Zambia (1966), *Report of the Commission Appointed to Review the Grading Structure of the Civil Service and the Salary Scales of the Civil Service*, (Whelan Commission) Lusaka.

Zambia (1966), *Report of the Commission of Inquiry into the Mining Industry* (Brown Commission Report) Lusaka.

Zambia (1969), *Report of the Second National Convention on Rural Development, Incomes, Wages and Prices in Zambia*, Lusaka.

Zambia (1971), *Report of the Commission Appointed to Review the Salaries, Salary Structure and Conditions of the Service of the Zambia Public Service*, (O' Riordan Commission Report), Lusaka.

Zambia, *Second National Development Plan, 1972–6*, Lusaka.

Zambia (1972), *The Leadership Code*, Lusaka.

Zambia (1975), *Report of the Commission of Inquiry into Salaries, Salary Structure and Conditions of Service*, (Mwanakatwe Commission), Lusaka.

Zambia, *Economic Report*, annual.

Zambia, *Draft Statement of Education for Development*, Lusaka.

Zambia, *Budget Addresses by the Minister of Finance*, annual.

General

Amey, A.B. and Leonard, D.K. (1979), 'Public policy, class and inequality in Kenya and Tanzania', *Africa Today*, Vol. 26, no. 4.

Bequelle, A. and van der Hoeven, R. (1980), 'Poverty and inequality in Sub-Saharan Africa', *International Labour Review*, Vol. 119, no. 3.

Chenery, H. *et al.* (1974), *Redistribution with Growth*, Oxford University Press, London.

Cliffe, L., (1975), 'Underdevelopment or socialism? A comparative analysis of Kenya and Tanzania', in Harris (ed.).

Court, D.. (1976), 'The education system as a response to inequality in Tanzania and Kenya', *Journal of Modern African Studies*, Vol. 14, no. 4.

Court, D. and Kinyanjui, K. (1980), 'Development policy and educational opportunity: the experience of Kenya and Tanzania', in Tarron and Chau.

Ghai, D., (1964), *Some Aspects of Income Distribution in East Africa*, mimeo, Makerere University, Kampala.

Gunning, J., (1979), *Income Distribution Models for Developing Countries; Kenya and Tanzania*, Thesis, Oxford.

Harris, R. (ed.) (1975), *The Political Economy of Africa*, Cambridge, Mass.

ILO (1976), *Employment, Growth, and Basic Needs*, Geneva.

Lewis, W.A., (1954), 'Economic development with unlimited supplies of labour', *Manchester School of Economic and Social Studies*, Vol. 22.

Selowsky, M., (1981), 'Income distribution, basic needs and trade-offs with growth: the case of semi-industrialized Latin American countries', *World Development*, Vol. 9.

Tarron, Gabriel and Chau, Ta Ngoc (1980), *Regional Disparities in Educational Development: Diagnosis and Policies for Reduction*, UNESCO, Paris.

Index